REPRESENTATIVE OPINIONS
OF
MR. JUSTICE HOLMES

REPRESENTATIVE OPINIONS
OF
MR. JUSTICE HOLMES

Arranged, with Introductory Notes, by
ALFRED LIEF

With a Foreword by
HAROLD J. LASKI
Professor of Political Science, London University

GREENWOOD PRESS, PUBLISHERS
WESTPORT, CONNECTICUT

Copyright 1931 by The Vanguard Press

Originally published in 1931 by The Vanguard Press, New York

Reprinted with the permission of Alfred Lief

Reprinted from an original copy in the collections of the University of Illinois Library

Reprinted in 1971 by Greenwood Press, a division of Congressional Information Service, 88 Post Road West, Westport, Connecticut 06881

Library of Congress catalog card number 76-156194

ISBN 0-8371-6143-6

Printed in the United States of America

10 9 8 7 6 5 4 3 2

CONTENTS

INTRODUCTION	ix
I. ON LEGISLATIVE FREEDOM.	1
MARGINAL SALE OF STOCK PROHIBITED.	3
RAILROADS AFFLICTING FARMERS WITH WEEDS	8
ASSESSED FOR UNWANTED IMPROVEMENTS	10
STEPS IN BEHALF OF EDUCATION	14
OBLIGATIONS OF THE BANKING BUSINESS	20
DISCOURAGING CHINESE HAND LAUNDRIES	25
DESTROYING LOCAL COMPETITION	28
WATER POWER A PUBLIC USE	31
A DISCRIMINATORY ATTEMPT TO CHECK MONOPOLY	34
SHIFTING THE BURDEN OF ACCIDENTS	41
TAXING HOLDING COMPANIES	44
GRADE CROSSINGS AND THE POLICE POWER	46
CONTROL OF RENT IN EMERGENCIES	53
EMERGENCY LEGISLATION IN NEW YORK	59
DESTROYING VALUES WITHOUT PAYMENT	62
STERILIZATION OF IMBECILES	67
REGULATING THE EYEGLASS BUSINESS	71
II. ON THE STATES AND THE NATION.	73
CONTEMPT OF A STATE COURT	75
A STATE'S CONTROL OVER ITS WATERS	80
A BURDEN ON INTERSTATE COMMERCE	86
EXECUTIVE PROCESS DURING AN INSURRECTION	91
EXTENDING CONGRESSIONAL AUTHORITY	96
JURISDICTION OVER MIGRATORY BIRDS	101
TAXING A RAILROAD'S PROPERTY	106
PIPE LINES IN INTERSTATE COMMERCE	109
STATE LAWS AND NATIONAL BANKS	113
INCONVENIENCES OF DAYLIGHT SAVING	116
ABUSING THE COMMERCE CLAUSE	119

CONTENTS

III. ON TRADE COMBINATIONS AND BOYCOTTS. . . . 123

    A COMBINATION TO MONOPOLIZE MEAT 125
    CONSPIRACY IN RESTRAINT OF TRADE 137
    "MISTAKEN NOTIONS" ON PRICE-FIXING 143
    CRIMINAL PROSECUTION UNDER THE SHERMAN ACT 147
    CONTROL OF PRICE IN A COMPLEX WORLD . . . 153
    WARFARE AGAINST COUNTRY BANKS. 158
    A COMBINATION OF LABOR 163
    BOYCOTTING A PRODUCERS' COOPERATIVE . . . 166

IV. ON INTERPRETING STATUTES 169

    SOLICITING POLITICAL FUNDS 171
    A MUSIC ROLL NOT A "COPY" 175
    UNION LEADER PUNISHED FOR CONTEMPT. . . . 177
    TAXING THE TRANSFER OF ESTATES 185
    AVOIDING THE CONSTITUTIONAL QUESTION . . . 190

V. ON CONSTITUTIONAL GUARANTIES 193

    EXCLUDING CHINESE WITHOUT A COURT HEARING 195
    USING ILLEGALLY SEIZED PAPERS. 201
    MOB DOMINATION OF A COURT 204
    BARRING NEGROES FROM PRIMARIES. 210
    A SELF-INCRIMINATING TAX RETURN 213

VI. ON TORTS AND CRIMINAL LAW 215

    LIBEL BY PHOTOGRAPH. 217
    PRESUMPTION OF GOOD CHARACTER 221
    A JUDGE INFLUENCING A JURY 224
    THE OBLIGATION TO RETREAT 228
    CHILDREN AS TRESPASSERS 232
    WITHOUT CONSENT OF CONVICT 236
    TRAFFICKING IN NARCOTICS 239

VII. ON REGULATION OF PUBLIC UTILITIES 243

    RATE-MAKING A LEGISLATIVE FUNCTION 245
    FIXING A MAXIMUM PRICE FOR GAS 255
    RATES UNDER MUNICIPAL OWNERSHIP 259

CONTENTS

VIII. ON STATE TAXATION 263
    TAXING A STOCK EXCHANGE SEAT 265
    TAXING A TRUST FUND IN ANOTHER STATE . . . 267
    ANOTHER TAX ACROSS STATE LINES 270
    A SKY-LIMIT TO "DUE PROCESS" 273

IX. EXCERPTS FROM VARIOUS OPINIONS 275

X. SELECTED MASSACHUSETTS OPINIONS 289
    IN DEFENSE OF LABOR LEGISLATION 291
    A POLICEMAN IN POLITICS 294
    A REFERENDUM ON WOMAN SUFFRAGE 297
    LICENSES FOR SPEECHES ON BOSTON COMMON . . 301
    COMBINATIONS OF LABOR AGAINST CAPITAL . . . 304
    INDUCING A BREACH OF CONTRACT 311
    UNLAWFUL METHODS OF UNIONIZING 314

INTRODUCTION

I

In the last decade, it has become generally recognized that not since Mr. Chief Justice Marshall has the United States possessed a jurist of the insight and distinction of Mr. Justice Holmes. Wherever the writ of the Common Law runs, there his opinions have won for him a standing which places him among the classic figures of Anglo-American legal history. It is not merely that what he has chosen to say has about it an unforgettable literary power. It is not merely, either, that he has had a learning and an historical penetration unsurpassed on the British and, I venture to think, unequalled upon the American, bench. It is not even because of his remarkable ability to penetrate through the mass of facts to the essential principles they imply. In one or other of these qualities, Mansfield and Bowen, Shaw and Jessel, Story and Blackburn, have been at least worthy rivals of his eminence.

The peculiar importance of Mr. Justice Holmes lies in the marriage of these qualities to a temperament capable of a detachment almost unique in judicial history. It is not that he does not possess a considered and emphatic philosophy. Aristocratic, conservative, sceptical, these marks of a deliberate outlook can be seen in almost everything he has written. But he has never allowed his own special attitude to balance unduly his approach to the law. He has worked within the framework of a judicial system which limits the power of the judge to make himself the master of the legislature; and, unlike not a few of his colleagues, he has been scrupulous to respect the implications of the system.

INTRODUCTION

And this is because he has realized the many-sidedness of truth, the possibility that men may genuinely differ upon evidence about the desirability of legislative action, and that the judge has no right, unless the Constitution is flagrantly violated, to make of his private convictions the measure of legality. Judicial history does not suggest that this is an easy task; and it is, above all, in his power of detachment that Mr. Justice Holmes has been able to win the respect of men in the most varied camps of opinion.

The keynote of his thought is not less important in this context. It lies, I venture to think, in a refusal to work with absolute concepts. Truth for him is not eternally given; it changes with the changing categories of space and time. Thus the *laissez-faire* philosophy of Spencer, upon which he was nourished as a young man, does not seem to him necessarily relevant to an age of which the industrial conditions are utterly different from any that Spencer can have imagined. Men are entitled to experiment; and novelty has never been for him an index to original sin. He is sceptical of rigid formulae of any kind because he has seen that the things we are inclined to accept as obviously true are not necessarily the inescapable laws of the universe. He has disliked a temper of confident dogmatism because it tends to make the judge the prisoner of private convictions which he cannot surrender before the realities of a changing world. He has seen, too, how various are the multitudinous desires in society, how impossible it is to reduce them to a single will. And from this he has drawn the inference that so long as order is maintained, and the clear prescriptions of the Constitution observed, a decision which has public opinion upon its side is entitled to its letters of credit.

Put baldly in this way is to omit the impact of the candor and integrity of mind which lies behind the attitude. And these are the vital qualities to which his power of intellectual detachment gives birth. They enable him to show a habit of tolerance in the consideration of opinions he dislikes which is rare and precious. I have said that in matters economic and political Mr. Justice Holmes is a conservative; but if every conservative judge upon the bench were to be as open-minded as he has been in the Lochner and Adair cases, for example, the attitude of organized labor to the American courts would have been very different in the last generation. If his dissents in the Abrams and Schwimmer cases had prevailed, one would have felt more hopeful that vital social differences do not necessarily lead to social conflict but admit of peaceful compromise. In this aspect, I believe, the temper in which he has approached his task is a lesson to radical and conservative alike. It is, I would add, the only temper that is compatible with a faith in the right of reason to adjust the opinions of mankind to the reality they confront.

II

I HAVE sought elsewhere to trace the broad outlines of Mr. Justice Holmes' philosophy,[1] and I may not here repeat the substance of that effort. But here I would emphasize certain essential characteristics of its quality without which he cannot be understood. There is in him the temper of a proud Stoic aware from the outset that he fights a losing battle with fate. He seeks to know the ground-plan of the universe even while he is aware that its inner secret will, to the end, be unrevealed. He attempts to measure rightness in matters of social constitution even while he insists that by rightness we mean the realization of the desires we feel intensely. Politics, for him, is a philosophy of the second best, and wisdom in social matters consists of such an adjustment of our wills as to make them accord with what is possible of attainment. We must realize the contingency of all that we claim as truth. We must avoid the danger of equating our incomplete principles with ultimate panaceas. We must recognize how partial and fragmentary is our experience, how unlikely, therefore, it is

---

[1] 40 *Yale Law Journal* (March, 1931), p. 683.

that they can claim the distinction of universality. We must remember that in the adjustment of the individual to his environment, the criterion of social welfare is the inevitable test of adequacy. If we would avoid what he has happily termed "the fallacy of logical form," we must remember that the historic process represents, not the conquest of necessary truth, but the imposition as desirable of those objectives which had the big battalions on their side. As I have elsewhere said, there is in his philosophy a likeness that is remarkable to the tenets of Hobbes and Spinoza; and it is from his insistence on their central concept of power as right that there comes the astonishing note of realism which pervades his pages.

It is well known that sociological jurists, Professor Frankfurter, for instance, and Dean Pound, acclaim him as their master; perhaps no one since Montesquieu has the same title to that place. For if, like Hobbes, he writes consistently of law as the fiat of a sovereign, the pronouncement which will, if it can, enforce itself upon the multitude, he has seen always with exceptional clarity the wide ambit of the sources which go to make the substance of that pronouncement. He has never spoken of law as the equivalent of justice. He has seen that, in any society, it is merely the will that has known how to get itself accepted. He has never sought, like Hegel, to confound the real with the rational, the legally valid with the ethically just. His sense of the category of time has always been too keen to claim for the dicta of the state more than that they preserve order and security, upon the one hand, and that they have an important chance of being right upon the other. The true justification of a statute, he has somewhere written, lies "in some help which the law brings towards reaching a social end which the governing power of the community has made up its mind that it wants." The remark opens up wide vistas; and it bears upon its face that empirical method of valuation which has made him always so remarkably appreciative of the contingent value of social postulates.

INTRODUCTION

It is, I think, important also that his practical work as a judge has followed upon long years of devotion to the study of legal history. To seek the key of events in the moulding of institutions is not the least certain path to wisdom. For the great historian —and the author of the *Common Law* is a very great historian— learns the significant lesson of being patient with the mutabilities of human nature. More, he learns the littleness of men, and the greatness of the web of circumstances in which they are caught. He comes to see the significance of causal sequence, to realize that the great event is never born suddenly but always prepared by an infinite series of vital minutiae. From this, if he will, he can learn, as Mr. Justice Holmes has learned, the lessons of charity and patience. He can see that anger, violence, wrongheadedness, error, are not born of wilful obstinacy or original sin in men, but are the outcome of events which produce a sense of pity and not of condemnation.

But to appreciate the possibilities of his art, the historian must have a sense of responsibility for their application. That is where one finds the significance of Mr. Justice Holmes' half-century upon the bench. The tendency of historians in general has been towards conservatism because so much of their attention is directed to the dubiety of change deliberately attempted, particularly to change deliberately attempted by average and ordinary men. They tend, like Burke, to pin their faith in the unconscious wisdom of the species and to belittle the value of the deliberate inventiveness of a particular generation. They recognize the inevitability of change; they doubt whether its conscious introduction can be successful. From that temper of hesitant paralysis, which one sees in men like Burke and Savigny and Maure, Mr. Justice Holmes has been delivered not merely by judicial experience, but by the special character of that experience.

For he was passing judgment upon the legislative work of an America still partly engaged in wresting civilization from a wilderness. He was not dealing with age-long traditions and in-

[xiii]

stitutions which had become part almost of the instinctive composition of mankind. He was dealing with a world more than half the modern history of which he has himself lived; in which nearly half the constituent states entered the Union in his own lifetime. His work has in no small part consisted in judging whether the experiments of legislators in the building of social and political institutions conformed to the essential principles of the American Constitution. He has been intensely conscious of the responsibility of the task; and he has seen that in a civilization so various it was impossible to limit experiment by insisting that it conform to his own conception of social wisdom. That is where his training as an historian has been of high creative value; for it has made him act upon his own insistence that "history sets us free, and enables us to make up our minds dispassionately whether the survival we are enforcing answers any new purpose when it has ceased to answer the old." Compare his decisions with those of Mr. Justice Brewer or Mr. Justice Peckham—to name only the dead—writing in the same epoch as himself—and the significance of his historical equipment is obvious. It has enabled him to see that the intent of the Constitution is always perverted when it is used to prevent the victory of a dominant opinion on whose behalf the plea of reasonableness may be maintained upon evidence.

III

THE temper in which Mr. Justice Holmes has done his work is the natural outcome of a view of legal science upon which it is worthwhile to say a word. Broadly, he may be described as a legal pragmatist; legal doctrines and institutions, for him, are to be explained in terms of the convenience they represent. The past has no necessary sanctity about it; its interest derives only from the light it can throw upon the present. What gives it its essential substance is the complex of social forces which deposit certain claims to which men feel they must respond. It is shaped, he has

INTRODUCTION

written, "by the felt necessities of the time, the prevalent moral and political theories, intuitions of public policy, avowed or unconscious, even the prejudices which judges share with their fellow-men." Law, so to say, is not for him a factor outside society, but a resultant of its processes, given shape and color by men's efforts to satisfy their wants.

This perception has always made him the enemy of legal formalism, and he has never had sympathy with the view that the predictions of law can be mathematical in character. For he has seen that behind their logic of form there is always, however unconsciously, a deliberate scheme of social preferences, a judgment upon the validity of competing social policies, which gives in fact the key to the decision made. The lawyer cannot, therefore, avoid "the duty of weighing considerations of social advantage." Legal rules are always seeking to accomplish an end deemed desirable by some group of men, and it is only by the conscious formulation of what that end is that we can obtain a realistic jurisprudence. We may not rely upon mere tradition, for each generation, however linked to the past, has the right to govern itself as best it can. To do so, we must draw our postulates from the widest area of facts likely to throw light upon the nature of our problems. We cannot rest content with the substance of decided cases. "For the rational study of law," he has written, "the black letter man may be the man of the present, but the man of the future is the man of statistics and the master of economics."

There, indeed, is the root of that sympathy for experiment which has been so striking a feature of Mr. Justice Holmes' decisions. It has enabled him to take a generous view of constitutional construction; the principles of 1787 must not be used as a strait-jacket for the twentieth century. It has enabled him, also, to see that phrases like "liberty of contract" have no absolute meaning, but depend for their content on the time and place to which they are applied. No one, I think, since Marshall has done so much as Mr. Justice Holmes to prevent the American Consti-

INTRODUCTION

tution from becoming the prisoner of a narrow individualism. And that is because, as its problems have come before him, he has deliberately sought to discover what interests were involved in them and what end a proposed solution was seeking to serve. He has realized that new knowledge means new potentialities of action, and that these, in their turn, cannot be denied the status of constitutionality merely because they could not have occurred to the legislators of sixty years ago. He may have disliked the purpose involved, on occasion, even, have indicated with some sharpness his conviction of its folly. But by refusing to make his private convictions the measure of legislative possibility, his influence has been one of the most considerable emancipating forces in the America of our time.

For the true impact of his work has been to release us from the illusion of certainty, to make us see that, if the problems are different, the solutions cannot be the same. He has seen how important is what Burke called "the little minor of circumstances" in the play of legal battle. He has emphasized that principles laid down for the agricultural society of Washington and Jefferson must have elasticity of interpretation in the industrial civilization of Rockefeller and Ford. He has recognized that in the conflict of interests nothing is so easy or so fatal as to confer upon the results we desire to see prevail the dignity and the claims of Absolute Justice or Absolute Truth. They are in fact imperfect generalizations offering themselves for acceptance less upon the ground of the reason they embody than of the driving power of the interest which has conceived them as desirable. The judge's task is to apply to them the acid test of proportionality, to see them in the perspective of that knowledge which blunts the sharp arrogance of their claim. And, to that end, as Mr. Justice Holmes has said, the lawyer must cease to be satisfied that the explanation of a dogma is resident in its history only. He must seek "an understanding of economics. The present divorce between the schools of political economy and law seems to me an evidence of

INTRODUCTION

how much progress in philosophical study still remains to be made."

Here, forty years before our time, is the realization that it is at the boundaries between the social disciplines that the great discoveries are to be made, the insistence that the law, especially, must be restated and that its new form will be wholly different from what we are now able to imagine. No one acquainted with contemporary developments in legal science will deny the remarkable character of this prediction.

IV

THERE is an anecdote in one of Hazlitt's essays in which a conversation is reported between Ayrton and Charles Lamb. The former had said that of all great names in English literature the two he would most wish to have seen were Locke and Newton. "Yes, the greatest names," Lamb stammered out hastily, "but they were not persons—not persons. . . . What we want to see anyone *bodily* for is when there is something peculiar, striking in the individuals, more than we can learn from their writings, and yet are curious to know."

No one acquainted with Mr. Justice Holmes is likely to deny that he is a person in the full sense of Lamb's phrase. Talk with him is one of the delights of our time; and, indeed, the late Lord Morley put him among the three best conversationalists he had ever known. For, in the first place, he never seeks to impose himself; there is nothing authoritarian in the expression of his views. He argues upon the basis of equality with his neighbor, and he enters vividly upon any battle of mind. And the very quickness of his rapier brings out the best in his opponent. He does not talk for victory, or the glamour of a phrase. He seems to join with you in a mutual search for truth, ready always to acknowledge a good point made, sharing your pride in a happy illustration, or a nimble turn of words. He does not let you escape lightly from

INTRODUCTION

his net. You must define your terms; you must not cease the journey of exploration until you have arrived at its end. You learn to appreciate the scientific temper as you watch the care with which he examines evidence, the precision in his choice of words, the attraction for him of a man who knows how to dig deep into a vital theme. A night with him in the book-lined study at Washington is an education in what is meant by love of truth for its own sake.

And in becoming a great lawyer he has not ceased to be a great man. He can still feel the thrill that comes to us at our first encounter with the giants of literature; and I can still catch the echo of that gust of helpless laughter that has come from some precious absurdity of Mr. P. G. Wodehouse. I have seen the glint in his eye at some line of *Macbeth* that stings its way to the inmost part of us, and the furtive tear when I have read to him of the quickened beat in Amelia's heart when the smoke of Captain Dobbin's steamer rises vaguely above the horizon. For it is one of the secrets of Mr. Justice Holmes that he has adventured life with the whole of his being. Law perhaps most profoundly; but law only as one clue to the undiscoverable labyrinth of the universe. Art, literature, the theater, philosophy, nothing that exhibits man in the context of life has been alien from his interest. And as he has touched life, so he has sought irresistibly to grasp its secret. With him, to examine is to generalize, and then to be impatient with the imperfection of his effort. But he is a soldier to his finger-tips, and he will fight for his hypothesis until his locker is exhausted. I have heard talk between him and Professor Morris Cohen which I would have pitted for depth and brilliance against even the historic encounters of Burke and Dr. Johnson at The Club. Neither is a respecter of persons; each is a devotee of logic. Professor Cohen, with the unending subtlety of the Talmudist, would wind his way into the subject like a serpent; and the judge would meet each twist of that darting sinuosity with

INTRODUCTION

exactly the acid question which brought it up squarely against the facts.

He is always eager and invariably interested, and, if he has pride in his work, there is an ultimate humility in him before which one can have no feeling save silent respect. I have never met a man less conscious of great place, and none better able to enter into the mind of the younger generation. He has, indeed, an almost instinctive understanding of the young; and I think the long procession of his Harvard secretaries would say that no year in their lives was richer in contact with seminal experience. His talk is so amply stored with memory of the great men of his time that one feels, as one listens, part of the supreme pageant of nineteenth century intelligence. He has the gift of friendship; and I know of few things more moving than his delight in the successes of his friends. Indeed, they are so widely flung a company that there is a sense in which friendship with him is like a League of Nations passport; and it is inevitable that, as they meet, his friends should seek to measure the depth of their affection for him.

He has the temperament of the soldier, and like most such men, the stoic outlook is rooted in him. One feels at once that he has made his bargain with fate, and met its demands without repining. He is a rationalist who admits that man is a creature of imagination and passion, an agnostic who does not crave the certitude to which reason does not entitle us. Conservative in all matters of social constitution, he is too inherently sceptical to deny to the radical the possibility that he may be right. And because he is sceptical, he is tolerant to the very roots of his being in the field where intelligence holds sway. That emerged nobly in cases like those of Abrams and Rosika Schwimmer where he fought with passion for beliefs in which he had not even a desire to share. He has directness and simplicity in all that he does; I have rarely, indeed, known a man of his eminence in whom there was less of conscious sophistication. He has not, perhaps, Mr. Justice Brandeis' power of attentive observation to the results of a complex machine, his width of information about the world of affairs, his power authoritatively to measure the value of its operations. But he has a power to dig through the mass of fact to their energizing principle which has been rarely equalled in our time.

It was said, I think of Burke, by Hazlitt, that there was no single speech of his which could convey a satisfactory idea of his powers of mind, that, to do him justice, one would have to quote the whole of his works. There is a sense in which this is true, also, of Mr. Justice Holmes. The big case may give you the realization of his powers; it cannot convey a sense of their range. For he has the secret, which I believe to be the index to the really supreme lawyer, of making the little case illustrate pivotal principle, of making insignificant events a highway to the wider universe. This is because he has passed his life in seeking to think in terms of its foundations, has found inescapable the passion for making knowledge ever more general in character. I would not argue that his reasons are conclusive; I would at least claim that there is always weight and the provocation to thought upon their side. And because he has felt the manysidedness of truth, he has never claimed for his conclusions more than a contingent validity; and even where time has decided against his view, his work has the outstanding merit of making possible new vistas upon the way. One can go to him with the assurance of finding in what he says the kind of legislative wisdom which illuminates the recesses of a subject. He has not that gift which Marshall possessed of so stating the results at which he has arrived that a course of immediate action seems to be indicated. He does not convey, as the opinions of Mr. Justice Brandeis convey, the sense that what the Supreme Court has gained, the Presidency of the United States has lost. He does not impress one, as Mansfield, as possessed of an overmastering desire to see the triumph of certain principles about the legal urgency of which he has made up his mind.

He seems rather to be above, or aloof, from the battle, than

INTRODUCTION

immersed in its tactics, to be concerned always with the larger principles of the campaign. It is law as science and philosophy, rather than law as politics, that has interested him. Indeed, I should have been tempted to say that laws, for him as for Montesquieu, represented the necessary relations of things, were it not that the idea of necessity connotes a recognition of inevitability from which the temper of his mind is aloof. But perhaps I can convey best what I am seeking to imply by saying that whereas, with Mr. Justice Brandeis, one feels that his whole heart is engaged in winning the victory for his side, Mr. Justice Holmes has known not less how to be a spectator of, than an actor in, the events to which his work has made him a party. In Mr. Justice Brandeis there is, almost explicitly a noble moralist with something of the prophet's passionate insight; Mr. Justice Holmes is rather the intellectual analyst whose interest is most deeply engaged in the discovery of causal relations. Where Mr. Justice Brandeis, profoundly moved by the consequences of the results at which he has arrived, must seek, as the price of his nature, to make the strongest impression upon his hearers, Mr. Justice Holmes retains a remoteness from the end he effects; it seems outside, rather than inside, himself. What Mr. Justice Brandeis urges is moulded into a logical whole by a fire he himself contributes to its being; with Mr. Justice Holmes the fire comes from the internal consistency of the selection of facts made.

This is not to say that Mr. Justice Holmes' detachment in matters of law must be interpreted as a detachment from life. No man can give what he has given to his friends without having warmed his hands at its central fire. He has a passionate love of his country; yet he has found that compatible with a high regard for other nations. Without sentimentality, he has a warm and glowing humanity which breaks into instant flame. He judges the motives of his friends with generosity and he is liberal to a degree in estimating those of his opponents. He has known with quickness how to give friendship; he has found it difficult only to dislike. If, like most soldiers, he rates the worth of human life less high than some of us would wish, like most soldiers also, his responsive admiration for courage is instant and profound. There is a pervasive humanity about him such as one would expect from a very great gentleman.

But I approach the frontiers of friendship, and, at this distance, the tribute it exacts is silence. Let me only say that when I look for words in which to describe the impact of Mr. Justice Holmes upon this generation my mind goes back to certain sentences written of Fox by the greatest of his contemporaries at a time when differences of outlook had not impaired his clarity of vision. "To his great and masterly understanding," wrote Burke, "he joined the utmost possible degree of moderation; he was of the most artless, candid, open and benevolent disposition; disinterested in the extreme; of a temper mild and placable even to a fault; and without one drop of gall in his constitution." I believe those words are the quintessence of Mr. Justice Holmes' secret; and they perhaps explain why he has so fully gained the respectful attention of men so diverse in views and the reverent love of friends so different in complexion.

HAROLD J. LASKI.

The London School of Economics and Political Science.

The series of dots which recur in the Opinions indicate the citations of Court decisions. As these are only of technical interest, the editor has thought best to omit them for the sake of smooth reading. Where asterisks appear, they indicate omissions that occur in the original, except in the excerpts, where they denote editorial selection.

I. ON LEGISLATIVE FREEDOM

Marginal Sale of Stock Prohibited

(*Otis* v. *Parker*, 1903)

THIS is an action in three counts, for money had and received, for money paid and promised to be repaid, and for margins paid to the defendants as stock brokers on contracts to buy and sell mining stocks, respectively. The answers to the first two counts are general denials and other matters now immaterial. The answer to the third count, beside a general denial, sets up that the count is based upon a provision in Article IV, § 26, of the constitution of California, that that provision is contrary to the first section of the Fourteenth Amendment of the Constitution of the United States. It appears by the record that the only cause of action was that stated specifically in the third count, and that the defendants interposed the constitutional objection at the trial and that it was overruled. The plaintiff had a general verdict on all three counts. The case was taken from the Superior to the Supreme Court of California on appeal, and the judgment of the Superior Court was affirmed, with an immaterial modification. It is now brought here by a writ of error to the Supreme Court of the State.

We must take it as established that the plaintiff did enter into transactions prohibited by the constitution of California, and that he had a right to his judgment under that constitution if the clause relied upon is not contrary to the Constitution of the United States. There is no question that the parties were subject to the provisions of the latter Constitution, and no doubt that the question whether it invalidated the State constitution necessarily was passed upon, and was answered in the negative by the State court. . . .

The provision of the State constitution is as follows: "All contracts for the sales of shares of the capital stock of any corporation or association, on margin, or to be delivered at a future day, shall be void, and any money paid on such contracts may be recovered by the party paying it by suit in any court of competent jurisdiction." There was some suggestion that these words might be narrowed by construction to contracts not contemplating a *bona fide* acquisition of the stock, but intended to cover only a wager or contemplated settlement of differences. Of course, if they were construed in that sense there would be no doubt of their validity. . . . But while the Supreme Court of California says in this case that it "will always see that legitimate business transactions are not brought under the ban," in the same sentence it leaves open the hypothesis that the provision "fails to distinguish between *bona fide* contracts and gambling contracts," and sustains it as a proper police regulation, even if it does fail as supposed. Therefore it may be held hereafter that ordinary contracts for the sale of stocks on margin are not legitimate transactions, and it would not be safe for us to take the words in any other than their literal meaning, or to assume in advance of a decision that they will be taken in a narrow sense. In this case the jury were instructed broadly to find for the plaintiff if he had paid any money to the defendants as a margin for the purchase of stock of a corporation, and this instruction was sustained.

The objection urged against the provision in its literal sense is that this prohibition of all sales on margin bears no reasonable relation to the evil sought to be cured, and therefore falls within the first section of the Fourteenth Amendment. It is said that it unduly limits the liberty of adult persons in making contracts which concern only themselves, and cuts down the value of a class of property that often must be disposed of under contracts of the prohibited kind if it is to be disposed of to advantage, thus depriving persons of liberty and property without due process of law, and that it unjustifiably discriminates against property of that class, while other familiar objects of speculation, such as cotton or grain, are not touched, thus depriving persons of the equal protection of the laws.

It is true, no doubt, that neither a State legislature nor a State constitution can interfere arbitrarily with private business or transactions, and that the mere fact that an enactment purports to be for the protection of public safety, health or morals, is not conclusive upon the courts. . . . But general propositions do not carry us far. While the courts must exercise a judgment of their own, it by no means is true that every law is void which may seem to the judges who pass upon it excessive, unsuited to its ostensible end, or based upon conceptions of morality with which they disagree. Considerable latitude must be allowed for differences of view, as well as for possible peculiar conditions which this Court can know but imperfectly, if at all. Otherwise a constitution, instead of embodying only relatively fundamental rules of right, as generally understood by all English-speaking communities, would become the partisan of a particular set of ethical or economical opinions, which by no means are held *semper ubique et ab omnibus.*

Even if the provision before us should seem to us not to have been justified by the circumstances locally existing in California at the time when it was passed, it is shown by its adoption to have expressed a deep-seated conviction on the part of the people concerned as to what that policy required. Such a deep-seated conviction is entitled to great respect. If the State thinks that an admitted evil cannot be prevented except by prohibiting a calling or transaction not in itself necessarily objectionable, the courts cannot interfere, unless, in looking at the substance of the matter, they can see that it "is a clear, unmistakable infringement of rights secured by the fundamental law." *Booth* v. *Illinois,*

184 U. S. 425, 429. No court would declare a usury law unconstitutional, even if every member of it believed that Jeremy Bentham had said the last word on that subject, and had shown for all time that such laws did more harm than good. The Sunday laws, no doubt, would be sustained by a bench of judges, even if every one of them thought it superstitious to make any day holy. Or, to take cases where opinion has moved in the opposite direction, wagers may be declared illegal without the aid of statute, or lotteries forbidden by express enactment, although at an earlier day they were thought pardonable at least. The case would not be decided differently if lotteries had been lawful when the Fourteenth Amendment became law, as indeed they were in some civilized States. . . .

We cannot say that there might not be conditions of public delirium in which at least a temporary prohibition of sales on margins would be a salutary thing. Still less can we say that there might not be conditions in which it reasonably might be thought a salutary thing, even if we disagreed with the opinion. Of course, if a man can buy on margin he can launch into a much more extended venture than where he must pay the whole price at once. If he pays the whole price he gets the purchased article, whatever its worth may turn out to be. But if he buys stocks on margin he may put all his property into the venture, and being unable to keep his margins good if the stock market goes down, a slight fall leaves him penniless, with nothing to represent his outlay, except that he has had the chances of a bet. There is no doubt that purchases on margin may be and frequently are used as a means of gambling for a great gain or a loss of all one has. It is said that in California, when the constitution was adopted, the whole people were buying mining stocks in this way with the result of infinite disaster. . . . If at that time the provision of the constitution, instead of being put there, had been embodied in a temporary act, probably no one would have questioned it, and it would be hard to take a distinction solely on the ground of its more permanent form. Inserting the provision in the constitution showed, as we have said, the conviction of the people at large that prohibition was a proper means of stopping the evil. And as was said with regard to a prohibition of option contracts in *Booth* v. *Illinois,* 184 U. S. 425, 431, we are unwilling to declare the judgment to have been wholly without foundation.

With regard to the objection that this provision strikes at only some, not all, of the objects of possible speculation, it is enough to say that probably in California the evil sought to be stopped was confined in the main to stocks in corporations. California is a mining State, and mines offer the most striking temptations to people in a hurry to get rich. Mines generally are represented by stocks. Stock is convenient for purposes of speculation, because of the ease with which it is transferred from hand to hand, as well as for other reasons. If stopping the purchase and sale of stocks on margin would stop the gambling which it was desired to prevent, it was proper for the people of California to go no farther in what they forbade. The circumstances disclose a reasonable ground for the classification, and thus distinguish the case from *Connolly* v. *Union Sewer Pipe Co.,* 184 U. S. 540. We cannot say that treating stocks of corporations as a class subject to special restrictions was unjust discrimination or the denial of the equal protection of the laws.

Judgment affirmed.

[Justices Brewer and Peckham dissented without opinion.]

Otis v. *Parker*
187 U. S. 606

Railroads Afflicting Farmers with Weeds

(*Missouri, Kansas & Texas Ry. Co.* v. *May,* 1904)

This is an action to recover a penalty of twenty-five dollars, brought by the owner of a farm contiguous to the railroad of the plaintiff in error, on the ground that the latter has allowed Johnson grass to mature and go to seed upon its road. The penalty is given to contiguous owners by a Texas statute of 1901, ch. 117, directed solely against railroad companies for permitting such grass or Russian thistle to go to seed upon their right of way, subject, however, to the condition that the plaintiff has not done the same thing. The case is brought here on the ground that the statute is contrary to the Fourteenth Amendment of the Constitution of the United States.

It is admitted that Johnson grass is a menace to crops, that it is propagated only by seed, and that a general regulation of it for the protection of farming would be valid. It is admitted also that legislation may be directed against a class when any fair ground for the discrimination exists. But it is said that this particular subjection of railroad companies to a liability not imposed on other owners of land on which Johnson grass may grow, is so arbitrary as to amount to a denial of the equal protection of the laws. There is no dispute about general principles. The question is whether this case lies on one side or the other of a line which has to be worked out between cases differing only in degree. With regard to the manner in which such a question should be approached, it is obvious that the legislature is the only judge of the policy of a proposed discrimination. The principle is similar to that which is established with regard to a decision of Congress that certain means are necessary and proper to carry out one of its express powers. *McCulloch* v. *Maryland*, 4 Wheat. 316. When a State legislature has declared that in its opinion policy requires a certain measure, its action should not be disturbed by the courts under the Fourteenth Amendment, unless they can see clearly that there is no fair reason for the law that would not require with equal force its extension to others whom it leaves untouched.

Approaching the question in this way we feel unable to say that the law before us may not have been justified by local conditions. It would have been more obviously fair to extend the regulation at least to highways. But it may have been found, for all that we know, that the seed of the Johnson grass is dropped from the cars in such quantities as to cause special trouble. It may be that the neglected strips occupied by railroads afford a ground where noxious weeds especially flourish, and that whereas self-interest leads the owners of farms to keep down pests, the railroad companies have done nothing in a matter which concerns their neighbors only. Other reasons may be imagined. Great constitutional provisions must be administered with caution. Some play must be allowed for the joints of the machine, and it must be remembered that legislatures are ultimate guardians of the liberties and welfare of the people in quite as great a degree as the courts.

Judgment affirmed.

[Mr. Justice Brown dissented, saying that the discrimination against the railway seemed "purely arbitrary"; he pointed out that the desired result could be reached if the law applied generally. Justices White and McKenna also dissented.]

Missouri, Kansas & Texas Railway Co. v. *May*
194 U. S. 267

Assessed for Unwanted Improvements

(*Louisville & Nashville* v. *Barber Asphalt Co.*, 1905)

This is a proceeding under the Kentucky Statutes, § 2834, to enforce a lien upon a lot adjoining a part of Frankfort avenue, in Louisville, for grading, curbing and paving with asphalt the carriageway of that part of the avenue. The defendant, the plaintiff in error, pleaded that its only interest in the lot was a right of way for its main roadbed, and that neither the right of way nor the lot would or could get any benefit from the improvement, but on the contrary rather would be hurt by the increase of travel close to the defendant's tracks. On this ground it set up that any special assessment would deny to it the equal protection of the laws, contrary to the Fourteenth Amendment of the Constitution of the United States. It did not object to the absence of the parties having any reversionary interest, but defended against any special assessment on the lot. The answer was demurred to, judgment was rendered for the plaintiff, and this judgment was affirmed by the Kentucky Court of Appeals. 76 S. W. Rep. 1097. A writ of error was taken out, and the case was brought to this Court. It will be noticed that the case concerns only grading, curbing and paving, and what we shall have to say is confined to a case of that sort.

The State of Kentucky created this lien by a statute entitled "An act for the government of cities of the first class." Louisville is the only city of the first class at present in Kentucky, and the general principles of the act are taken verbatim from the part of the charter of Louisville which was considered and upheld by this Court in *Watson* v. *Nevin*, 128 U. S. 578. But we take the statute as a general prospective law, and not as a legislative adjudication concerning a particular place and a particular plan such as may have existed in *Spencer* v. *Merchant*, 125 U. S. 345, and as was thought to exist in *Smith* v. *Worcester*, 182 Massachusetts, 232, referred to at the argument.

The law provides in the case of original construction, such as this improvement was, that it shall be made at the exclusive cost of the adjoining owners, to be equally apportioned according to the number of feet owned by them. In the case of a square or subdivision of land bounded by principal streets, which the land including the defendant's lot was held to be, see *Cooper* v. *Nevin*, 90 Kentucky, 85; *Nevin* v. *Roach*, 86 Kentucky, 492, 499, the land is assessed half way back from the improvement to the next street. Act of 1898, c. 48. Ky. Stat. § 2833. A lien is imposed upon the land, and "the general council, or the courts in which suits may be pending, shall make all corrections, rules, and orders to do justice to all parties concerned." Section 2834. The principle of this mode of taxation seems to have been familiar in Kentucky for the better part of a hundred years. . . .

The argument for the plaintiff in error oscillates somewhat between the objections to the statute and the more specific grounds for contending that it cannot be applied constitutionally to the present case. So far as the former are concerned they are disposed of by the decisions of this Court. There is a look of logic when it is said that special assessments are founded on special benefits and that a law which makes it possible to assess beyond the amount of the special benefit attempts to rise above its source. But that mode of argument assumes an exactness in the premises which does not exist. The foundation of this familiar form of taxation is a question of theory. The amount of benefit which an improvement will confer upon particular land, indeed whether it is a benefit at all, is a matter of forecast and estimate. In its general aspects at least it is peculiarly a thing to be decided by those who make the law. The result of the supposed constitutional principle is simply to shift the burden to a somewhat larger taxing district, the municipality, and to disguise rather than to answer the theoretic doubt. It is dangerous to tie down legislatures too closely by judicial constructions not necessarily arising from the words of the Constitution. Particularly, as was intimated in *Spencer* v. *Merchant*, 125 U. S. 345, it is important for this Court to avoid extracting from the very general language of the Fourteenth Amendment a system of delusive exactness in order to destroy methods of taxation which were well known when that Amendment was adopted and which it is safe to say that no one then supposed would be disturbed. It now is established beyond permissible controversy that laws like the one before us are not contrary to the Constitution of the United States. . . .

A statute like the present manifestly might lead to the assessment of a particular lot for a sum larger than the value of the benefits to that lot. The whole cost of the improvement is distributed in proportion to area, and a particular area might receive no benefits at all, at least if its present and probable use be taken into account. If that possibility does not invalidate the act it would be surprising if the corresponding fact should invalidate an assessment. Upholding the act as embodying a principle generally fair and doing as nearly equal justice as can be expected seems to import that if a particular case of hardship arises under it in its natural and ordinary application, that hardship must be borne as one of the imperfections of human things. And this has been the implication of the cases. . . .

But in this case it is not necessary to stop with these general considerations. The plea plainly means that the improvement will not benefit the lot because the lot is occupied for railroad purposes and will continue so to be occupied. Compare *Chicago, Burlington & Quincy R. R.* v. *Chicago*, 166 U. S. 226, 257, 258. That, apart from the specific use to which this land is devoted,

ON LEGISLATIVE FREEDOM

land in a good-sized city generally will get a benefit from having the streets about it paved, and that this benefit generally will be more than the cost, are propositions which, as we already have implied, a legislature is warranted in adopting. But, if so, we are of opinion that the legislature is warranted in going one step further and saying that on the question of benefit or no benefit the land shall be considered simply in its general relations and apart from its particular use. See *Illinois Central R. R.* v. *Decatur,* 147 U. S. 190. On the question of benefits the present use is simply a prognostic, and the plea of prophecy. If an occupant could not escape by professing his desire for solitude and silence, the legislature may make a similar desire fortified by structures equally ineffective. It may say that it is enough that the land could be turned to purposes for which the paving would increase its value. Indeed, it is apparent that the prophecy in the answer cannot be regarded as absolute, even while the present use of the land continues—for no one can say that changes might not make a station desirable at this point; in which case the advantages of a paved street could not be denied. We are not called on to say that we think the assessment fair. But we are compelled to declare that it does not go beyond the bounds set by the Fourteenth Amendment of the Constitution of the United States.

Judgment affirmed.

[Justices White and Peckham dissented without opinion.]

Louisville & Nashville R. R. Co. v. *Barber Asphalt Paving Co.*
197 U. S. 430

Steps in Behalf of Education

(*Interstate Ry. Co.* v. *Massachusetts,* 1907)

This was a complaint against the plaintiff in error for refusing to sell tickets for the transportation of pupils to and from the public schools at one-half the regular fare charged by it, as required by Mass. Rev. Laws, c. 112, § 72. At the trial the Railway Company admitted the fact, but set up that the statute was unconstitutional, in that it denied to the company the equal protection of the laws and deprived it of its property without just compensation and without due process of law. In support of this defense it made an offer of proof which may be abridged into the propositions that the regular fare was five cents; that during the last fiscal year the actual and reasonable cost of transportation per passenger was 3.86 cents, or, including taxes, 4.10 cents; that pupils of the public schools formed a considerable part of the passengers carried by it, and that the one street railway expressly exempted by the law transported nearly one-half the passengers transported on street railways and received nearly one-half the revenue received for such transportation in the Commonwealth. The offer was stated to be made for the purpose of showing that the plaintiff in error could not comply with the statute without carrying passengers for less than a reasonable compensation and for less than cost. The offer of proof was rejected, and a ruling that the statute was repugnant to the Fourteenth Amendment was refused. The plaintiff in error excepted and, after a verdict of guilty and sentence, took the case to the Supreme Judicial Court.

187 Massachusetts, 436. That court overruled the exceptions, whereupon the plaintiff in error brought the case here.

This Court is of opinion that the decision below was right. A majority of the Court considers that the case is disposed of by the fact that the statute in question was in force when the plaintiff in error took its charter, and confines itself to that ground. The section of the Revised Laws (c. 112, § 72), was a continuation of St. 1900, c. 197. Rev. Laws, c. 226, § 2. . . . The Act of incorporation went into effect March 15, 1901. St. 1901, c. 159. By the latter Act the plaintiff in error was "subject to all the duties, liabilities and restrictions set forth in all general laws now or hereafter in force relating to street railway companies, except," &c., § 1. See also § 2. There is no doubt that, by the law as understood in Massachusetts, at least, the provisions of Rev. L. c. 112, § 72, St. 1900, c. 197, if they had been inserted in the charter in terms, would have bound the corporation, whether such requirements could be made constitutionally of an already existing corporation or not. The railroad company would have come into being and have consented to come into being subject to the liability and could not be heard to complain. . . .

If the charter, instead of writing out the requirements of Rev. L. 112, § 72, referred specifically to another document expressing them, and purported to incorporate it, of course the charter would have had the same effect as if it itself contained the words. If the document was identified, it would not matter what its own nature or effect might be, as the force given to it by reference and incorporation would be derived wholly from the charter. The document, therefore, might as well be an unconstitutional as a constitutional law. See *Commonwealth* v. *Melville*, 160 Massachusetts, 307, 308. But the contents of a document may be incorporated or adopted as well by generic as by specific reference, if only the purport of the adopting statute is clear. . . .

Speaking for myself alone, I think that there are considerations on the other side from the foregoing argument that make it unsafe not to discuss the validity of the regulation apart from the supposition that the plaintiff in error has accepted it. See *W. W. Cargill Co.* v. *Minnesota,* 180 U. S. 452, 468. Therefore I proceed to state my grounds for thinking the statute constitutional irrespective of any disabilities to object to its terms.

The discrimination alleged is the express exception from the Act of 1900 of the Boston Elevated Railway Company and the railways then owned, leased or operated by it. But, in the first place, this was a legislative adjudication concerning a specific road, as in *Wight* v. *Davidson,* 181 U. S. 371, not a general prospective classification as in *Martin* v. *District of Columbia,* 205 U. S. 135, 138. A general law must be judged by public facts, but a specific adjudication may depend upon many things not judicially known. Therefore the law must be sustained on this point unless the facts offered in evidence clearly show that the exception cannot be upheld. But the local facts are not before us, and it follows that we cannot say that the legislature could not have been justified in thus limiting its action. . . . In the next place, if the only ground were that the charter of the Elevated Railway contained a contract against the imposition of such a requirement, it would be attributing to the Fourteenth Amendment an excessively nice operation to say that the immunity of a single corporation prevented the passage of an otherwise desirable and wholesome law. It is unnecessary to consider what would be the effect on the statute by construction in Massachusetts if the exception could not be upheld. For, if in order to avoid the Scylla of unjustifiable class legislation, the law were read as universal, (see *Dunbar* v. *Boston & Providence R. R. Co.,* 181 Massachusetts, 383, 386) it might be thought by this Court to fall into the Charybdis of impairing the obligation of a contract with the elevated road, although that objection might perhaps be held not to be open to the plaintiff in error here. . . .

The objection that seems to me, as it seemed to the court below, most serious is that the statute unjustifiably appropriates

ON LEGISLATIVE FREEDOM

the property of the plaintiff in error. It is hard to say that street railway companies are not subjected to a loss. The conventional fare of five cents presumably is not more than a reasonable fare, and it is at least questionable whether street railway companies would be permitted to increase it on the ground of this burden. It is assumed by the statute in question that the ordinary fare may be charged for these children or some of them when not going to or from school. Whatever the fare, the statute fairly construed means that children going to or from school must be carried for half the sum that would be reasonable compensation for their carriage, if we looked only to the business aspect of the question. Moreover, while it may be true that in some cases rates or fares may be reduced to an unprofitable point in view of the business as a whole or upon special considerations, *Minneapolis & St. Louis R. R. Co.* v. *Minnesota*, 186 U. S. 256, 267, it is not enough to justify a general law like this, that the companies concerned still may be able to make a profit from other sources, for all that appears. . . .

Notwithstanding the foregoing considerations I hesitatingly agree with the State court that the requirement may be justified under what commonly is called the police power. The obverse way of stating this power in the sense in which I am using the phrase would be that constitutional rights like others are matters of degree and that the great constitutional provisions for the protection of property are not to be pushed to a logical extreme, but must be taken to permit the infliction of some fractional and relatively small losses without compensation, for some at least of the purposes of wholesome legislation. . . .

If the Fourteenth Amendment is not to be a greater hamper upon the established practices of the States in common with other governments than I think was intended, they must be allowed a certain latitude in the minor adjustments of life, even though by their action the burdens of a part of the community are some-

[17]

what increased. The traditions and habits of centuries were not intended to be overthrown when that amendment was passed. Education is one of the purposes for which what is called the police power may be exercised. . . . Massachusetts always has recognized it as one of the first objects of public care. It does not follow that it would be equally in accord with the conceptions at the base of our constitutional law to confer equal favors upon doctors, or workingmen, or people who could afford to buy 1000-mile tickets. Structural habits count for as much as logic in drawing the line. And, to return to the taking of property, the aspect in which I am considering the case, general taxation to maintain public schools is an appropriation of property to a use in which the taxpayer may have no private interest, and, it may be, against his will. It has been condemned by some theorists on that ground. Yet no one denies its constitutionality. People are accustomed to it and accept it without doubt. The present requirement is not different in fundamental principle, although the tax is paid in kind and falls only on the class capable of paying that kind of tax—a class of *quasi*-public corporations specially subject to legislative control.

Thus the question narrows itself to the magnitude of the burden imposed—to whether the tax is so great as to exceed the limits of police power. Looking at the law without regard to its special operation I should hesitate to assume that its total effect, direct and indirect, upon the roads outside of Boston amounted to a more serious burden than a change in the law of nuisance, for example, might be. See further, *Williams* v. *Parker*, 188 U. S. 491. Turning to the specific effect, the offer of proof was cautious. It was simply that a "considerable percentage" of the passengers carried by the company consisted of pupils of the public schools. This might be true without the burden becoming serious. I am not prepared to overrule the decision of the legislature and of the highest court of Massachusetts that the requirement is reasonable under the conditions existing there, upon evidence that goes no higher than this. It is not enough that a statute goes to the verge of constitutional power. We must be able to see clearly that it goes beyond that power. In case of real doubt a law must be sustained.

Mr. Justice Harlan is of opinion that the constitutionality of the Act of 1900 is necessarily involved in the determination of this case. He thinks the Act is not liable to the objection that it denies to the railway company the equal protection of the laws. Nor does he think it can be held, upon any showing made by this record, to be unconstitutional as depriving the plaintiff in error of its property without due process of law. Upon these grounds alone, and independent of any other question discussed, he joins in a judgment of affirmance.

Judgment affirmed.

Interstate Consolidated Street Railway Co.
v. Commonwealth of Massachusetts
207 U. S. 79

Obligations of the Banking Business

(Noble State Bank v. Haskell, 1911)

THIS is a proceeding against the Governor of the State of Oklahoma and other officials who constitute the State Banking Board, to prevent them from levying and collecting an assessment from the plaintiff under an Act approved December 17, 1907. This Act creates the Board and directs it to levy upon every bank existing under the laws of the State an assessment of one percent of the bank's average daily deposits, with certain deductions, for the purpose of creating a Depositors' Guaranty Fund. There are provisos for keeping up the fund, and by an Act passed March 11, 1909, since the suit was begun, the assessment is to be five percent. The purpose of the fund is shown by its name. It is to secure the full repayment of deposits. When a bank becomes insolvent and goes into the hands of the Bank Commissioner, if its cash immediately available is not enough to pay depositors in full, the Banking Board is to draw from the Depositors' Guaranty Fund (and from additional assessments if required) the amount needed to make up the deficiency. A lien is reserved upon the assets of the failing bank to make good the sum thus taken from the fund. The plaintiff says that it is solvent and does not want the help of the Guaranty Fund, and that it cannot be called upon to contribute toward securing or paying the depositors in other banks consistently with Article I, § 10, and the Fourteenth Amendment of the Constitution of the United States. The petition was dismissed on demurrer by the Supreme Court of the State. . . .

ON LEGISLATIVE FREEDOM

The reference to Article I, § 10, does not strengthen the plaintiff's bill. The only contract that it relies upon is its charter. That is subject to alteration or repeal, as usual, so that the obligation hardly could be said to be impaired by the Act of 1907 before us, unless that statute deprives the plaintiff of liberty or property without due process of law. See *Sherman* v. *Smith*, 1 Black, 587, Whether it does so or not is the only question in the case.

In answering that question we must be cautious about pressing the broad words of the Fourteenth Amendment to a drily logical extreme. Many laws which it would be vain to ask the Court to overthrow could be shown, easily enough, to transgress a scholastic interpretation of one or another of the great guaranties in the Bill of Rights. They more or less limit the liberty of the individual or they diminish property to a certain extent. We have few scientifically certain criteria of legislation, and as it often is difficult to mark the line where what is called the police power of the States is limited by the Constitution of the United States, judges should be slow to read into the latter a *nolumus mutare* as against the law-making power

The substance of the plaintiff's argument is that the assessment takes private property for private use without compensation. And while we should assume that the plaintiff would retain a reversionary interest in its contribution to the fund so as to be entitled to a return of what remained of it if the purpose were given up (see *Receiver of Danby Bank* v. *State Treasurer*, 39 Vermont, 92, 98), still there is no denying that by this law a portion of its property might be taken without return to pay debts of a failing rival in business. Nevertheless, notwithstanding the logical form of the objection, there are more powerful considerations on the other side. In the first place it is established by a series of cases that an ulterior public advantage may justify a comparatively insignificant taking of private property for what, in its immediate purpose, is a private use. . . . And in the next, it would seem that there may be other cases beside the every day one of taxation, in which the share of each party in the benefit of a scheme of mutual protection is sufficient compensation for a correlative burden that it is compelled to assume. See *Ohio Oil Co. v. Indiana*, 177 U. S. 190. At least, if we have a case within the reasonable exercise of the police power as above explained, no more need be said.

It may be said in a general way that the police power extends to all the great public needs. . . . It may be put forth in aid of what is sanctioned by usage, or held by the prevailing morality or strong and preponderant opinion to be greatly and immediately necessary to the public welfare. Among matters of that sort probably few would doubt that both usage and preponderant opinion give their sanction to enforcing the primary conditions of successful commerce. One of those conditions at the present time is the possibility of payment by checks drawn against bank deposits, to such an extent do checks replace currency in daily business. If then the legislature of the State thinks that the public welfare requires the measure under consideration, analogy and principle are in favor of the power to enact it. Even the primary object of the required assessment is not a private benefit as it was in the cases above cited of a ditch for irrigation or a railway to a mine, but it is to make the currency of checks secure, and by the same stroke to make safe the almost compulsory resort of depositors to banks as the only available means of keeping money on hand. The priority of claim given to depositors is incidental to the same object and is justified in the same way. The power to restrict liberty by fixing a minimum of capital required of those who would engage in banking is not denied. The power to restrict investments to securities regarded as relatively safe seems equally plain. It has been held, we do not doubt rightly, that inspections may be required and the cost thrown on the bank. See *Charlotte, Columbia & Augusta R. R. Co. v. Gibbes*, 142 U. S. 386. The power to compel, beforehand, cooperation, and thus, it is believed, to make a failure unlikely

ON LEGISLATIVE FREEDOM

and a general panic almost impossible, must be recognized, if government is to do its proper work, unless we can say that the means have no reasonable relation to the end. . . . So far is that from being the case that the device is a familiar one. It was adopted by some States the better part of a century ago, and seems never to have been questioned until now. . . . Recent cases going not less far are *Lemieux* v. *Young*, 211 U. S. 489, 496. *Kidd, Dater & Price Co.*, v. *Musselman Grocer Co.*, 217 U. S. 461.

It is asked whether the State could require all corporations or all grocers to help to guarantee each other's solvency, and where we are going to draw the line. But the last is a futile question, and we will answer the others when they arise. With regard to the police power, as elsewhere in the law, lines are pricked out by the gradual approach and contact of decisions on the opposing sides. . . . It will serve as a datum on this side, that in our opinion the statute before us is well within the State's constitutional power, while the use of the public credit on a large scale to help individuals in business has been held to be beyond the line. . . .

The question that we have decided is not much helped by propounding the further one, whether the right to engage in banking is or can be made a franchise. But as the latter question has some bearing on the former and as it will have to be considered in the following cases, if not here, we will dispose of it now. It is not answered by citing authorities for the existence of the right at common law. There are many things that a man might do at common law that the States may forbid. He might embezzle until a statute cut down his liberty. We cannot say that the public interests to which we have adverted, and others, are not sufficient to warrant the State in taking the whole business of banking under its control. On the contrary we are of opinion that it may go on from regulation to prohibition except upon such conditions as it may prescribe. In short, when the Oklahoma legislature declares by implication that free banking is a public danger, and that incorporation, inspection and the above-described cooperation are necessary safeguards, this Court certainly cannot say that it is wrong. . . . Some further details might be mentioned, but we deem them unnecessary. Of course objections under the State constitution are not open here.

Judgment affirmed.

LEAVE to file application for rehearing is asked in this case. We see no reason to grant it, but, as the judgment delivered [above] seems to have conveyed a wrong impression of the opinion of the Court in some details, we add a few words to what was said when the case was decided. We fully understand the practical importance of the question and the very powerful argument that can be made against the wisdom of the legislation, but on that point we have nothing to say, as it is not our concern. *Clark* v. *Nash* 198 U. S. 361, *Strickley* v. *Highland Boy Mining Co.,* 200 U. S. 527, etc., were cited to establish, not that property might be taken for a private use, but that among the public uses for which it might be taken were some which, if looked at only in their immediate aspect, according to the proximate effect of the taking, might seem to be private. This case, in our opinion, is of that sort. The analysis of the police power, whether correct or not, was intended to indicate an interpretation of what has taken place in the past, not to give a new or wider scope to the power. The propositions with regard to it, however, in any form, are rather in the nature of preliminaries. For in this case there is no out and out unconditional taking at all. The payment can be avoided by going out of the banking business, and is required only as a condition for keeping on, from corporations created by the State. We have given what we deem sufficient reasons for holding that such a condition may be imposed.

Leave to file petition denied.

Noble State Bank v. *Haskell*
219 U. S. 104 and 575

Discouraging Chinese Hand Laundries

(*Quong Wing* v. *Kirkendall*, 1912)

THIS is an action to recover ten dollars paid under duress and protest for a license to do hand laundry work. The plaintiff got judgment in the court of first instance, but this judgment was reversed by the Supreme Court of the State. 39 Montana, 64. The law under which the fee was exacted imposed the payment upon all persons engaged in laundry business other than the steam laundry business, with a proviso that it should not apply to women so engaged where not more than two women were employed. . . . The only question is whether this is an unconstitutional discrimination depriving the plaintiff of the equal protection of the laws. United States Constitution, Amendment XIV.

The case was argued upon the discrimination between the instrumentalities employed in the same business and that between men and women. One like the former was held bad in *In re Yot Sang*, 75 Fed. Rep. 983, and while the latter was spoken of by the Supreme Court of the State as an exemption of one or two women, it is to be observed that in 1900 the census showed more women than men engaged in hand laundry work in that State. Nevertheless we agree with the Supreme Court of the State so far as these grounds are concerned. A State does not deny the equal protection of the laws merely by adjusting its revenue laws and taxing system in such a way as to favor certain industries or forms of industry. Like the United States, although with more restriction and in less degree, a State may carry out a policy, even a policy with which we might disagree. . . . It may make discriminations, if founded on distinctions that we cannot pronounce unreasonable and purely arbitrary, as was illustrated in *American Sugar Refining Co.* v. *Louisiana,* 179 U. S. 89, 92, 95; *Williams* v. *Fears,* 179 U. S. 270, 276; *W. W. Cargill Co.* v. *Minnesota,* 180 U. S. 452, 469. It may favor or discourage the liquor traffic, or trusts. The criminal law is a whole body of policy on which States may and do differ. If the State sees fit to encourage steam laundries and discourage hand laundries that is its own affair. And if again it finds a ground of distinction in sex, that is not without precedent. It has been recognized with regard to hours of work. *Muller* v. *Oregon,* 208 U. S. 412. It is recognized in the respective rights of husband and wife in land during life, in the inheritance after the death of the spouse. Often it is expressed in the time fixed for coming of age. If Montana deems it advisable to put a lighter burden upon women than upon men with regard to employment that our people commonly regard as more appropriate for the former, the Fourteenth Amendment does not interfere by creating a fictitious equality where there is a real difference. The particular points at which that difference shall be emphasized by legislation are largely in the power of the State.

Another difficulty suggested by the statute is that it is impossible not to ask whether it is not aimed at the Chinese; which would be a discrimination that the Constitution does not allow. . . . It is a matter of common observation that hand laundry work is a widespread occupation of Chinamen in this country while on the other hand it is so rare to see men of our race engaged in it that many of us would be unable to say that they ever had observed a case. But this ground of objection was not urged and rather was disclaimed when it was mentioned from the Bench at the argument. It may or may not be that if the facts were called to our attention in a proper way the objection would prove to be real. But even if when called to our attention the facts should be taken notice of judicially, whether because they are only the premise for a general proposition of law, *Prentis v. Atlantic Coast Line Co.,* 211 U. S. 210, 227; *South Ottawa v. Perkins,* 94 U. S. 260; *Telfair v. Stead,* 2 Cranch, 407, 418, or for any other reason, still there are many things that courts would notice if brought before them that beforehand they do not know. It rests with counsel to take the proper steps, and if they deliberately omit them, we do not feel called upon to institute inquiries on our own account. Laws frequently are enforced which the Court recognizes as possibly or probably invalid if attacked by a different interest or in a different way. Therefore without prejudice to the question that we have suggested, when it shall be raised, we must conclude that so far as the present case is concerned the judgment must be affirmed.

Judgment affirmed.

[Mr. Justice Hughes concurred in the result. Mr. Justice Lamar dissented from the conclusions in the first part of the opinion on the ground that the statute was a revenue measure making an arbitrary discrimination "founded on the personal attributes of those engaged in the same occupation."]

Quong Wing v. Kirkendall, Treasurer of Lewis and Clark County, Montana
223 U. S. 59

Destroying Local Competition

(*Central Lumber Co.* v. *South Dakota*, 1912)

The plaintiff in error was found guilty of unfair discrimination under Session Laws of South Dakota for 1907, c. 131, and was sentenced to a fine of two hundred dollars and costs. It objected in due form that the statute was contrary to the Fourteenth Amendment, but on appeal the judgment of the trial court was sustained. 24 So. Dak. 136. By the statute anyone "Engaged in the production, manufacture or distribution of any commodity in general use, that intentionally, for the purpose of destroying the competition of any regular established dealer in such commodity, or to prevent the competition of any person who in good faith intends and attempts to become such dealer, shall discriminate between different sections, communities, or cities of this state, by selling such commodity at a lower rate in one section . . . than such person . . . charges for such commodity in another section, . . . after equalizing the distance from the point of production," &c., shall be guilty of the crime and liable to the fine.

The subject-matter, like the rest of the criminal law, is under the control of the legislature of South Dakota, by virtue of its general powers, unless the statute conflicts as alleged with the Constitution of the United States. The grounds on which it is said to do so are that it denies the equal protection of the laws, because it affects the conduct of only a particular class— those selling goods in two places in the State—and is intended for the protection of only a particular class—regular established dealers; and also because it unreasonably limits the liberty of people to make such bargains as they like.

On the first of these points it is said that an indefensible classification may be disguised in the form of a description of the acts constituting the offense, and it is urged that to punish selling goods in one place lower than at another in effect is to select the class of dealers that have two places of business for a special liability, and in real fact is a blow aimed at those who have several lumber yards along a line of railroad, in the interest of independent dealers. All competition, it is added, imports an attempt to destroy or prevent the competition of rivals, and there is no difference in principle between the prohibited act and the ordinary efforts of traders at a single place. The premises may be conceded without accepting the conclusion that this is an unconstitutional discrimination. If the legislature shares the now prevailing belief as to what is public policy and finds that a particular instrument of trade war is being used against that policy in certain cases, it may direct its law against what it deems the evil as it actually exists without covering the whole field of possible abuses, and it may do so none the less that the forbidden act does not differ in kind from those that are allowed. . . .

That is not the arbitrary selection that is condemned in such cases as *Southern Ry. Co. v. Greene,* 216 U. S. 400. The Fourteenth Amendment does not prohibit legislation special in character. . . . It does not prohibit a State from carrying out a policy that cannot be pronounced purely arbitrary, by taxation or penal laws. . . . If a class is deemed to present a conspicuous example of what the legislature seeks to prevent, the Fourteenth Amendment allows it to be dealt with although otherwise and merely logically not distinguishable from others not embraced in the law. . . . We must assume that the legislature of South Dakota considered that people selling in two places made the prohibited use of their opportunities and that such use was harmful, although the usual efforts of competitors were desired. It might have been argued to the legislature with more force than it can be to us that recoupment in one place of losses in another is merely an instance of financial ability to compete. If the legislature thought that that particular manifestation of ability usually came from great corporations whose power it deemed excessive and for that reason did more harm than good in their State, and that there was no other case of frequent occurrence where the same could be said, we cannot review their economics or their facts. That the law embodies a widespread conviction appears from the decisions in other States. . . .

What we have said makes it unnecessary to add much on the second point, if open, that the law is made in favor of regular established dealers—but the short answer is simply to read the law. It extends on its face also to those who intend to become such dealers. If it saw fit not to grant the same degree of protection to parties making a transitory incursion into the business, we see no objection. But the Supreme Court says that the statute is aimed at preventing the creation of a monopoly by means likely to be employed, and certainly we should read the law as having in view ultimately the benefit of buyers of the goods.

Finally, as to the statute's depriving the plaintiff in error of its liberty because it forbids a certain class of dealings, we think it enough to say that as the law does not otherwise encounter the Fourteenth Amendment, it is not to be disturbed on this ground. The matter has been discussed so often in this Court that we simply refer to *Chicago, Burlington & Quincy R. R. Co.* v *McGuire,* 219 U. S. 549, 567, 568, and the cases there cited to illustrate how much power is left in the States. See also *Granada Lumber Co.* v. *Mississippi,* 217 U. S. 433, 442. *Lemieux* v. *Young,* 211 U. S. 489, 496. *Otis* v. *Parker,* 187 U. S. 606, 609.

Judgment affirmed.

Central Lumber Co. v. *State of South Dakota*
226 U. S. 157

Water Power a Public Use

(*Mt. Vernon Cotton Co.* v. *Alabama Power Co.*, 1916)

THIS is a petition for a writ of prohibition to prevent the Probate Court of Tallapoosa County from taking jurisdiction of condemnation proceedings instituted by the Alabama Interstate Power Company to take land, water and water rights belonging to the petitioner. An alternative writ was issued but the Supreme Court of the State ordered it to be quashed and the writ to be dismissed. 186 Alabama, 622. The grounds of the petition are that the statutes of Alabama do not authorize the proceedings and that if they do they contravene the Fourteenth Amendment of the Constitution of the United States. The Supreme Court upheld the statutes and the jurisdiction of the Probate Court, but left the sufficiency of the petition for condemnation, whether every subject of which condemnation was sought could be condemned, and the ability of the Power Company to prove its case, to be determined in the condemnation case. There is a motion to dismiss the writ of error on the ground that the present decision is not final because it does not determine the merits; but this motion must be denied. Prohibition is a distinct suit and the judgment finally disposing of it is a final judgment within the meaning of the Judicial Code, Act of March 3, 1911, c. 231, § 237, 36 Stat. 1087, 1156, under the statutes of Alabama, and by the common law. Code of 1907, §§ 4864-4867, 4872. . . . The fact that it does not decide the merits of the principal suit is immaterial. It is not devoted to that point, but only to the preliminary question of the jurisdiction of the court in which that suit is brought.

The argument in favor of granting the writ presented by the plaintiffs in error, is addressed in great part to matters with which this Court has no concern. It is argued that the Probate Court could not be given jurisdiction of the condemnation proceedings consistently with the constitution of the State; that under the same instrument the State legislature had no power to pass the condemnation acts, that the petition was insufficient to found jurisdiction of the case and was defective in various ways; that a part of the condemnation sought was bad under the statutes in any event; and that certain words in the Alabama Code under which it is sought to condemn rights below the contemplated dam of the Power Company, never were properly enacted by the legislature of the State. All these points must be taken to have been decided adversely to the plaintiff in error by the Supreme Court of Alabama so far as they might furnish grounds for prohibition, and they are all matters on which this Court follows the Supreme Court of the State.

The principal argument presented that is open here, is that the purpose of the condemnation is not a public one. The purpose of the Power Company's incorporation and that for which it seeks to condemn property of the plaintiff in error is to manufacture, supply, and sell to the public, power produced by water as a motive force. In the organic relations of modern society it may sometimes be hard to draw the line that is supposed to limit the authority of the legislature to exercise or delegate the power of eminent domain. But to gather the streams from waste and to draw from them energy, labor without brains, and so to save mankind from toil that it can be spared, is to supply what, next to intellect, is the very foundation of all our achievements and all our welfare. If that purpose is not public we should be at a loss to say what is. The inadequacy of use by the general public as a universal test is established. . . . The respect due to the judgment of the State would have great weight if there were a doubt. . . . But there is none. . . . We perceive no ground for the distinction attempted between the taking of rights below the contemplated dam, such as these are, and those above. Compensation is provided for according to rules that the court below declares to be well settled and that appear to be adequate. The details as to what may be taken and what not under the statutes and petition are not open here. Before a corporation can condemn rights it is required to have obtained, by other means, at least an acre on each side of the stream for a dam site, and this is supposed to show that the use is not public. It is only a reasonable precaution to insure good faith. A hardly consistent argument is that the dam should be built before the necessity of taking waters below can be shown. But a plan may show the necessity beforehand. All that we decide is that no general objection based on these grounds affects the jurisdiction of the Probate Court or the constitutionality of the act.

Certain exceptions from the powers conferred, such as private residences, lands of other corporations having similar powers, and cotton factories, subject to the taking of the excess of water over that in actual use or capable of use at normal stages of the stream, are too plainly reasonable so far as they come in question here to need justification. Discrimination is alleged but not argued. We see nothing that runs against the Fourteenth Amendment. The right given to take possession before the compensation is finally determined also is not argued. . . . Without further discussion of the minutiae, we are of opinion that the decision of the Supreme Court of Alabama upon the questions arising under the Constitution of the United States was correct.

Judgment affirmed.

Mt. Vernon Cotton Co. v. Alabama Interstate Power Co.
240 U. S. 30

A Discriminatory Attempt to Check Monopoly

(*McFarland* v. *American Sugar Co.*, 1916)

This is a bill in equity brought by a New Jersey corporation, the appellee, against the Inspector of Sugar Refining, the Governor and the Attorney General of Louisiana, to prevent the enforcement of Act No. 10 of the Extra Session of the General Assembly of that State for 1915. The grounds of relief are the commerce clause and the Fourteenth Amendment of the Constitution of the United States.

The plaintiff was granted a preliminary injunction by three judges in the District Court and the defendants appealed. . . .

A summary of the statute is as follows: The business of refining sugar is declared to be impressed with a public interest "by reason of the nature and by reason of the monopolization thereof," and on that footing the regulations are made. After providing for elaborate reports and inspection of books by the Inspector, the Act imposes for the benefit of the Inspection Fund a tax of one-half cent for every three hundred and fifty pounds of granulated sugar made. It then makes it unlawful to buy sugar on an *ex parte* test of quality, &c., and proceeds to authorize the Inspector to make such reasonable regulations not only concerning that, but affecting any branch of the business of sugar refining, as he may deem proper and as may be conducive to the public interest, and to the prevention of monopoly in the business or to the protection of the public from its consequences. Then come the provisions chiefly in issue here. By § 7 "any person engaged in the business of refining sugar within this State who shall systematically pay in Louisiana a less price for sugar than he pays in any other State shall be *prima facie* presumed to be a party to a monopoly or combination or conspiracy in restraint of trade and commerce, and upon conviction thereof shall be subject to a fine of five hundred dollars a day for the period during which he is adjudged to have done so"; his license to do business in the State is to be revoked, and any foreign corporation (such as the plaintiff is) is to be ousted from the State and its property sold. If irreparable injury to the public interest is shown in such a case the court may appoint a receiver at any stage of the proceedings, &c. By § 8 if shown by affidavit or otherwise either *in limine* or after trial that any refinery has been closed or kept idle for more than one year it shall be presumed to have been done for the purpose of violating this Act or the laws against monopoly, &c., and if the counter evidence does not rebut the presumption the court shall order the owner to sell the refinery within six months and if that is not done shall appoint a receiver to do it within twelve months. In computing the year of idleness any plant shall be treated as idle that has not been operating *bona fide*. By § 9 in suits for ouster, &c., upon showing by the State that the monopoly, &c., are detrimental to the public welfare, an injunction may be issued or a receiver appointed, after a hearing, subject to an appeal returnable within five days to be determined within forty days, &c. By § 10 a fine of from fifty to twenty-five hundred dollars a day is imposed for violations of the Act not otherwise provided for or of any of the regulations promulgated by the Inspector. By § 11, in suits under the Act, books, letters and other documents, "or apparent copies thereof," of the defendant shall be given effect as being what they purport to be and "as establishing the facts carried on their face" unless sufficiently rebutted, upon proof of their having been in the possession or control of the defendant; and any report of any legislative committee of the State, or of the Senate or House of Representatives of the United States, or of any bureau, department, or commission acting under the authority either of the State or of the Senate or the House of Representatives of the United States, and the records of any court of any State, or of the United States are made *prima facie* evidence of the facts set forth therein, subject to rebuttal. In conclusion, by § 15 the business of refining sugar is defined to be "that of any concern that buys and refines raw or other sugar exclusively, or that refines raw or other sugar from sugar taken on toll, or that buys or refines more raw or other sugar than the aggregate of the sugar produced by it from cane grown and purchased by it."

Besides the allegations that bring the plaintiff within the purview of the Act, the claims of the protection of the Constitution, and the invocation of the principle of *Ex parte Young*, 209 U. S. 123, for equitable relief, the bill sets forth some facts that throw special light upon the case. First, for the bearing of § 8, it shows that formerly the plaintiff purchased a consolidated refinery called the Louisiana Refinery, increased its capacity to 2,500,000 pounds daily and worked it until 1909. It then built at the cost of about six million dollars a new refinery at Chalmette with a daily melting capacity of 3,000,000 pounds since increased to 3,500,000. It then closed the Louisiana Refinery as it could not distribute from New Orleans more refined sugar than could be made at Chalmette. The machinery of the Louisiana Refinery is comparatively antiquated and could not be operated economically, although in case of the destruction of the Chalmette plant it could be used as a substitute at considerable expense and after some delay.

As to the presumption created from the systematic paying in Louisiana a less price for sugar than is paid in any other State, the bill alleges that the plaintiff purchases on an average less than one-half of the Louisiana sugar crop, of which half over a third is shipped as bought, to the plaintiff's northern refineries, so that not much over thirty percent is melted at Chalmette. In fact only a comparatively small portion of the plaintiff's meltings in Louisiana is of sugar produced in Louisiana, the remainder having been imported. The chief port for the receipt of raw sugar imported is New York, at or near which there are seven large refineries now in operation. The Louisiana sugar customarily has been brought on the market in November and December, during which months it is pressed for sale in amounts far in excess of the requirements of all the refineries in the State. Purchasers therefore had either to ship a part north or to store it with consequent loss from deterioration and in weight, interest, and cost of storage and insurance, and at the risk of a decline in the market. These elements necessarily affect the price, which cannot be higher than that in the ultimate market less the cost of transportation, and which has been approximately that. Furthermore the period of storage is a time when the market for raw sugar generally declines and the price of refined sugar follows that of raw to the refiner's loss.

Formerly a large part of the sugar manufactured in Louisiana by the plaintiff was sold in the Middle West and in Minnesota, Iowa, the Dakotas, &c., and it was to meet that market that the Chalmette refinery was built. But the great and rapid increase in the production of beet sugar, which now forms one-sixth of all the sugar consumed in the United States and is sold at prices below those of cane sugar, has driven the plaintiff out of those markets to a great extent. The result frequently has been that the plaintiff has derived little or no advantage from the purchase of Louisiana sugar even when bought at a less price than that in New York on the same day.

The bill also shows fully that the plaintiff melts solely on its own account so that its only contact with the public is as a buyer of raw and a seller of refined sugar and its business is affected with a public interest not otherwise than as any other business is, according to its importance and size. It also shows that much the greater part of its Chalmette commerce both in purchase and sale is foreign or among the States. There are other allegations besides those that we have summed up but enough has been stated to disclose the plaintiff's case.

The answer alleges that the plaintiff is a monopoly and combination in restraint of trade in buying, refining and selling sugar throughout the United States and completely controls the sugar trade in Louisiana and sets forth a long series of letters thought to show efforts to obtain and keep such control. It obliquely intimates that the plaintiff can fix prices on occasion even in the New York market, admitted to be the ruling one in the United States. It alleges that suits have been brought against the plaintiff by sugar planters under the Sherman Act, for a total of near $200,000,000, and that after the exposure of the plaintiff's criminality in a suit by the United States that seems to have come to nothing, this law was passed. All of the foregoing, the main portion of the answer, is offered as ground for denying to the plaintiff any equitable relief.

In the alternative, if the plaintiff has a standing in equity, the answer denies the plaintiff's explanation of the idleness of the Louisiana Refinery, and avers that the statement that it buys less than half the Louisiana crop is deceptive, and that it buys seventy percent of the raw sugar sold to refiners. It alleges that the shipping of raw sugar north is due to artificial conditions created by the plaintiff and that but for them the whole would be "handled locally." It also alleges that the difference between the Louisiana and the New York price has been made less by the plaintiff since 1911, in order to prevent a repetition of the one successful combination made by the planters. Finally it alleges that the shipments to New York arrive when there is no sugar on hand or when the first sugar from Cuba is coming in, and enable the plaintiff to influence downward the price of the Cuban sugar that it needs. Most of the allegations of the bill are denied, and it is said that the rush to sell in November and December would have found a market but for the plaintiff's wrongful deeds.

The answer is signed by the Attorney General of the State; and if he were authorized to interpret the meaning of the other voice of the State heard in Act No. 10, would seem to import that the latter was a bill of pains and penalties disguised in general words. For the first division of the answer shows that the plaintiff is the only one to whom the Act could apply and that the statute was passed in view of the plaintiff's conduct, to meet it. It is upon the assumption of the latter fact that the argument is pressed that the plaintiff has no standing in equity since it made the legislation necessary. If the connection were admitted it would be so much the worse for the constitutionality of the Act. We deem it enough to say that neither that supposed connection nor the general intimation of the plaintiff's wickedness in the answer deprive it of its constitutional rights or prevent it from asserting them in the only practicable and adequate way.

The statute bristles with severities that touch the plaintiff alone, and raises many questions that would have to be answered before it could be sustained. We deem it sufficient to refer to those that were mentioned by the District Court; a classification which, if it does not confine itself to the American Sugar Refinery, at least is arbitrary beyond possible justice,—and a creation of presumptions and special powers against it that can have no foundation except the intent to destroy. As to the classification, if a powerful rival of the plaintiff should do no refining within the State it might systematically pay a less price for sugar in Louisiana than it paid elsewhere with none of the consequences attached to doing so in the plaintiff's case. So of anyone who purchases but does not refine. So of any concern that does not buy and refine more sugar "than the aggregate of the sugar produced by it from cane grown and purchased by it" as easily might happen with a combination of planters such as the answer gives us to understand has been attempted heretofore.

As to the presumptions, of course the legislature may go a good way in raising one or in changing the burden of proof, but there are limits. It is "essential that there shall be some rational connection between the fact proved and the ultimate fact presumed, and that the inference of one fact from proof of another shall not be so unreasonable as to be a purely arbitrary mandate." *Mobile, Jackson & Kansas City R. R.* v. *Turnipseed,* 219 U. S. 35, 43. The presumption created here has no relation in experience to general facts. It has no foundation except with tacit reference to the plaintiff. But it is not within the province of a legislature to declare an individual guilty or presumptively guilty of a crime. If the statute had said what it was argued that it means, that the plaintiff's business was affected with a public interest by reason of the plaintiff's monopolizing it and that therefore the plaintiff should be *prima facie* presumed guilty upon proof that it was carrying on business as it does, we suppose that no one would contend that the plaintiff was given the equal protection of the laws. We agree with the court below that the Act must fall as a whole, as it falls in the sections without which there is no reason to suppose that it would have been passed.

Decree affirmed.

McFarland, Supervisor of Public Accounts of Louisiana
v. *American Sugar Refining Co.*
241 U. S. 79

Shifting the Burden of Accidents

(*Arizona Employers' Liability Cases*, 1919, *Concurring Opinion*)

THE plaintiff (defendant in error) was employed in the defendant's mine, was hurt in the eye in consequence of opening a compressed air valve and brought the present suit. The injury was found to have been due to risks inherent to the business and so was within the Employers' Liability Law of Arizona, Rev. Stats. 1913, Title 14, c. 6. By that law as construed the employer is liable to damages for injuries due to such risks in specified hazardous employments when guilty of no negligence. Par. 3158. There was a verdict for the plaintiff, judgment was affirmed by the Supreme Court of the State, 19 Arizona, 151, and the case comes here on the single question whether, consistently with the Fourteenth Amendment, such liability can be imposed. It is taken to exclude "speculative, exemplary and punitive damages," but to include all loss to the employee caused by the accident, not merely in the way of earning capacity, but of disfigurement and bodily or mental pain. See *Arizona Copper Co.* v. *Burciaga*, 177 Pac. Rep. 29, 33.

There is some argument made for the general proposition that immunity from liability when not in fault is a right inherent in free government and the *obiter dicta* of Mr. Justice Miller in *Citizens' Savings & Loan Association* v. *Topeka*, 20 Wall. 655 are referred to. But if it is thought to be public policy to put certain voluntary conduct at the peril of those pursuing it, whether in the interest of safety or upon economic or other grounds, I know of nothing to hinder. A man employs a servant at the peril of what that servant may do in the course of his employment and there is nothing in the Constitution to limit the principle to that instance. . . . There are cases in which even the criminal law requires a man to know facts at his peril. Indeed, the criterion which is thought to be free from constitutional objection, the criterion of fault, is the application of an external standard, the conduct of a prudent man in the known circumstances, that is, in doubtful cases, the opinion of the jury, which the defendant has to satisfy at his peril and which he may miss after giving the matter his best thought. . . . Without further amplification so much may be taken to be established by the decisions. . . .

I do not perceive how the validity of the law is affected by the fact that the employee is a party to the venture. There is no more certain way of securing attention to the safety of the men, an unquestionably constitutional object of legislation, than by holding the employer liable for accidents. Like the crimes to which I have referred they probably will happen a good deal less often when the employer knows that he must answer for them if they do. I pass, therefore, to the other objection urged and most strongly pressed. It is that the damages are governed by the rules governing in action of tort—that is, as we have said, that they may include disfigurement and bodily or mental pain. Natural observations are made on the tendency of juries when such elements are allowed. But if it is proper to allow them of course no objection can be founded on the supposed foibles of the tribunal that the Constitution of the United States and the States have established. Why then, is it not proper to allow them? It is said that the pain cannot be shifted to another. Neither can the loss of a leg. But one can be paid for as well as the other. It is said that these elements do not constitute an economic loss, in the sense of diminished power to produce. They may. . . . But whether they do or not they are as much part of the workman's loss as the loss of a limb. The legislature may have reasoned thus. If a business is unsuccessful it means that the public does not care enough for it to make it pay. If it is successful the public pays its expenses and something more. It is reasonable that the public should pay the whole cost of producing what it wants and a part of that cost is the pain and mutilation incident to production. By throwing that loss upon the employer in the first instance we throw it upon the public in the long run and that is just. If a legislature should reason in this way and act accordingly it seems to me that it is within constitutional bounds. . . . It is said that the liability is unlimited, but this is not true. It is limited to a conscientious valuation of the loss suffered. Apart from the control exercised by the judge it is to be hoped that juries would realize that unreasonable verdicts would tend to make the business impossible and thus to injure those whom they might wish to help. But whatever they may do we must accept the tribunal, as I have said, and are bound to assume that they will act rightly and confine themselves to the proper scope of the law.

It is not urged that the provision allowing twelve percent interest on the amount of the judgment from the date of filing the suit, in case of an unsuccessful appeal, is void. . . .

Mr. Justice Brandeis and Mr. Justice Clarke concur in this statement of additional reasons that lead me to agree with the opinion just delivered by my brother Pitney.

[Mr. Justice McKenna, dissenting, said: "It seems to me to be of the very foundation of right—of the essence of liberty as it is of morals—to be free from liability if one is free from fault." Mr. Justice McReynolds also wrote a dissenting opinion. Chief Justice White and Mr. Justice Van Devanter sided with the dissenters.]

Arizona Employers' Liability Cases
250 U. S. 400, 431

Taxing Holding Companies

(*Ft. Smith Lumber Co.* v. *Arkansas*, 1920)

THIS is a suit by the State of Arkansas against the plaintiff in error, a corporation of the State, to recover back taxes alleged to be due upon a proper valuation of its capital stock. The corporation owned stock in two other corporations of this State each of which paid full taxes and it contended that it was entitled to omit the value of such stock from the valuation of its own. This omission is the matter in dispute. The corporation defends on the ground that individuals are not taxed for such stock or subject to suit for back taxes, and that the taxation is double, setting up the Fourteenth Amendment. The case was heard on demurrer to the answer and agreed facts, and the statute levying the tax was sustained by the Supreme Court of the State.

The objection to the taxation as double may be laid on one side. That is a matter of State law alone. The Fourteenth Amendment no more forbids double taxation than it does doubling the amount of a tax, short of confiscation or proceedings unconstitutional on other grounds. . . . We are of opinion that it also is within the power of a State, so far as the Constitution of the United States is concerned, to tax its own corporations in respect of the stock held by them in other domestic corporations, although unincorporated stockholders are exempt. A State may have a policy in taxation. *Quong Wing* v. *Kirkendall* [see page 25]. If the State of Arkansas wished to discourage but not to forbid the holding of stock in one corporation by another and sought to attain the result by this tax, or if it simply saw fit to make corporations pay for the privilege, there would be nothing in the Constitution to hinder. A discrimination between corporations and individuals with regard to a tax like this cannot be pronounced arbitrary, although we may not know the precise ground of policy that led the State to insert the distinction in the law.

The same is true with regard to confining the recovery of back taxes to those due from corporations. It is to be presumed, until the contrary appears, that there were reasons for more strenuous efforts to collect admitted dues from corporations than in other cases, and we cannot pronounce it an unlawful policy on the part of the State. See *New York State* v. *Barker,* 179 U. S. 279, 283. We have nothing to do with the supposed limitations upon the power of the State legislature in the constitution of the State. Those must be taken to be disposed of by the decisions of the State court. As this case properly comes here by writ of error, an application for a writ of certiorari that was presented as a precaution will be denied.

Judgment affirmed.

[Justices McKenna, Day, Van Devanter and McReynolds dissented without opinion.]

Fort Smith Lumber Co. v. *State of Arkansas*
ex. rel. Arbuckle, Attorney General
251 U. S. 532

Grade Crossings and the Police Power

(*Erie R. R. Co.* v. *Public Utility Commrs.*, 1921)

These are writs of error brought by parties interested in an order of the Board of Public Utility Commissioners of New Jersey, dated April 20, 1915, directing a change in fifteen places in the City of Paterson, where the Erie Railroad now crosses that number of streets at grade. The order was reviewed on writs of certiorari and affirmed by the Supreme Court, and on appeal by the Court of Errors and Appeals. . . . The Erie Railroad Company made two applications to the Supreme Court, the second being based upon a refusal by the Board to grant a rehearing of its order. Accordingly it has two writs of error here. But the second adds nothing to the first as we could not say that the Board unreasonably refused further delay. Those of the other parties are to the judgments affirming the original order of the Board. The Erie Railroad was ordered to make the change by carrying fourteen of the crossings under, and one, at Madison avenue, over the railroad. It will also have to bear the cost, subject to a charge to the Public Service Railway Company of ten per centum of the cost of changing three crossings used by its road. The most important questions arise in the Erie Railroad Company's case and we take that up first.

The order was made under an Act of March 12, 1913, c. 57, P.L. 1913, p. 91, which is construed by the State courts to authorize it, subject to the constitutional questions to be dealt with here. The Erie Railroad's line in Paterson is over tracks originally

[46]

belonging to the President and Directors of the Paterson and Hudson River Railroad Company and the Paterson and Ramapo Railroad Company, but now held by the Erie Railroad, by assignment of perpetual leases upon the terms that if in any unforeseen way the leases terminate the value of erections and improvements must be repaid by the lessors. They however are small corporations having no assets except their roads and the rentals received from the Erie Company. The leases were ratified by an Act of March 14, 1853, providing that they should not be held to confer any privilege or right not granted to the lessors by their charters. It is admitted that the statute must be taken to impose the duty of making the changes upon the company operating the road, the plaintiff in error, which is an interstate road. It put in evidence that it did not have assets sufficient to make the changes, at least without interfering with the proper development of its interstate commerce, and also contended that the whole evidence did not justify the finding of the Board that the crossings were dangerous to public safety but at most showed that the change would be a public convenience. It is said that the order must be reasonable to be upheld and that it is not reasonable to require an expenditure for such a purpose of over two million dollars from a company that has not more than $100,000 available, and that the order and the statute when construed to justify it not only interfere unwarrantably with interstate commerce and impair the obligation of contracts but take the Erie Company's property without due process of law.

Most of the streets concerned were laid out later than the railroads and this fact is relied upon, so far as it goes, as an additional reason for denying the power of the State to throw the burden of this improvement upon the railroad. That is the fundamental question in the case. It might seem to be answered by the summary of the decisions given in *Chicago, Milwaukee & St. Paul Ry. Co.* v. *Minneapolis*, 232 U. S. 430, 438. "It is well settled that railroad corporations may be required, at their own expense, not only to abolish existing grade crossings but also to build and maintain suitable bridges or viaducts to carry highways, newly laid out, over their tracks or to carry their tracks over such highways." ... For although the statement is said to be explained as a matter of State law by the previous decisions in Minnesota, it is made without reference to those decisions or to any local rule, and moreover the intimation of the judgment in the present case is that whatever may have been the earlier rulings the law of New Jersey now adopts the same view.

But it is argued that the order is unreasonable in the circumstances to which we have adverted, the principle applied to the regulation of public service corporations being invoked. ... But the extent of the States' power varies in different cases from absolute to qualified, somewhat as the privilege in respect of inflicting pecuniary damage varies. The power of the State over grade crossings derives little light from cases on the power to regulate trains.

Grade crossings call for a necessary adjustment of two conflicting interests—that of the public using the streets and that of the railroads and the public using them. Generically the streets represent the more important interest of the two. There can be no doubt that they did when these railroads were laid out, or that the advent of automobiles has given them an additional claim to consideration. They always are the necessity of the whole public, which the railroads, vital as they are, hardly can be called to the same extent. Being places to which the public is invited and that it necessarily frequents, the State, in the care of which this interest is and from which, ultimately, the railroads derive their right to occupy the land, has a constitutional right to insist that they shall not be made dangerous to the public, whatever may be the cost to the parties introducing the danger. That is one of the most obvious cases of the police power, or to put the same proposition in another form, the authority of the railroads to project their moving masses across thoroughfares must be taken to be subject to the implied limitation that it may be cut down whenever and so far as the safety of the public requires. It is said that if the same requirement were made for the other grade crossings of the road it would soon be bankrupt. That the States might be so foolish as to kill a goose that lays golden eggs for them, has no bearing on their constitutional rights. If it reasonably can be said that safety requires the change it is for them to say whether they will insist upon it, and neither prospective bankruptcy nor engagement in interstate commerce can take away this fundamental right of the sovereign of the soil. . . . To engage in interstate commerce the railroad must get on to the land and to get on to it must comply with the conditions imposed by the State for the safety of its citizens. Contracts made by the road are made subject to the possible exercise of the sovereign right. . . . If the burdens imposed are so great that the road cannot be run at a profit it can stop, whatever the misfortunes of stopping may produce. . . . Intelligent self-interest should lead to a careful consideration of what the road is able to do without ruin, but this is not a constitutional duty. In the opinion of the courts below the evidence justified the conclusion of the Board that the expense would not be ruinous. Many details as to the particular situation of this road are disposed of without the need of further mention by what we have said thus far.

The plaintiff in error discusses with considerable detail the effect of the changes upon private sidings. But its rights in respect of these are at least no greater than those in respect of the main line and are covered by the preceding discussion. So are the objections that if the leases ever are terminated it has no chance of being repaid the value of its improvements because of the smallness of the lessor corporations. They would have this property in that event and it would be subject to their obligation—but the answer to the complaint of the plaintiff in error in all its forms is that which we have made. Whatever the cost, it may be required by New Jersey not to imperil the highways if it does business there. We agree with the decisions below that as the railroad company might have been charged with the whole expense the fact that no more than ten per centum of the cost of three crossings is thrown upon a street railway company is a matter of which it cannot complain.

If we could see that the evidence plainly did not warrant a finding that the particular crossings were dangerous there might be room for the argument that the order was so unreasonable as to be void. The number of accidents shown was small and if we went upon that alone we well might hesitate. But the situation is one that always is dangerous. The Board must be supposed to have known the locality and to have had an advantage similar to that of a judge who sees and hears the witnesses. The courts of the State have confirmed its judgment. The tribunals were not bound to await a collision that might cost the road a sum comparable to the cost of the change. If they were reasonably warranted in their conclusion their judgment must stand. We cannot say that they were not. At some crossings the danger was less than at others, but it was necessary or at least prudent to proceed on a general plan. Upon the whole matter while it is difficult to avoid the apprehension that the State officials hardly gave due weight to the situation of the company as a whole in their anxiety for the well-being of the State, we are of opinion that they did not exceed their constitutional powers. The order should be regarded as stating a condition that must be complied with if the company continues to use the New Jersey soil. Probably the conclusion that we have reached could be supported upon the narrower ground that a continuing obligation was imposed by the charters of the plaintiff in error's lessors, and was assumed by the plaintiff in error, but that which we have stated seems to us free from doubt.

Some argument is based upon a discretion supposed to be left to the Board by the statute, which reads that when it appears to the Board that the crossing is dangerous it may order, &c. The

State courts seem to regard the words as imposing a positive duty, but upon either construction we perceive no infraction of the company's constitutional rights. If the words are imperative the reasons that we have given apply. If they leave a discretion it is subject to review by the courts, and this Court has no concern with the question how far legislative or *quasi*-legislative powers may be delegated to a commission or board. . . . We deem it unnecessary to give our reasons in greater detail for deciding that the judgment against the Erie Railroad Company must be affirmed.

While the Railroad Company contends that the Public Service Railway Company should be charged more, the latter company comes here upon the proposition that it should be charged nothing. We agree with the courts below that a street railway crossing the tracks of a steam road at grade in a public street increases the danger and may be required to bear a part of the expense of removing it. The amount charged does not appear to be excessive and upon the principles that we have laid down the payment of it may be made a condition of the continued right to use the streets. . . .

The Passaic Water Company contends that the expense of moving its pipes cannot be thrown wholly upon it—mainly on the ground that the change of grade was unlawful. This ground fails and the company must adjust itself to the lawfully changed conditions. It also contends that it does not receive the equal protection of the laws because the street railway instead of being charged the expense of moving its tracks is charged ten per centum of the total expense at its crossings. Presumably this charge is greater than the mere adjustment of tracks to a new surface. It is based upon the share of the street railroad in creating the danger. As the street railroad cannot complain, certainly the Water Company cannot.

The Western Union Telegraph Company makes similar objections and also says that its interstate commerce is interfered with and presents from its own point of view arguments dealt with so far as they seem to us to need mention in disposing of the principal case. The other plaintiffs in error own side tracks which will be dislocated by the change and they will be put to further expense if the plan is carried out according to what the New Jersey court decides to be suggestions, not commands. The rights in the side tracks are subordinate to changes in the main track otherwise lawful. As against these as against the others the judgment of the Court of Errors and Appeals is affirmed.

Judgment affirmed.

[Chief Justice White and Justices Van Devanter and McReynolds dissented without opinion.]

Erie Railroad Company v. *Board of Public Utility Commissioners, et al.*
254 U. S. 394

Control of Rent in Emergencies

(*Block* v. *Hirsh*, 1921)

THIS is a proceeding brought by the defendant in error, Hirsh, to recover possession of the cellar and first floor of a building on F Street in Washington which the plaintiff in error, Block, holds over after the expiration of a lease to him. Hirsh bought the building while the lease was running, and on December 15, 1919, notified Block that he should require possession on December 31, when the lease expired. Block declined to surrender the premises, relying upon the Act of October 22, 1919, c. 80, Title II, "District of Columbia Rents"; especially § 109, 41 Stat. 297, 298, 301. That is also the ground of his defense in this Court, and the question is whether the statute is constitutional, or, as held by the Court of Appeals, an attempt to authorize the taking of property not for public use and without due process of law, and for this and other reasons void.

By § 109 of the Act the right of a tenant to occupy any hotel, apartment, or "rental property," i. e., any building or part thereof, other than hotel or apartment, (§ 101), is to continue notwithstanding the expiration of his term, at the option of the tenant, subject to regulation by the Commission appointed by the Act, so long as he pays the rent and performs the conditions as fixed by the lease or as modified by the Commission. It is provided in the same section that the owner shall have the right to possession "for actual and bona fide occupancy by himself, or his wife, children, or dependents . . . upon giving thirty days' notice in writing." According to his affidavit Hirsh wanted the premises for his own use, but he did not see fit to give thirty days' notice because he denied the validity of the Act. The statute embodies a scheme or code which it is needless to set forth, but it should be stated that it ends with the declaration in § 122 that the provisions of Title II are made necessary by the emergencies growing out of the war, resulting in rental conditions in the District dangerous to the public health and burdensome to public officers, employees and accessories, and thereby embarrassing the Federal Government in the transaction of the public business. As emergency legislation the Title is to end in two years unless sooner repealed.

No doubt it is true that a legislative declaration of facts that are material only as the ground for enacting a rule of law, for instance, that a certain use is a public one, may not be held conclusive by the courts. . . . But a declaration by a legislature concerning public conditions that by necessity and duty it must know, is entitled at least to great respect. In this instance Congress stated a publicly notorious and almost world-wide fact. That the emergency declared by the statute did exist must be assumed, and the question is whether Congress was incompetent to meet it in the way in which it has been met by most of the civilized countries of the world.

The general proposition to be maintained is that circumstances have clothed the letting of buildings in the District of Columbia with a public interest so great as to justify regulation by law. Plainly circumstances may so change in time or so differ in space as to clothe with such an interest what at other times or in other places would be a matter of purely private concern. It is enough to refer to the decisions as to insurance, in *German Alliance Insurance Co.* v. *Lewis,* 233 U. S. 389; irrigation, in *Clark* v. *Nash,* 198 U. S. 361; and mining, in *Strickley* v. *Highland Boy Gold Mining Co.,* 200 U. S. 527. They sufficiently illustrate what hardly would be denied. They illustrate also that the use by the public generally of each specific thing affected cannot be made the test of public interest, *Mt. Vernon-Woodberry Cotton Duck Co.* v. *Alabama Interstate Power Co.* [see page 31], and that the public interest may extend to the use of land. They dispel the notion that what in its immediate aspect may be only a private transaction may not be raised by its class or character to a public affair. See also *Noble State Bank* v. *Haskell* [page 20 of this volume].

The fact that tangible property is also visible tends to give a rigidity to our conception of our rights in it that we do not attach to others less concretely clothed. But the notion that the former are exempt from legislative modification required from time to time in civilized life is contradicted not only by the doctrine of eminent domain, under which what is taken is paid for, but by that of the police power in its proper sense, under which property rights may be cut down, and to that extent taken, without pay. Under the police power the right to erect buildings in a certain quarter of a city may be limited to from eighty to one hundred feet.... Safe pillars may be required in coal mines.... Billboards in cities may be regulated.... Watersheds in the country may be kept clear.... These cases are enough to establish that a public exigency will justify the legislature in restricting property rights in land to a certain extent without compensation. But if to answer one need the legislature may limit height, to answer another it may limit rent. We do not perceive any reason for denying the justification held good in the foregoing cases to a law limiting the property rights now in question if the public exigency requires that. The reasons are of a different nature but they certainly are not less pressing. Congress has stated the unquestionable embarrassment of government and danger to the public health in the existing conditions of things. The space in Washington is necessarily monopolized in comparatively few hands, and letting portions of it as much a business as any other. Housing is a necessary of life. All the elements of a public interest justifying some degree of public control are present. The only matter that seems to us open to debate is whether the statute goes too far. For just as there comes a point at which the police power ceases and leaves only that of eminent domain, it may be conceded that regulations of the present sort pressed to a certain height might amount to a taking without due process of law. . . .

Perhaps it would be too strict to deal with this case as concerning only the requirement of thirty days' notice. For although the plaintiff alleged that he wanted the premises for his own use the defendant denied it and might have prevailed upon that issue under the Act. The general question to which we have adverted must be decided, if not in this then in the next case, and it should be disposed of now.— The main point against the law is that tenants are allowed to remain in possession at the same rent that they have been paying, unless modified by the Commission established by the Act, and that thus the use of the land and the right of the owner to do what he will with his own and to make what contracts he pleases are cut down. But if the public interest be established the regulation of rates is one of the first forms in which it is asserted, and the validity of such regulation has been settled since *Munn* v. *Illinois*, 94 U. S. 113. It is said that a grain elevator may go out of business whereas here the use is fastened upon the land. The power to go out of business, when it exists, is an illusory answer to gas companies and waterworks, but we need not stop at that. The regulation is put and justified only as a temporary measure. See *Wilson* v. *New*, 243 U. S. 332, 345, 346. *Fort Smith & Western R.R. Co.* v. *Mills*, 253 U. S. 206. A limit in time, to tide over a passing trouble, well may justify a law that could not be upheld as a permanent change.

Machinery is provided to secure to the landlord a reasonable rent. § 106. It may be assumed that the interpretation of "reasonable" will deprive him in part at least of the power of profiting by the sudden influx of people to Washington caused by the needs of government and the war, and thus of a right usually incident to fortunately situated property—of a part of the value of his property as defined in *International Harvester Co. v. Kentucky*, 234 U. S. 222 [see page 153]. . . . But while it is unjust to pursue such profits from a national misfortune with sweeping denunciations, the policy of restricting them has been embodied in taxation and is accepted. It goes little if at all farther than the restriction put upon the rights of the owner of money by the more debatable usury laws. The preference given to the tenant in possession is an almost necessary incident of the policy and is traditional in English law. If the tenant remained subject to the landlord's power to evict, the attempt to limit the landlord's demands would fail.

Assuming that the end in view otherwise justifies the means adopted by Congress, we have no concern of course with the question whether those means were the wisest, whether they may not cost more than they come to, or will effect the result desired. It is enough that we are not warranted in saying that legislation that has been resorted to for the same purpose all over the world, is futile or has no reasonable relation to the relief sought. . . .

The statute is objected to on the further ground that landlords and tenants are deprived by it of a trial by jury on the right to possession of the land. If the power of the Commission established by the statute to regulate the relation is established, as we think it is, by what we have said, this objection amounts to little. To regulate the relation and to decide the facts affecting it are hardly separable. While the Act is in force there is little to decide except whether the rent allowed is reasonable, and upon that question the courts are given the last word. A part of the exigency is to secure a speedy and summary administration of the law and we are not prepared to say that the suspension of ordinary remedies was not a reasonable provision of a statute reasonable in its aim and intent. The plaintiff obtained a judgment on the ground tHat the statute was void, root and branch. That judgment must be reversed.

Judgment reversed.

[Mr. Justice McKenna, joined by Chief Justice White and Justices Van Devanter and McReynolds, dissented, holding that private property was protected by the Constitution against taking without compensation and that Congress impaired the obligation of a contract by passing the law. "Of what concern is it to the public health or the operations of the Federal Government who shall occupy a cellar, and a room above it, for business purposes in the City of Washington?" Justice McKenna asked. "Have conditions come *** that are not amenable to passing palliatives, so that socialism or some form of socialism, is the only permanent corrective or accommodation?" The prohibitions of the Constitution, he said, "are as absolute as axioms."]

Block, trading under the name of Whites, v. Hirsh
256 U. S. 135

Emergency Legislation in New York

(*Marcus Brown Co.* v. *Feldman*, 1921)

THIS is a bill in equity brought by the Marcus Brown Holding Company, the appellant, owner of a large apartment house in the City of New York, against the tenants of an apartment in the house and the District Attorney of the County of New York. The tenants are holding over after their lease has expired, which it did on September 30, 1920, claiming the right to do so under cc. 942 and 947 of the laws of New York of 1920. The object of the bill is to have these and other connected laws declared unconstitutional. The District Attorney is joined in order to prevent his enforcing by criminal proceedings cc. 131 and 951 of the acts of the same year, which make it a misdemeanor for the lessor or any agent or janitor intentionally to fail to furnish such water, heat, light, elevator, telephone, or other service as may be required by the terms of the lease and necessary to the proper or customary use of the building. The case was heard in the District Court by three judges upon the bill, answer, affidavits and some public documents, all of which may be summed up in a few words. The bill alleges at length the rights given to a lessor by the common law and statutes of New York before the enactment of the statutes relied upon by the tenants, a covenant by the latter to surrender possession at the termination of their lease, and due demand, and claims protection under Article I, § 10, and the Fourteenth Amendment of the Constitution of the United States. An affidavit alleges that before the passage of the new statutes another lease of the premises had been made, to go into effect on October 1,

1920. The answer of the tenants relies upon the new statutes and alleges a willingness to pay a reasonable rent and any reasonable increase as the same may be determined by a court of competent jurisdiction. It also alleges that they made efforts to obtain another suitable apartment but failed. The District Attorney moved to dismiss the bill. The judges considered the case upon the merits, upheld the laws and ordered the bill to be dismissed.

By the above-mentioned cc. 942 and 947, a public emergency is declared to exist and it is provided by c. 947 that no action "shall be maintainable to recover possession of real property in a city of a population of one million or more or in a city in a county adjoining such city, occupied for dwelling purposes, except an action to recover such possession upon the ground that the person is holding over and is objectionable, . . . or an action where the owner of record of the building, being a natural person, seeks in good faith to recover possession of the same or a room or rooms therein for the immediate and personal occupancy by himself and his family as a dwelling; or an action to recover premises for the purposes of demolishing the same with the intention of constructing a new building. . . ." The earlier c. 942 is similar with some further details. Both Acts are to be in effect only until November 1, 1922. It is unnecessary to state the provisions of c. 944 for disputes as to what is a reasonable rent. They are dealt with in the decisions of the Court of Appeals cited below and in *Edgar A. Levy Leasing Co., Inc.,* v. *Siegel*, 230 N. Y. 834, by the same court. In this as in the previous case of *Block* v. *Hirsh, ante,* [see page 53 of this volume], we shall assume in accordance with the statutes, the finding of the court below and of the Court of Appeals of the State, in *People ex. rel. Durham Realty Corporation* v. *La Fetra*, 230 N. Y. 429, and *Guttag* v. *Shatzkin*, 230 N. Y. 647, that the emergency declared exists. . . .

The chief objections to these Acts have been dealt with in *Block* v. *Hirsh*. In the present case more emphasis is laid upon the impairment of the obligation of the contract of the lessees to surrender possession and of the new lease which was to have gone into effect upon October 1, last year. But contracts are made subject to this exercise of the power of the State when otherwise justified, as we have held this to be. . . . It is said too that the laws are discriminating, in respect of the cities affected and the character of the buildings, the laws not extending to buildings occupied for business purposes, hotel property or buildings now in course of erection, &c. But as the evil to be met was a very pressing want of shelter in certain crowded centers the classification was too obviously justified to need explanation, beyond repeating what was said below as to new buildings, that the unknown cost of completing them and the need to encourage such structures sufficiently explain the last item on the excepted list.

It is objected finally that c. 951, above stated, in so far as it required active services to be rendered to the tenants, is void on the rather singular ground that it infringes the Thirteenth Amendment. It is true that the traditions of our law are opposed to compelling a man to perform strictly personal services against his will even when he has contracted to render them. But the services in question although involving some activities are so far from personal that they constitute the universal and necessary incidents of modern apartment houses. They are analogous to the services that in the old law might issue out of or be attached to land. We pereceive no additional difficulties in this statute, if applicable as assumed. The whole case was well discussed below and we are of opinion that the decree should be affirmed.

Decree affirmed.

[Mr. Justice McKenna, Chief Justice White and Justices Van Devanter and McReynolds dissented on the same grounds as in *Block* v. *Hirsh*, adding that the preeminence of the Constitution ought not to be weakened by "refined dialectics."]

Marcus Brown Holding Co., Inc., v. Feldman, et al.
256 U. S. 170

Destroying Values without Payment

(Penna. Coal Co. v. Mahon, 1922)

This is a bill in equity brought by the defendants in error to prevent the Pennsylvania Coal Company from mining under their property in such way as to remove the supports and cause a subsidence of the surface and of their house. The bill sets out a deed executed by the Coal Company in 1878, under which the plaintiffs claim. The deed conveys the surface, but in express terms reserves the right to remove all the coal under the same, and the grantee takes the premises with the risk, and waives all claims for damages that may arise from mining out the coal. But the plaintiffs say that whatever may have been the Coal Company's rights, they were taken away by an Act of Pennsylvania, approved May 27, 1921, P. L. 1198, commonly known as the Kohler Act. The Court of Common Pleas found that if not restrained the defendant would cause the damage to prevent which the bill was brought, but denied an injunction, holding that the statute if applied to this case would be unconstitutional. On appeal the Supreme Court of the State agreed that the defendant had contract and property rights protected by the Constitution of the United States, but held that the statute was a legitimate exercise of the police power and directed a decree for the plaintiffs. A writ of error was granted bringing the case to this Court.

The statute forbids the mining of anthracite coal in such way as to cause the subsidence of, among other things, any structure used as a human habitation, with certain exceptions, including among them land where the surface is owned by the owner of the underlying coal and is distant more than one hundred and fifty feet from any improved property belonging to any other person. As applied to this case the statute is admitted to destroy previously existing rights of property and contract. The question is whether the police power can be stretched so far.

Government hardly could go on if to some extent values incident to property could not be diminished without paying for every such change in the general law. As long recognized, some values are enjoyed under an implied limitation and must yield to the police power. But obviously the implied limitation must have its limits, or the contract and due process clauses are gone. One fact for consideration in determining such limits is the extent of the diminution. When it reaches a certain magnitude, in most if not in all cases there must be an exercise of eminent domain and compensation to sustain the Act. So the question depends upon the particular facts. The greatest weight is given to the judgment of the legislature, but it always is open to interested parties to contend that the legislature has gone beyond its constitutional power.

This is the case of a single private house. No doubt there is a public interest even in this, as there is in every purchase and sale and in all that happens within the commonwealth. Some existing rights may be modified even in such a case. . . . But usually in ordinary private affairs the public interest does not warrant much of this kind of interference. A source of damage to such a house is not a public nuisance even if similar damage is inflicted on others in different places. The damage is not common or public. . . . The extent of the public interest is shown by the statute to be limited, since the statute ordinarily does not apply to land when the surface is owned by the owner of the coal. Furthermore, it is not justified as a protection of personal safety. That could be provided for by notice. Indeed the very foundation of this bill is that the defendant gave timely notice of its intent to mine under the house. On the other hand the extent of the taking is great. It purports to abolish what is recognized in Pennsylvania as an estate in land—a very valuable estate—and what is declared by the court below to be a contract hitherto binding the plaintiffs. If we were called upon to deal with the plaintiff's position alone, we should think it clear that the statute does not disclose a public interest sufficient to warrant so extensive a destruction of the defendant's constitutionally protected rights.

But the case has been treated as one in which the general validity of the Act should be discussed. The Attorney General of the State, the City of Scranton, and the representatives of other extensive interests were allowed to take part in the argument below and have submitted their contentions here. It seems, therefore, to be our duty to go farther in the statement of our opinion, in order that it may be known at once, and that further suits should not be brought in vain.

It is our opinion that the Act cannot be sustained as an exercise of the police power, so far as it affects the mining of coal under streets or cities in places where the right to mine such coal has been reserved. As said in a Pennsylvania case, "For practical purposes, the right to coal consists in the right to mine it." *Commonwealth* v. *Clearview Coal Co.*, 256 Pa., 328, 331. What makes the right to mine coal valuable is that it can be exercised with profit. To make it commercially impracticable to mine certain coal has very nearly the same effect for constitutional purposes as appropriating or destroying it. This we think that we are warranted in assuming that the statute does.

It is true that in *Plymouth Coal Co.* v. *Pennsylvania*, 232 U. S. 531, it was held competent for the legislature to require a pillar of coal to be left along the line of adjoining property, that, with the pillar on the other side of the line, would be a barrier sufficient for the safety of the employees of either mine in case the other should be abandoned and allowed to fill with water. But that was a requirement for the safety of employees invited into the mine, and secured an average reciprocity of advantage that has been recognized as a justification of various laws.

The rights of the public in a street purchased or laid out by eminent domain are those that it has paid for. If in any case its representatives have been so short sighted as to acquire only surface rights without the right of support, we see no more authority for supplying the latter without compensation than there was for taking the right of way in the first place and refusing to pay for it because the public wanted it very much. The protection of private property in the Fifth Amendment presupposes that it is wanted for public use, but provides that it shall not be taken for such use without compensation. A similar assumption is made in the decisions upon the Fourteenth Amendment. . . . When this seemingly absolute protection is found to be qualified by the police power, the natural tendency of human nature is to extend the qualification more and more until at last private property disappears. But that cannot be accomplished in this way under the Constitution of the United States.

The general rule at least is, that while property may be regulated to a certain extent, if regulation goes too far it will be recognized as a taking. It may be doubted how far exceptional cases, like the blowing up of a house to stop a conflagration, go—and if they go beyond the general rule, whether they do not stand as much upon tradition as upon principle. . . . In general it is not plain that a man's misfortunes or necessities will justify his shifting the damages to his neighbor's shoulders. . . . We are in danger of forgetting that a strong public desire to improve the public condition is not enough to warrant achieving the desire by a shorter cut than the constitutional way of paying for the change. As we have already said, this is a question of degree— and therefore cannot be disposed of by general propositions. But we regard this as going beyond any of the cases decided by this Court. The late decisions upon laws dealing with the congestion of Washington and New York, caused by the war, dealt with laws intended to meet a temporary emergency and providing for compensation determined to be reasonable by an impartial board. They went to the verge of the law but fell far short of the present Act. . . .

We assume, of course, that the statute was passed upon the conviction that an exigency existed that would warrant it, and we assume that an exigency exists that would warrant the exercise of eminent domain. But the question at bottom is upon whom the loss of the changes desired should fall. So far as private persons or communities have seen fit to take the risk of acquiring only surface rights, we cannot see that the fact that their risk has become a danger warrants the giving to them greater rights than they bought.

Decree reversed.

[Mr. Justice Brandeis, reasoning that the right of an owner to use his land is not absolute and that "uses, once harmless, may, owing to changed conditions, seriously threaten the public welfare," argued that a restriction imposed by a legislature to protect the public was not a taking. As for diminution in value, "values are relative," and "I suppose no one would contend that by selling his interest above one hundred feet from the surface he could prevent the State from limiting, by the police power, the height of structures in a city. And why should a sale of underground rights bar the State's power?" Then again, "the value of the coal kept in place by the restriction may be negligible as compared with the value of the whole property." Brandeis further suggested that the Court should defer to the State court's greater knowledge of local conditions; that contracts between private individuals could not preclude the exercise of the police power; that there was no room here for considering "reciprocity of advantage," except that the coal operators were given "the advantage of living and doing business in a civilized community."]

Pennsylvania Coal Co. v. Mahon, et al.
260 U. S. 393

Sterilization of Imbeciles

(*Buck* v. *Bell*, 1927)

This is a writ of error to review a judgment of the Supreme Court of Appeals of the State of Virginia, affirming a judgment of the Circuit Court of Amherst County, by which the defendant in error, the superintendent of the State Colony for Epileptics and Feeble Minded, was ordered to perform the operation of salpingectomy upon Carrie Buck, the plaintiff in error, for the purpose of making her sterile. 143 Va. 310. The case comes here upon the contention that the statute authorizing the judgment is void under the Fourteenth Amendment as denying to the plaintiff in error due process of law and the equal protection of the laws.

Carrie Buck is a feeble minded white woman who was committed to the State Colony above mentioned in due form. She is the daughter of a feeble minded mother in the same institution, and the mother of an illegitimate feeble minded child. She was eighteen years old at the time of the trial of her case in the Circuit Court, in the latter part of 1924. An Act of Virginia, approved March 20, 1924, recites that the health of the patient and the welfare of society may be promoted in certain cases by the sterilization of mental defectives, under careful safeguard, &c.; that the sterilization may be effected in males by vasectomy and in females by salpingectomy, without serious pain or substantial danger to life; that the Commonwealth is supporting in various institutions many defective persons who if now discharged would become a menace but if incapable of procreating might be discharged with safety and become self-supporting with benefit to themselves and to society; and that experience has shown that heredity plays an important part in the transmission of insanity, imbecility, &c. The statute then enacts that whenever the superintendent of certain institutions including the above named State Colony shall be of opinion that it is for the best interests of the patients and of society that the inmate under his care should be sexually sterilized, he may have the operation performed upon any patient afflicted with hereditary forms of insanity, imbecility, &c., on complying with the very careful provisions by which the Act protects the patients from possible abuse.

The superintendent first presents a petition to the special board of directors of his hospital or colony, stating the facts and the grounds for his opinion, verified by affidavit. Notice of the petition and of the time and place of the hearing in the institution is to be served upon the inmate, and also upon his guardian, and if there is no guardian the superintendent is to apply to the Circuit Court of the County to appoint one. If the inmate is a minor notice also is to be given to his parents if any with a copy of the petition. The board is to see to it that the inmate may attend the hearings if desired by him or his guardian. The evidence is all to be reduced to writing, and after the board has made its order for or against the operation, the superintendent, or the inmate, or his guardian, may appeal to the Circuit Court of the County. The Circuit Court may consider the record of the board and the evidence before it and such other admissible evidence as may be offered, and may affirm, revise, or reverse the order of the board and enter such order as it deems just. Finally any party may apply to the Supreme Court of Appeals, which, if it grants the appeal, is to hear the case upon the record of the trial in the Circuit Court and may enter such order as it thinks the Circuit Court should have entered. There can be no doubt that so far as procedure is concerned the rights of the patient are most carefully considered, and as every step in this case was taken in scrupulous compliance with the statute and after months of observation, there is no doubt that in that respect the plaintiff in error has had due process of law.

The attack is not upon the procedure but upon the substantive law. It seems to be contended that in no circumstances could such an order be justified. It certainly is contended that the order cannot be justified upon the existing grounds. The judgment finds the facts that have been recited and that Carrie Buck "is the probable potential parent of socially inadequate offspring, likewise afflicted, that she may be sexually sterilized without detriment to her general health and that her welfare and that of society will be promoted by her sterilization," and thereupon makes the order. In view of the general declarations of the legislature and the specific findings of the court, obviously we cannot say as matter of law that the grounds do not exist, and if they exist they justify the result. We have seen more than once that the public welfare may call upon the best citizens for their lives. It would be strange if it could not call upon those who already sap the strength of the State for these lesser sacrifices, often not felt to be such by those concerned, in order to prevent our being swamped with incompetence. It is better for all the world, if instead of waiting to execute degenerate offspring for crime, or to let them starve for their imbecility, society can prevent those who are manifestly unfit from continuing their kind. The principle that sustains compulsory vaccination is broad enough to cover cutting the Fallopian tubes. . . . Three generations of imbeciles are enough.

But, it is said, however it might be if this reasoning were applied generally, it fails when it is confined to the small number who are in the institutions named and is not applied to the multitudes outside. It is the usual last resort of constitutional arguments to point out shortcomings of this sort. But the answer is that the law does all that is needed when it does all that it can, indicates a policy, applies to all within the lines, and seeks to bring within the lines all similarly situated so far and so fast as its means allow. Of course so far as the operations enable those who otherwise must be kept confined to be returned to the world, and thus open the asylum to others, the equality aimed at will be more nearly reached.

Judgment affirmed.

[Mr. Justice Butler dissented without opinion.]

Buck v. *Bell, Superintendent*
274 U. S. 200

Regulating the Eyeglass Business

(*Roschen* v. *Ward,* 1929)

THESE are suits brought by dealers in eye glasses for an injunction prohibiting the enforcement of chapter 379 of the New York Laws of 1928, which amends the Education Law by inserting two sections, of which the material portion makes it unlawful to sell at retail in any store or established place of business "any spectacles, eye glasses, or lenses for the correction of vision, unless a duly licensed physician or duly qualified optometrist, certified under this article, be in charge of and [in] personal attendance at the booth, counter or place, where such articles are sold in such store or established place of business." The complainants moved for a preliminary injunction, a statutory court of three judges was convened and after a hearing the injunction was refused and the bills were dismissed on the ground that no cause of action was shown. . . .

The complainants sell only ordinary spectacles with convex spherical lenses, which merely magnify and which it is said can do no harm. The customers select for themselves without being examined and buy glasses for a relatively small sum. It is said that the cost of employing an optometrist would make the complainants' business impossible, and that in the common case of eyes only grown weaker by age the requirement is unreasonable. But the argument most pressed is that the statute does not provide for an examination by the optometrist in charge of the counter. This as it is presented seems to us a perversion of the Act. When the statute requires a physician or optometrist to be in charge of the place of sale and in personal attendance at it, obviously it means in charge of it by reason of and in the exercise of his professional capacity. If we assume that an examination of the eye is not required in every case, it plainly is the duty of the specialist to make up his mind whether one is necessary and, if he thinks it necessary, to make it. We agree to all the generalities about not supplying criminal laws with what they omit, but there is no canon against using common sense in construing laws as saying what they obviously mean. Moreover, as pointed out below, wherever the requirements of the Act stop, there can be no doubt that the presence and superintendence of the specialist tend to diminish an evil. A statute is not invalid under the Constitution because it might have gone farther than it did, or because it may not succeed in bringing about the result that it tends to produce.

Of course we cannot suppose the Act to have been passed for sinister motives. We will assume that there are strong reasons against interference with the business as now done—but it is obvious that much good will be accomplished if eyes were examined in a great many cases where hitherto they have not been, and the balance of the considerations of advantage and disadvantage is for the legislature not for the courts. We cannot say, as the complainants would have us say, that the supposed benefits are a cloak for establishing a monopoly and a pretence.

Decree affirmed.

Roschen v. Ward, Attorney General of New York, et al.;
S. S. Kresge Co. v. Same
279 U. S. 337

II. ON THE STATES AND THE NATION

Contempt of a State Court

(*Patterson* v. *Colorado*, 1907)

This is a writ of error to review a judgment upon an information for contempt. The contempt alleged was the publication of certain articles and a cartoon, which, it was charged, reflected upon the motives and conduct of the Supreme Court of Colorado in cases still pending and were intended to embarrass the court in the impartial administration of justice. There was a motion to quash on grounds of local law and the State constitution and also of the Fourteenth Amendment to the Constitution of the United States. This was overruled and thereupon an answer was filed, admitting the publication, denying the contempt, also denying that the cases referred to were still pending, except that the time for motions for rehearing had not elapsed, and averring that the motions for rehearing subsequently were overruled, except that in certain cases the orders were amended so that the Democratic officeholders concerned could be sooner turned out of their offices. The answer went on to narrate the transactions commented on, at length, intimating that the conduct of the court was unconstitutional and usurping, and alleging that it was in aid of a scheme, fully explained, to seat various Republican candidates, including the governor of the State, in place of Democrats who had been elected, and that two of the judges of the court got their seats as a part of the scheme. Finally, the answer alleged that the respondent published the articles in pursuance of what he regarded as a public duty, repeated the previous objections to the information, averred the truth of the articles, and set up and claimed the right to prove the truth under the Constitution of the United States. Upon this answer the court, on motion, ordered judgment fining the plaintiff in error for contempt.

The foregoing proceedings are set forth in a bill of exceptions, and several errors are alleged. The difficulty with those most pressed is that they raise questions of local law, which are not open to reexamination here. The requirement in the Fourteenth Amendment of due process of law does not take up the special provisions of the State constitution and laws into the Fourteenth Amendment for the purposes of the case, and in that way subject a State decision that they have been complied with to revision by this Court. . . . For this reason, if for no other, the objection that the information was not supported by an affidavit until after it was filed cannot be considered. See further *Ex parte Wall*, 107 U. S. 265. The same is true of the contention that the suits referred to in the article complained of were not pending. Whether a case shall be regarded as pending while it is possible that a petition for rehearing may be filed, or, if in an appellate court, until the *remittitur* is issued, are questions which the local law can settle as it pleases without interference from the Constitution of the United States. It is admitted that this may be true in some other sense, but it is not true, it is said, for the purpose of fixing the limits of possible contempts. But here again the plaintiff in error confounds the argument as to the common law, or as to what it might be wise and humane to hold, with that concerning the State's constitutional power. If a State should see fit to provide in its constitution that conduct otherwise amounting to a contempt should be punishable as such if occurring at any time while the court affected retained authority to modify its judgment, the Fourteenth Amendment would not forbid. The only question for this Court is the power of the State. . . .

It is argued that the decisions criticized, and in some degree that in the present case, were contrary to well-settled previous adjudications of the same court, and this allegation is regarded as giving some sort of constitutional right to the plaintiff in error. But while it is true that the United States courts do not always hold themselves bound by State decisions in cases arising before them, that principle has but a limited application to cases brought from the State courts here on writs of error. Except in exceptional cases, the grounds on which the Circuit Courts are held authorized to follow an earlier State decision rather than a later one, or to apply the rules of commercial law as understood by this Court, rather than those laid down by the local tribunals, are not grounds of constitutional right, but considerations of justice and expediency. There is no constitutional right to have all general propositions of law once adopted remain unchanged. Even if it be true, as the plaintiff in error says, that the Supreme Court of Colorado departed from earlier and well-established precedents to meet the exigencies of this case, whatever might be thought of the justice or wisdom of such a step, the Constitution of the United States is not infringed. It is unnecessary to lay down an absolute rule beyond the possibility of exception. Exceptions have been held to exist. But in general the decision of a court upon a question of law, however wrong and however contrary to previous decisions, is not an infraction of the Fourteenth Amendment merely because it is wrong or because earlier decisions are reversed.

It is argued that the articles did not constitute a contempt. In view of the answer, which sets out more plainly and in fuller detail what the articles insinuate and suggest, and in view of the position of the plaintiff in error that he was performing a public duty, the argument for a favorable interpretation of the printed words loses some of its force. However, it is enough for us to say that they are far from showing that innocent conduct has been laid hold of as an arbitrary pretense for an arbitrary punishment. Supposing that such a case would give the plaintiff in error a standing here, anything short of that is for the State court to decide. What constitutes contempt, as well as the time during which it may be committed, is a matter of local law.

The defense upon which the plaintiff in error most relies is raised by the allegation that the articles complained of are true and the claim of the right to prove the truth. He claimed this right under the constitutions of both the State and of the United States, but the latter ground alone comes into consideration here, for reasons already stated. . . . We do not pause to consider whether the claim was sufficient in point of form, although it is easier to refer to the Constitution generally for the supposed right than to point to the clause from which it springs. We leave undecided the question whether there is to be found in the Fourteenth Amendment a prohibition similar to that in the First. But even if we were to assume that freedom of speech and freedom of the press were protected from abridgment on the part not only of the United States but also of the States, still we should be far from the conclusion that the plaintiff in error would have us reach. In the first place, the main purpose of such constitutional provisions is "to prevent all such *previous restraints* upon publications as had been practiced by other governments," and they do not prevent the subsequent punishment of such as may be deemed contrary to the public welfare. . . . The preliminary freedom extends as well to the false as to the true; the subsequent punishment may extend as well to the true as to the false. This was the law of criminal libel apart from statute in most cases, if not in all. . . .

In the next place, the rule applied to criminal libels applies yet more clearly to contempts. A publication likely to reach the eyes of a jury, declaring a witness in a pending cause a perjurer, would be none the less a contempt that it was true. It would tend to obstruct the administration of justice, because even a correct conclusion is not to be reached or helped in that way, if our system of trials is to be maintained. The theory of our system is that the conclusions to be reached in a case will be induced only by evidence and argument in open court, and not by any outside influence, whether of private talk or public print.

What is true with reference to a jury is true also with reference to a court. Cases like the present are more likely to arise, no doubt, when there is a jury and the publication may affect their judgment. Judges generally, perhaps, are less apprehensive that publications impugning their own reasoning or motives will interfere with their administration of the law. But if a court regards, as it may, a publication concerning a matter of law pending before it, as tending toward such an interference, it may punish it as in the instance put. When a case is finished, courts are subject to the same criticism as other people, but the propriety and necessity of preventing interference with the course of justice by premature statement, argument or intimidation hardly can be denied. . . . It is objected that the judges were sitting in their own case. But the grounds upon which contempts are punished are impersonal. . . . No doubt judges naturally would be slower to punish when the contempt carried with it a personally dishonoring charge, but a man cannot expect to secure immunity from punishment by the proper tribunal, by adding to illegal conduct a personal attack. It only remains to add that the plaintiff in error had his day in court and opportunity to be heard. We have scrutinized the case, but cannot say that it shows an infraction of rights under the Constitution of the United States, or discloses more than the formal appeal to that instrument in the answer to found the jurisdiction of this Court.

Writ of error dismissed.

[In the dissenting opinion of Mr. Justice Harlan the point was made that free speech and a free press were rights belonging to citizens before the Fourteenth Amendment was adopted and that legislatures could not impair those rights. "The public welfare cannot override constitutional privileges." Dissenting separately, Mr. Justice Brewer felt that the Court had jurisdiction and should determine the alleged rights of the plaintiff in error.]

Patterson v. *Colorado, ex. rel. Attorney General of the State of Colorado*
205 U. S. 454

A State's Control Over Its Waters

(*Hudson Water Co.* v. *McCarter*, 1908)

This is an information, alleging that the defendant (the plaintiff in error), under a contract with the City of Bayonne in New Jersey, has laid mains in that city for the purpose of carrying water to Staten Island in the State of New York. By other contracts it is to get the water from the Passaic River, at Little Falls, where the East Jersey Water Company has a large plant by which the water is withdrawn. On May 11, 1905, the State of New Jersey, reciting the need of preserving the fresh water of the State for the health and prosperity of the citizens, enacted that "It shall be unlawful for any person or corporation to transport or carry, through pipes, conduits, ditches or canals, the waters of any fresh water lake, pond, brook, creek, river or stream of this State into any other State, for use therein." By a second section a proceeding like the present was authorized, in order to enforce the act. Laws of 1905, c. 238, p. 461. After the passage of this statute the defendant made a contract with the City of New York to furnish a supply of water adequate for the Borough of Richmond, and of not less than three million gallons a day. Thereupon this information was brought, praying that, pursuant to the above act and otherwise, the defendant might be enjoined from carrying the waters of the Passaic River out of the State. There are allegations as to the amount of water and the probable future demand upon which the parties are not wholly agreed, but the essential facts are not denied. The defendant sets up that the statute, if applicable to it, is contrary to the Constitution of the United States, that it impairs the obligation of contracts, takes property without due process of law, interferes with commerce between New Jersey and New York, denies the privileges of citizens of New Jersey to citizens of other States, and denies to them the equal protection of the laws. An injunction was issued by the Chancellor, 70 N. J. Eq. 525, the decree was affirmed by the Court of Errors and Appeals, 70 N. J. Eq. 695, and the case then was brought here.

The courts below assumed or decided and we shall assume that the defendant represents the rights of a riparian proprietor, and on the other hand, that it represents no special chartered powers that give it greater rights than those. On these assumptions the Court of Errors and Appeals pointed out that a riparian proprietor has no right to divert waters for more than a reasonable distance from the body of the stream or for other than the well-known ordinary uses, and that for any purpose anywhere he is narrowly limited in amount. It went on to infer that his only right in the body of the stream is to have the flow continue, and that there is a residuum of public ownership in the State. It reinforced the State's rights by the State's title to the bed of the stream where flowed by the tide, and concluded from the foregoing and other considerations that, as against the rights of riparian owners merely as such, the State was warranted in prohibiting the acquisition of the title to water on a larger scale.

We will not say that the considerations that we have stated do not warrant the conclusion reached; and we shall not attempt to revise the opinion of the local court upon the local law, if, for the purpose of decision, we accept the argument of the plaintiff in error that it is open to revision when constitutional rights are set up. Neither shall we consider whether such a statute as the one before us might not be upheld, even if the lower riparian proprietors collectively were the absolute owners of the stream, on the ground that it authorized a suit by the State in their interest where it does not appear that they all have released their rights. See *Kansas* v. *Colorado,* 185 U. S. 125, 142. But we prefer to put the authority which cannot be denied to the State upon a broader ground than that which was emphasized below, since in our opinion it is independent of the more or less attenuated residuum of title that the State may be said to possess.

All rights tend to declare themselves absolute to their logical extreme. Yet all in fact are limited by the neighborhood of principles of policy which are other than those on which the particular right is founded, and which become strong enough to hold their own when a certain point is reached. The limits set to property by other public interests present themselves as a branch of what is called the police power of the State. The boundary at which the conflicting interests balance cannot be determined by any general formula in advance, but points in the line, or helping to establish it, are fixed by decisions that this or that concrete case falls on the nearer or farther side. For instance, the police power may limit the height of buildings, in a city, without compensation. To that extent it cuts down what otherwise would be the rights of property. But if it should attempt to limit the height so far as to make an ordinary building lot wholly useless, the rights of property would prevail over the other public interest, and the police power would fail. To set such a limit would need compensation and the power of eminent domain.

It sometimes is difficult to fix boundary stones between the private right of property and the police power when, as in the case at bar, we know of few decisions that are very much in point. But it is recognized that the State as *quasi*-sovereign and representative of the interests of the public has a standing in court to protect the atmosphere, the water and the forests within its territory, irrespective of the assent or dissent of the private owners of the land most immediately concerned. . . . What it may protect by suit in this Court from interference in the name of property outside the State's jurisdiction, one would think that it could protect by statute from interference in the same name within. On this principle of public interest and the police power, and not merely as the inheritor of a royal prerogative, the State may make laws for the preservation of game, which seems a stronger case. . . .

The problems of irrigation have no place here. Leaving them on one side, it appears to us that few public interests are move obvious, indisputable and independent of particular theory than the interest of the public of a State to maintain the rivers that are wholly within it substantially undiminished, except by such drafts upon them as the guardian of the public welfare may permit for the purpose of turning them to a more perfect use. This public interest is omnipresent wherever there is a State, and grows more pressing as population grows. It is fundamental, and we are of opinion that the private property of riparian proprietors cannot be supposed to have deeper roots. Whether it be said that such an interest justifies the cutting down by statute, without compensation, in the exercise of the police power, of what otherwise would be private rights of property, or that apart from statute those rights do not go to the height of what the defendant seeks to do, the result is the same. But we agree with the New Jersey courts, and think it quite beyond any rational view of riparian rights that an agreement, of no matter what private owners, could sanction the diversion of an important stream outside the boundaries of the State in which it flows. The private right to appropriate is subject not only to the rights of lower owners but to the initial limitation that it may not substantially diminish one of the great foundations of public welfare and health.

We are of opinion, further, that the constitutional power of the State to insist that its natural advantages shall remain unimpaired by its citizens is not dependent upon any nice estimate of the extent of present use or speculation as to future needs. The legal conception of the necessary is apt to be confined to somewhat rudimentary wants, and there are benefits from a great river that might escape a lawyer's view. But the State is not required to submit even to an aesthetic analysis. Any analysis may be inadequate. It finds itself in possession of what we all admit to be a great public good, and what it has it may keep and give no one a reason for its will.

The defense under the Fourteenth Amendment is disposed of by what we have said. That under Article I, § 10, needs but a few words more. One whose rights, such as they are, are subject to State restriction, cannot remove them from the power of the State by making a contract about them. The contract will carry with it the infirmity of the subject-matter. . . . But the contract, the execution of which is sought to be prevented here, was illegal when it was made.

The other defenses also may receive short answers. A man cannot acquire a right to property by his desire to use it in commerce among the States. Neither can he enlarge his otherwise limited and qualified right to the same end. The case is covered in this respect by *Geer* v. *Connecticut,* 161 U. S. 519, and the same decision disposes of the argument that the New Jersey law denies equal protection to the citizens of New York. It constantly is necessary to reconcile and to adjust different constitutional principles, each of which would be entitled to possession of the disputed ground but for the presence of the others, as we already have said that it is necessary to reconcile and to adjust different principles of the common law. See *Asbell* v. *Kansas,* 209 U. S. 251. The right to receive water from a river through pipes is subject to territorial limits by nature, and those limits may be fixed by the State within which the river flows, even if they are made to coincide with the State line. Within the boundary citizens of New York are as free to purchase as citizens of New Jersey. But this question does not concern the defendant, which is a New Jersey corporation. There is nothing else that needs mention.

ON THE STATES AND THE NATION

We are of opinion that the decision of the Court of Errors and Appeals was right.

Decree affirmed.

[Justice McKenna dissented without opinion.]

Hudson County Water Co. v. McCarter, Attorney
General of the State of New Jersey
209 U. S. 349

A Burden on Interstate Commerce

(*Galveston, Harrisburg &c. Ry. Co.* v. *Texas,* 1908)

This is an action against certain railroads to recover taxes and penalties. The Supreme Court of the State held the penalties to be void under the State constitution, but upheld the tax. . . . The railroads bring the case here mainly on the ground that the law upon which the action is based is an attempt to regulate commerce among the States.

The act in question is entitled, "An Act imposing a tax upon railroad corporations . . . and other persons . . . owning . . . or controlling any line of railroad in this State . . . equal to one per cent. of their gross receipts . . . and repealing the existing tax on the gross passenger earnings of railroads." It proceeds in § 1 to impose upon such railroads "an annual tax for the year 1905, and for each calendar year thereafter, equal to one per centum of its gross receipts, if such line of railroad lies wholly within the State." In § 2 a report, under oath, of "the gross receipts of such line of railroad, from every source whatever, for the year ending on the thirtieth day of June last preceding," and immediate payment of the tax "calculated on the gross receipts so reported," are required. The comptroller is given power to call for other reports, and is to "estimate such tax on the true gross receipts thereby disclosed," etc. The lines of the railroads concerned are wholly within the State, but they connect with other lines, and a part, in some instances much the larger part, of their gross receipts is derived from the carriage of passengers and freight coming from, or destined to, points without the State. In view of this portion of their business, the railroads contend that the case is governed by *Philadelphia & Southern Mail Steamship Co.* v. *Pennsylvania,* 122 U. S. 326. The counsel for the State rely upon *Maine* v. *Grand Trunk Ry. Co.,* 142 U. S. 217, and maintain, if necessary, that the later overrules the earlier case.

In *Philadelphia & Southern Mail S. S. Co.* v. *Pennsylvania,* 122 U. S. 326, it was decided that a tax upon the gross receipts of a steamship corporation of the State, when such receipts were derived from commerce between the States and with foreign countries, was unconstitutional. We regard this decision as unshaken and as stating established law. It cites the earlier cases to the same effect. Late ones are *Ratterman* v. *Western Union Telegraph Co.,* 127 U. S. 411; *Western Union Telegraph Co.* v. *Pennsylvania,* 128 U. S. 39; *Western Union Telegraph Co.* v. *Seay,* 132 U. S. 472. . . . In *Maine* v. *Grand Trunk Ry. Co.,* 142 U. S. 217, the authority of the *Philadelphia Steamship Company Case* was accepted without question, and the decision was justified by the majority as not in any way qualifying or impairing it. The validity of the distinction was what divided the Court.

It being once admitted, as of course it must be, that not every law that affects commerce among the States is a regulation of it in a constitutional sense, nice distinctions are to be expected. Regulation and commerce among the States both are practical rather than technical conceptions, and, naturally, their limits must be fixed by practical lines. As the property of companies engaged in such commerce may be taxed, *Pullman's Palace Car Co.* v. *Pennsylvania,* 141 U. S. 18, and may be taxed at its value as it is, in its organic relations, and not merely as congeries of unrelated items, taxes on such property have been sustained that took account of the augmentation of value from the commerce in which it was engaged. . . . So it has been held that a tax on the property and business of a railroad operated within the State might be estimated *prima facie* by gross income, computed by adding to the income derived from business within the State the proportion of interstate business equal to the proportion between the road over which the business was carried within the State to the total length of the road over which it was carried. . . .

Since the commercial value of property consists in the expectation of income from it, and since taxes ultimately, at least in the long run, come out of income, obviously taxes called taxes on property and those called taxes on income or receipts tend to run into each other somewhat as fair value and anticipated profits run into each other in the law of damages. The difficulty of distinguishing them became greater when it was decided, not without much debate and difference of opinion, that interstate carriers' property might be taxed as a going concern. In *Wisconsin & Michigan Ry. Co.* v. *Powers,* 191 U. S. 379, the measure of property by income purported only to be *prima facie* valid. But the extreme case came earlier. In *Maine* v. *Grand Trunk Ry. Co., supra,* "an annual excise tax for the privilege of exercising its franchise," was levied upon every one operating a railroad in the State, fixed by percentages, varying up to a certain limit, upon the average gross receipts per mile multiplied by the number of miles within the State when the road extended outside. This seems at first sight like a reaction from the *Philadelphia & Southern Mail Steamship Company Case.* But it may not have been. The estimated gross receipts per mile may be said to have been made a measure of the value of the property per mile. That the effort of the State was to reach that value and not to fasten on the receipts from transportation as such was shown by the fact that the scheme of the statute was to establish a system. The buildings of the railroad and its lands and fixtures outside of its right of way were to be taxed locally, as other property was taxed, and this excise with the local tax were to be in lieu of all taxes. The language shows that the local tax was not expected to include the additional value gained by the property being part of a going concern. That idea came in later. The excise was an attempt to reach that additional value. The two taxes together fairly may be called a commutation tax. See *Ficklen* v. *Taxing District of Shelby County,* 145 U. S. 1, 23; *Postal Telegraph Cable Co.* v. *Adams,* 155 U. S. 688, 697; *McHenry* v. *Alford,* 168 U. S. 651, 670, 671.

"By whatever name the exaction may be called, if it amounts to no more than the ordinary tax upon property or a just equivalent therefor, ascertained by reference thereto, it is not open to attack as inconsistent with the Constitution." *Postal Telegraph Cable Co.* v. *Adams,* 155 U. S. 688, 697. See *New York, Lake Erie & Western R. R. Co.* v. *Pennsylvania,* 158 U. S. 431, 438, 439. The question is whether this is such a tax. It appears sufficiently, perhaps from what has been said, that we are to look for a practical rather than a logical or philosophical distinction. The State must be allowed to tax the property and to tax it at its actual value as a going concern. On the other hand the State cannot tax the interstate business. The two necessities hardly admit of an absolute logical reconciliation. Yet the distinction is not without sense. When a legislature is trying simply to value property, it is less likely to attempt to or effect injurious regulation than when it is aiming directly at the receipts from interstate commerce. A practical line can be drawn by taking the whole scheme of taxation into account. That must be done by this Court as best it can. Neither the State courts nor the legislatures, by giving the tax a particular name or by the use of some form of words, can take away our duty to consider its nature and effect. If it bears upon commerce among the States so directly as to amount to a regulation in a relatively immediate way, it will not be saved by name or form. . . .

We are of opinion that the statute levying this tax does amount to an attempt to regulate commerce among the States. The distinction between a tax "equal to" one percent of gross receipts and a tax of one percent of the same, seems to us nothing, except where the former phrase is the index of an actual attempt to reach the property and to let the interstate traffic and the receipts from it alone. We find no such attempt or anything to qualify the plain inference from the statute taken by itself. On the contrary, we rather infer from the judgment of the State court and from the argument on behalf of the State that another tax on the property of the railroad is upon a valuation of that property taken as a going concern. This is merely an effort to reach the gross receipts, not even disguised by the name of an occupation tax, and in no way helped by the words "equal to."

Of course, it does not matter that the plaintiffs in error are domestic corporations or that the tax embraces indiscriminately gross receipts from commerce within as well as outside of the State. We are of opinion that the judgment should be reversed.

Judgment reversed.

[Mr. Justice Harlan wrote a dissenting opinion in which Chief Justice Fuller and Justices White and McKenna concurred. They felt that the State intended to impose only an occupation tax, and that "its operation on interstate commerce is only incidental, not direct."]

Galveston, Harrisburg & San Antonio Ry. Co.
v. *State of Texas*
210 U. S. 217

Executive Process During an Insurrection

(*Moyer* v. *Peabody*, 1909)

This is an action brought by the plaintiff in error against the former Governor of the State of Colorado, the former Adjutant General of the National Guard of the same State, and a captain of a company of the National Guard, for an imprisonment of the plaintiff by them while in office. The complaint was dismissed on demurrer, and the case comes here on a certificate that the demurrer was sustained solely on the ground that there was no jurisdiction in the Circuit Court. . . .

The complaint alleges that the imprisonment was continued from the morning of March 30, 1914, to the afternoon of June 15, and that the defendants justified under the constitution of Colorado making the Governor commander-in-chief of the State forces, and giving him power to call them out to execute laws, suppress insurrection and repel invasion. It alleges that his imprisonment was without probable cause, that no complaint was filed against plaintiff, and that (in that sense) he was prevented from having access to the courts of the State, although they were open during the whole time; but it sets out proceedings on *habeas corpus*, instituted by him before the Supreme Court of the State, in which that court refused to admit him to bail and ultimately discharged the writ. . . . In those proceedings it appeared that the Governor had declared a county to be in a state of insurrection, had called out troops to put down the trouble, and had ordered that the plaintiff should be arrested as a leader of the outbreak, and should be detained until he could be discharged with safety, and that then he should be delivered to the civil authorities to be dealt with according to law.

The jurisdiction of the Circuit Court, if it exists, is under Rev. Stat. § 629, Sixteenth. That clause gives original jurisdiction "of all suits authorized by law to be brought by any person to redress the deprivation, under color of any law, statute, ordinance, regulation, custom, or usage of any State, of any right, privilege, or immunity, secured by the Constitution of the United States, or of any right secured by any law providing for equal rights of citizens of the United States, or of all persons within the jurisdiction of the United States." The complaint purports to be founded upon the Constitution and on Rev. Stat. § 1979, which authorizes suit to be brought for such deprivation as above described. Therefore the question whether the complaint states a case upon the merits under § 1979 in this instance is another aspect of the question whether it states a case within the jurisdiction of the court under § 629, cl. 16. Taken either way, the question is whether this is a suit authorized by law, that is, by § 1979, or the Constitution, or both.

The plaintiff's position, stated in a few words, is that the action of the Governor, sanctioned to the extent that it was by the decision of the Supreme Court, was the action of the State and therefore within the Fourteenth Amendment; but that if that action was unconstitutional the Governor got no protection from personal liability for his unconstitutional interference with the plaintiff's rights. It is admitted, as it must be, that the Governor's declaration that a state of insurrection existed is conclusive of that fact. It seems to be admitted also that the arrest alone would not necessarily have given a right to bring this suit. . . . But it is said that a detention for so many days, alleged to be without probable cause, at a time when the courts were open, without an attempt to bring the plaintiff before them, makes a case on which he has a right to have a jury pass.

ON THE STATES AND THE NATION

We shall not consider all of the questions that the facts suggest, but shall confine ourselves to stating what we regard as a sufficient answer to the complaint, without implying that there are not others equally good. Of course the plaintiff's position is that he has been deprived of his liberty without due process of law. But it is familiar that what is due process of law depends on circumstances. It varies with the subject-matter and the necessities of the situation. Thus summary proceedings suffice for taxes, and executive decisions for exclusion from the country.... What, then, are the circumstances of this case? By agreement the record of the proceedings upon *habeas corpus* was made part of the complaint, but that did not make the averments of the petition for the writ averments of the complaint. The facts that we are to assume are that a state of insurrection existed and that the Governor, without sufficient reason but in good faith, in the course of putting the insurrection down, held the plaintiff until he thought that he safely could release him.

It would seem to be admitted by the plaintiff that he was president of the Western Federation of Miners, and that, whoever was to blame, trouble was apprehended with the members of that organization. We mention these facts not as material, but simply to put in more definite form the nature of the occasion on which the Governor felt called upon to act. In such a situation we must assume that he had a right under the State constitution and laws to call out troops, as was held by the Supreme Court of the State. The constitution is supplemented by an Act providing that "when an invasion of or an insurrection in the State is made or threatened the Governor shall order the National Guard to repel or suppress the same." Laws of 1897, c. 63, Art. 7, § 2, p. 204. That means that he shall make the ordinary use of soldiers to that end; that he may kill persons who resist and, of course, that he may use the milder measure of seizing the bodies of those whom he considers to stand in the way of restoring peace. Such arrests are not necessarily for punishment, but are by way of precaution to prevent the exercise of hostile power. So long as such arrests are made in good faith and in the honest belief that they are needed in order to head the insurrection off, the Governor is the final judge and cannot be subjected to an action after he is out of office on the ground that he had not reasonable ground for his belief. If we suppose a Governor with a very long term of office, it may be that a case could be imagined in which the length of the imprisonment would raise a different question. But there is nothing in the duration of the plaintiff's detention or in the allegations of the complaint that would warrant submitting the judgment of the Governor to revision by a jury. It is not alleged that his judgment was not honest, if that be material, or that the plaintiff was detained after fears of the insurrection were at an end.

No doubt there are cases where the expert on the spot may be called upon to justify his conduct later in court, notwithstanding the fact that he had sole command at the time and acted to the best of his knowledge. That is the position of the captain of a ship. But even in that case great weight is given to his determination and the matter is to be judged on the facts as they appear then and not merely in the light of the event. . . . When it comes to a decision by the head of the State upon a matter involving its life, the ordinary rights of individuals must yield to what he deems the necessities of the moment. Public danger warrants the substitution of executive process for judicial process. See *Keely v. Sanders*, 90 U. S. 441, 446. This was admitted with regard to killing men in the actual clash of arms, and we think it obvious, although it was disputed, that the same is true of temporary detention to prevent apprehended harm. As no one would deny that there was immunity for ordering a company to fire upon a mob in insurrection, and that a State law authorizing the Governor to deprive citizens of life under such circumstances was consistent with the Fourteenth Amendment, we are of opinion that the same is true of a law authorizing by implication what was done in this case. As we have said already, it is unnecessary to consider whether there are other reasons why the Circuit Court was right in its conclusion. It is enough that in our opinion the declaration does not disclose a "suit authorized by law to be brought to redress the deprivation of any right secured by the Constitution of the United States." See *Dow* v. *Johnson,* 100 U. S. 158.

Judgment affirmed.

Moyer v. *Peabody*
212 U. S. 78

Extending Congressional Authority

(*Ruddy* v. *Rossi*, 1918)

[THE COURT HELD THE CONSTITUTIONALITY OF A PROVISION OF THE Homestead Act, which conferred on the property of a homesteader an exemption from execution to satisfy a judgment obtained against him after his final entry on the land, but before a patent had been issued. "Congress has plenary power to dispose of public lands," wrote Mr. Justice McReynolds; hence it might grant titles with exemption from certain debts. Mr. Justice Holmes dissented:]

THIS CASE involves a question of theory that may be important and I think it desirable to state the considerations that make me doubt. The facts needing to be mentioned are few. On August 26, 1912, the United States conveyed land in Idaho to Ruddy in fee simple, in pursuance of a homestead entry by Ruddy on August 6, 1903, final proof on October 4, 1909, and final receipt of the purchase price on November 12, 1909. In September, 1912, after the conveyance, Rossi began suits against Ruddy, attaching this land, and in June, 1914, levied executions upon the same. The debts for which the suits were brought were incurred before the issue of the patent and the present proceeding is to prevent Rossi from selling the land to satisfy the judgments. The question arises under Rev. Stats. § 2296, providing that no lands acquired under that chapter shall in any event become liable to the satisfaction of any debt contracted prior to the issuing of the patent therefor. The Supreme Court of Idaho narrowed the issue to the case of debts contracted after final proof, but that distinction is not important to the difficulty in my mind.

My question is this: When land has left the ownership and control of the United States and is part of the territory of a State not different from any other privately owned land within the jurisdiction and no more subject to legislation on the part of the United States than any other land, on what ground is a previous law of Congress supposed any longer to affect it in a way that a subsequent one could not? This land was levied upon not on the assertion that any lien upon it was acquired before the title passed to the United States, but merely as any other land might be attached for a debt that Rossi had a right to collect, after the United States had left the premises. I ask myself what the United States has to do with that. There is no condition, no reserved right of reentry, no reversion in the United States, saved either under the Idaho law as any private grantor might save it, or by virtue of antecedent title. All interest of the United States as owner is at an end. It is a stranger to the title. Even in case of an escheat the land would not go to it, but would go to the State. Therefore the statute must operate, if at all, purely by way of legislation, not as a qualification of a grant. If § 2296 is construed to apply to this case, there is simply the naked assumption of one sovereignty to impose its will after whatever jurisdiction or authority it had has ceased and the land has come fully under the jurisdiction of what for this purpose is a different power. It is a pure attempt to regulate the alienability of land in Idaho by law, without regard to the will of Idaho, which we must assume on this record to authorize the levy if it is not prevented by an Act of Congress occupying a paramount place.

I believe that this Court never has gone farther in the way of sustaining legislation concerning land within a State than to uphold a law forbidding the enclosure of public lands, which little, if at all, exceeded the rights of a private owner, although it was construed to prevent the erection of fences upon the defendants' own property manifestly for the sole purpose of enclosing land of the United States. . . . At most it was a protection of the present interests of the United States under a title paramount to the State. On the other hand, it is said in *Pollard* v. *Hagan*, 3 How. 212, 224, that no power in the nature of municipal sovereignty can be exercised by the United States within a State; that such power is repugnant to the Constitution. This case was referred to in *Withers* v. *Buckley*, 20 How. 84, and it was decided that an Act of Congress authorizing the formation of the State of Mississippi and providing that the Mississippi River should be forever free "could have no effect to restrict the new State in any of its necessary attributes as an independent sovereign government," and both these cases were cited upon this point with approval in *Ward* v. *Racehorse*, 163 U. S. 504, 511, 512. See also *Shively* v. *Bowlby*, 152 U. S. 1, 27. In *Irvine* v. *Marshall*, 20 How. 558, where it was held that the laws of a territory abolishing constructive trusts were ineffectual to protect the holder of a certificate from the United States against the establishment of such a trust, it was said that "when the subject, and all control over it, shall have passed from the United States, and have become vested in a citizen or resident of the territory, then indeed the territorial regulations may operate upon it," and later in the decision there is cited a passage from *Wilcox* v. *Jackson*, 13 Pet. 498, 517, to the same effect—a passage also cited and relied upon by the four justices who dissented and held that the territorial laws governed even then. It has been repeated ever since. . . .

Coming to the precise issue, the question of the power of the United States to restrict alienation of land within a State after it had conveyed the land in fee was left open in *Wright* v. *Morgan*, 191 U. S. 55, 58, but it was said that the clearest expression would be necessary before it would be admitted that such a restriction was imposed. In *Buchser* v. *Buchser*, 231 U. S. 157, it was held that the laws of the United States did not prevent homestead land becoming community property at the moment that title was acquired, and it was said that, the acquisition under the United States law being complete, that law had released its control. The statement in *Wilcox* v. *Jackson, supra,* that when the title has passed the land "like all other property in the State is subject to the state legislation," was repeated. In *Alabama* v. *Schmidt,* 232 U. S. 168, following *Cooper* v. *Roberts,* 18 How. 173, it was held that land conveyed to the State by the United States for the use of schools could be acquired by adverse possession under State law, and that the trust, although as was said in the earlier case "a sacred obligation imposed on its public faith" imposed only an honorary obligation on the State. *Northern Pacific Ry. Co.* v. *Townsend,* 190 U. S. 267, was distinguished as having been decided on the ground that in the grant to the Railway there was an implied condition of reverter in case the company ceased to hold the land for the purpose for which it was granted, a ground, which, as I have said, is absent here.

It is said that where a statute is susceptible of two constructions, by one of which grave constitutional questions arise and by the other of which they are avoided, our duty is to adopt the latter. . . . I am aware that this principle like some others more often is invoked in aid of a conclusion reached on other grounds than made itself the basis of decision, but it seems to me that it properly should govern here. It might without violence. When the Act of 1862, now Rev. Stats., § 2296, was passed, the United States owned territories to which it could be applied with full scope. . . . The greater part of the public land was in those territories. Without stopping to suggest other possibilities of construction this fact is enough to explain and give validity to the Act when passed. There is no need to import to it the intent to anticipate the future and to reach the States that were still in the bosom of time.

Of course the United States has power to choose appropriate means for exercising the authority given to it by the Constitution. But I see no sufficient ground for extending that authority to a case like this. It is not the business of the United States to determine the policy to be pursued concerning privately owned land within a State. According to all cases in this Court, so far as I know, when the patent issued its authority was at an end.

I am aware that my doubts are contrary to manifest destiny and to a number of decisions in the State courts. I know also that when common understanding and practice have established a way it is a waste of time to wander in bypaths of logic. But as I have a real difficulty in understanding how the congressional restriction is held to govern this case—a question which nothing that I have heard as yet appears to me to answer—I think it worth while to mention my misgivings, if only to show that they have been considered and are not shared.

Ruddy v. *Rossi*
248 U. S. 104, 107

Jurisdiction Over Migratory Birds

(*Missouri* v. *Holland*, 1920)

THIS is a bill in equity brought by the State of Missouri to prevent a game warden of the United States from attempting to enforce the Migratory Bird Treaty Act of July 3, 1918, c. 128, 40 Stat. 755, and the regulations made by the Secretary of Agriculture in pursuance of the same. The ground of the bill is that the statute is an unconstitutional interference with the rights reserved to the States by the Tenth Amendment, and that the acts of the defendant done and threatened under that authority invade the sovereign right of the State and contravene its will manifested in statutes. The State also alleges a pecuniary interest, as owner of the wild birds within its borders and otherwise, admitted by the Government to be sufficient, but it is enough that the bill is a reasonable and proper means to assert the alleged *quasi*-sovereign rights of a State. . . . A motion to dismiss was sustained by the District Court on the ground that the Act of Congress is constitutional. . . . The State appeals.

On December 8, 1916, a treaty between the United States and Great Britain was proclaimed by the President. It recited that many species of birds in their annual migrations traversed many parts of the United States and of Canada, that they were of great value as a source of food and in destroying insects injurious to vegetation, but were in danger of extermination through lack of adequate protection. It therefore provided for specified close seasons and protection in other forms, and agreed that the two powers would take or propose to their law-making bodies the necessary measures for carrying the treaty out. 39 Stat. 1702. The above mentioned Act of July 3, 1918, entitled "An Act to give effect to the convention," prohibited the killing, capturing or selling of any of the migratory birds included in the terms of the treaty except as permitted by regulations compatible with those terms, to be made by the Secretary of Agriculture. Regulations were proclaimed on July 31, and October 25, 1918. 40 Stat. 1812; 1863. It is unnecessary to go into any details, because, as we have said, the question raised is the general one whether the treaty and statute are void as an interference with the rights reserved to the States.

To answer this question it is not enough to refer to the Tenth Amendment, reserving the powers not delegated to the United States, because by Article II, § 2, the power to make treaties is delegated expressly, and by Article VI treaties made under the authority of the United States, along with the Constitution and laws of the United States made in pursuance thereof, are declared the supreme law of the land. If the treaty is valid there can be no dispute about the validity of the statute under Article I, § 8, as a necessary and proper means to execute the powers of the Government. The language of the Constitution as to the supremacy of treaties being general, the question before us is narrowed to an inquiry into the ground upon which the present supposed exception is placed.

It is said that a treaty cannot be valid if it infringes the Constitution, that there are limits, therefore, to the treaty-making power, and that one such limit is that what an Act of Congress could not do unaided, in derogation of the powers reserved to the States, a treaty cannot do. An earlier Act of Congress that attempted by itself and not in pursuance of a treaty to regulate the killing of migratory birds within the States had been held bad in the District Court. . . . Those decisions were supported by arguments that migratory birds were owned by the States in their sovereign capacity for the benefit of their people, and that under cases like *Geer* v. *Connecticut*, 161 U. S. 519, this control was one that Congress had no power to displace. The same argument is supposed to apply now with equal force.

Whether the two cases cited were decided rightly or not they cannot be accepted as a test of the treaty power. Acts of Congress are the supreme law of the land only when made in pursuance of the Constitution, while treaties are declared to be so when made under the authority of the United States. It is open to question whether the authority of the United States means more than the formal acts prescribed to make the convention. We do not mean to imply here that there are no qualifications to the treaty-making power; but they must be ascertained in a different way. It is obvious that there may be matters of the sharpest exigency for national well-being that an Act of Congress could not deal with but that a treaty followed by such an act could, and it is not lightly to be assumed that, in matters requiring national action, "a power which must belong to and somewhere reside in every civilized government" is not to be found. *Andrews* v. *Andrews*, 188 U. S. 14, 33. What was said in that case with regard to the powers of the States applies with equal force to the powers of the Nation in cases where the States individually are incompetent to act. We are not yet discussing the particular case before us but only are considering the validity of the test proposed. With regard to that we may add that when we are dealing with words that also are a constituent act, like the Constitution of the United States, we must realize that they have called into life a being the development of which could not have been foreseen completely by the most gifted of its begetters. It was enough for them to realize or to hope that they had created an organism; it has taken a century and has cost their successors much sweat and blood to prove that they created a Nation. The case before us must be considered in the light of our whole experience and not merely in that of what was said a hundred years ago. The treaty in question does not contravene any prohibitory words to be found in the Constitution. The only question is whether it is forbidden by some invisible radiation from the general terms of the Tenth Amendment. We must consider what this country has become in deciding what that Amendment has reserved.

The State as we have intimated founds its claim of exclusive authority upon an assertion of title to migratory birds, an assertion that is embodied in statute. No doubt it is true that as between a State and its inhabitants the State may regulate the killing and sale of such birds, but it does not follow that its authority is exclusive of paramount powers. To put the claim of the State upon title is to lean upon a slender reed. Wild birds are not in the possession of anyone; and possession is the beginning of ownership. The whole foundation of the State's rights is the presence within their jurisdiction of birds that yesterday had not arrived, tomorrow may be in another State and in a week a thousand miles away. If we are to be accurate we cannot put the case of the State upon higher ground than that the treaty deals with creatures that for the moment are within the State borders, that it must be carried out by officers of the United States within the same territory, and that but for the treaty the State would be free to regulate this subject itself.

As most of the laws of the United States are carried out within the States and as many of them deal with matters which in the silence of such laws the State might regulate, such general grounds are not enough to support Missouri's claim. Valid treaties of course "are as binding within the territorial limits of the States as they are effective throughout the dominion of the United States," *Baldwin* v. *Franks*, 120 U. S. 678, 683. No doubt the great body of private relations usually falls within the control of the State but a treaty may override its power. We do not have to invoke the later developments of constitutional law for this proposition; it was recognized as early as *Hopkirk* v. *Bell*, 3 Cranch, 454, with regard to statutes of limitation, and even earlier, as to confiscation, in *Ware* v. *Hylton*, 3 Dall. 199. It was assumed by Chief Justice Marshall with regard to the escheat of land to the State in *Chirac* v. *Chirac*, 2 Wheat. 259, 275. . . . So as to a limited jurisdiction of foreign consuls within a State. . . . Further illustration seems unnecessary, and it only remains to consider the application of established rules to the present case.

Here a national interest of very nearly the first magnitude is involved. It can be protected only by national action in concert with that of another power. The subject-matter is only transitorily within the State and has no permanent habitat therein. But for the treaty and the statute there soon might be no birds for any powers to deal with. We see nothing in the Constitution that compels the Government to sit by while a food supply is cut off and the protectors of our forests and our crops are destroyed. It is not sufficient to rely upon the States. The reliance is vain, and were it otherwise, the question is whether the United States is forbidden to act. We are of opinion that the treaty and statute must be upheld. . . .

Decree affirmed.

[Justices Van Devanter and Pitney dissented without opinion.]

Missouri v. *Holland, United States Game Warden*
252 U. S. 416

Taxing a Railroad's Property

(*Wallace* v. *Hines*, 1920)

This is an appeal from an order of three judges restraining the defendants, the appellants, from taking steps to enforce taxes imposed by an Act of North Dakota, approved March 7, 1919, (c. 222) until the further order of the court. The plaintiff railroads are corporations of other States with lines extending into North Dakota. The defendants are the State Tax Commissioner, the State Treasurer, the State Auditor, the Attorney General and the Secretary of State for North Dakota. As the tax is made a first lien upon all the property of the plaintiff railroads in the State and thus puts a cloud upon their title, and as delay in payment is visited with considerable penalties, there is jurisdiction in equity unless there is an adequate remedy at law against the State, to which the tax is to be paid. . . . The only ground for supposing that there is such a remedy is a provision that "an action respecting the title to property, or arising upon any contract, may be brought in the district court against the state the same as against a private person." Compiled Laws, N. Dak., § 8175. This case does not arise upon contract except in the purely artificial sense that some claims for money alleged to have been obtained wrongfully might have been enforced at common law by an action of *assumpsit*. Nothing could be more remote from an actual contract than the wrongful extortion of money by threats, and we ought not to leave the plaintiffs to a speculation upon what the State court might say if an action at law were brought. . . .

We quote the tax in full [in the margin]. It will be seen that it purports to be a special excise tax upon doing business in the State. As the law is administered, the tax commissioner fixes the value of the total property of each railroad by the total value of its stocks and bonds and assesses the proportion of this value that the main track mileage in North Dakota bears to the main track of the whole line. But on the allegations of the bill, which is all that we have before us, the circumstances are such as to make the mode of assessment indefensible. North Dakota is a State of plains, very different from the other States, and the cost of the roads there was much less than it was in mountainous regions that the roads had to traverse. The State is mainly agricultural. Its markets are outside its boundaries and most of the distributing centers from which it purchases also are outside. It naturally follows that the great and very valuable terminals of the roads are in other States. So looking only to the physical track the injustice of assuming the value to be evenly distributed according to main track mileage is plain. But that is not all.

The only reason for allowing a State to look beyond its borders when it taxes the property of foreign corporations is that it may get the true value of the things within it, when they are part of an organic system of wide extent, that gives them a value above what they otherwise would possess. The purpose is not to expose the heel of the system to a mortal dart—not, in other words, to open to taxation what is not within the State. Therefore no property of such an interstate road situated elsewhere can be taken into account unless it can be seen in some plain and fairly intelligible way that it adds to the value of the road and the rights exercised in the State. Hence the possession of bonds secured by mortgage of lands in other States, or of a land-grant in another State or of other property that adds to the riches of the corporation but does not affect the North Dakota part of the road is no sufficient ground for the increase of the tax—whatever it may be—whether a tax on property, or, as here, an excise upon doing business in the State. . . . In this case, it is alleged, the tax commissioner's valuation included items of the kind described to very large amounts. The foregoing considerations justify the preliminary injunction that was granted against what would appear to be an unwarranted interference with interstate commerce and a taking of property without due process of law. . . .

The Attorney General of the State in his very candid argument suggested that if the mode adopted by the tax commissioner were open to objections the statute might be construed to give him an election as to the method of distribution, and that he should take gross earnings, or, if more easily ascertainable, the property or mileage basis of distribution. As we are dealing only with a preliminary injunction we confine our consideration to a general view of the mode actually followed, and upon that we are of opinion that the decree should be affirmed.

Decree affirmed.

Wallace v. *Hines*
253 U. S. 66

Pipe Lines in Interstate Commerce

(*Eureka Pipe Line Co.* v. *Hallanan*, 1921)

THIS is a bill to prevent the enforcement against the plaintiff of a statute of West Virginia that forbids engaging in the business of transporting petroleum in pipe lines without the payment of a tax of two cents for each barrel of oil transported. Acts of 1919, Extraordinary Session, c. 5. It is set up that the statute is contrary to the Constitution of the United States in several ways, one of these being that as applied to the plaintiff it imposes a tax upon commerce among the States. The plaintiff owns a system of pipe lines in West Virginia connecting with other pipe lines in Ohio and Kentucky on the west and in Pennsylvania on the east of the State. Through the plaintiff's pipes oil flows in a continuous stream to the State line and beyond—in all amounting to over twenty-two million barrels in the year ending June 30, 1919. There are four grades of the oil thus moved. Two of these are produced partly in West Virginia. According to the figures accepted by the defendants in error, out of a total of 9,076,599.83 barrels of the Pennsylvania grade 6,510,081.51 barrels came from this State, upon over six millions of which the plaintiff made a charge of twenty, later thirty, cents for gathering, on an interstate tariff and also under a local statute. But all the oil of the same grade was mixed, regardless of source, and of the Pennsylvania grade only 1,239,099.55 barrels were used in West Virginia. It is admitted that the tax may be levied in respect of the last item, but the question before us is whether the tax can be laid upon the whole product of the State upon which was imposed the gathering charge.

The Circuit Court of the State held that the statute was void. The Supreme Court of Appeals sustained it so far as the oil produced in West Virginia was concerned. But as the court declared that the Act should be construed to apply only to commerce within the State, it is urged that there is no jurisdiction here of the writ of error because there is no question as to the validity of a statute so limited. The plaintiff in error also applied for a writ of certiorari so that the objection would be immaterial were we not required to determine upon which proceeding the decree should issue. In view of that necessity we dispose of the matter before going further. Upon the declaration of the court we may conjecture that if it had considered that the oil in question moved in interstate commerce it would have agreed with the court below, and on this ground it is argued that the mistake, if any, was not in approving the statute but in the court's conception of interstate commerce. But we must look at what the court has done, not at its mode of reaching the result. What it has done is to decide that the statute covers all the oil produced in West Virginia and that it shall be upheld in so doing. The nature of the mistake that induced the Act is immaterial. A case would not be withdrawn from the jurisdiction of this Court in error by a declaration that a statute was addressed only to intrastate commerce if it was applied wholesale to freight passing across the continent. The fact that the error was less does not affect the principle involved. But furthermore the court only confined the statute to intrastate commerce "as above defined," that is, to commerce that embraced what the plaintiff carried on.

We return to the facts affecting the merits. When oil is received from the producer he receives a credit on the books of the plaintiff pipe line, and thereafter is charged for storage, as it is called, the plaintiff being required by the laws of West Virginia to keep enough oil in its tanks and pipes to satisfy such credits. Code, 1913, § 3864. If the producer desires to deliver oil outside the State it hands to the pipe line company what is called a tender of shipment for so many barrels of the specified kind of oil, naming the consignee, and expressed to be subject to an identified tariff filed with the Interstate Commerce Commission. This is said to be a joint tariff in which the connecting carriers share, but they do not share in the twenty or thirty cents charged for gathering the oil. The argument for the defendants in error of course is that the producer is free to sell within or without the State and that the movement of gathering having taken place before any order is given and while the producer still can do as he likes, it must be regarded as intrastate.

It does not seem to matter for the question before us, whether the delivery to the pipe line be regarded as making it the owner of what it receives and a debtor for the amounts, as in the case of a bank, or as akin to those transactions that are held to make the recipient a bailee of the mingled mass and the bailors tenants in common, as seems to have been assumed. Whether debtor or bailee the pipe line controls the movement of any specific oil in its hands and the bailor assents to its doing so. The bailor assents to its becoming part of a stream that is pouring through and out of the State. Its only right is to call on the pipe line to divert a portion of that stream. So far as the oil that it calls for goes out of the State with the general current it seems to us not to be distinguishable from the rest admitted to move in interstate commerce. No bailor has title to any specific oil, and to deny the character of interstate commerce to the whole stream simply because some one might have called for a delivery that probably would have been made from it in an event that did not happen, is going too far. The charges for gathering and storage seem to us not to affect the case. The storage merely means that enough oil must be kept in the tanks and pipes to satisfy credits. The oil runs into a tank on one side and out on the other. The tank may be regarded as a pipe of larger size. Whether the plaintiff in error was right or wrong in relying upon State law for its gathering charge its attitude does not matter here.

As has been repeated many times, interstate commerce is a practical conception, and, as remarked by the court of first instance, a tax to be valid "must not in its practical effect and operation burden interstate commerce." It appears to us as a practical matter that the transmission of this stream of oil was interstate commerce from the beginning of the flow, and that it was none the less so that if different orders had been received by the pipe line it would have changed the destination upon which the oil was started and at which it in fact arrived. We repeat that the pipe line company not the producer was the master of the destination of any specific oil. Therefore its intent and action determined the character of the movement from its beginning, and neither the intent nor the direction of the movement changed.

Decree reversed.
Writ of certiorari denied.

[Mr. Justice Clarke thought that the Court's "practical conception" of what constitutes interstate commerce was "a too highly technical conception to find place in the world of practical business." Justices Pitney and Brandeis concurred in his dissent.]

Eureka Pipe Line Co. v. *Hallanan,*
State Tax Commissioner, et al.
257 U. S. 265

State Laws and National Banks

(*Missouri ex rel. Burnes Nat'l Bank* v. *Duncan*, 1924)

THE relator, the Burnes National Bank of St. Joseph, was appointed executor by a citizen of Missouri who died on November 27, 1922, leaving a will. The Bank applied to the proper Probate Court for letters testamentary, but was denied appointment on the ground that by the laws of Missouri national banks were not authorized to act as executors. Thereupon it applied to the Supreme Court of the State for a writ of *mandamus* to the judge of the Probate Court and an alternative writ was issued. The respondent demurred, the demurrer was sustained and the peremptory writ was denied. 302 Mo. 130. A writ of error was allowed by the Chief Justice of the State Court. The Bank claims the capacity to fill the office under the statutes of the United States.

By the Act of September 26, 1918, c. 177, § 2, 40 Stat. 967, 968, amending § 11 (k) of the Federal Reserve Act, the Federal Reserve Board was empowered "To grant by special permit to national banks applying therefor, when not in contravention of State or local law, the right to act as trustee, executor, administrator . . . or in any other fiduciary capacity in which State banks, trust companies, or other corporations which come into competition with national banks, are permitted to act under the laws of the State in which the national bank is located." If the section stopped there the decision of the State court might be final, but it adds the following paragraph, "Whenever the laws of such State authorize or permit the exercise of any or all of the foregoing powers by State banks, trust companies, or other corporations which compete with national banks, the granting to and the exercise of such powers by national banks shall not be deemed to be in contravention of State or local law within the meaning of this Act." This says in a roundabout and polite but unmistakable way that whatever may be the State law, national banks having the permit of the Federal Reserve Board may act as executors if trust companies competing with them have that power. The relator has the permit, competing trust companies can act as executors in Missouri, the importance of the power to the sustaining of competition in the banking business is so well known and has been explained so fully heretofore that it does not need to be emphasized, and thus the naked question presented is whether Congress had the power to do what it tried to do.

The question is pretty nearly answered by the decision and fully answered by the reasoning in *First National Bank of Bay City* v. *Fellows*, 244 U. S. 416. That case was decided before the amendment to the Federal Reserve Act that we have quoted and came here on the single issue of the power of Congress when the State law was not contravened. It was held that the power "was to be tested by the right to create the bank and the authority to attach to it that which was relevant in the judgment of Congress to make the business of the bank successful." 244 U. S. 420. Now that Congress has expressed its paramount will this language is more apposite than ever. The States cannot use their most characteristic powers to reach unconstitutional results. . . . There is nothing over which a State has more exclusive authority than the jurisdiction of its courts, but it cannot escape its constitutional obligations by the device of denying jurisdiction to courts otherwise competent. . . . So here—the State cannot lay hold of its general control of administration to deprive national banks of their power to compete that Congress is authorized to sustain.

The fact that Missouri has regulations to secure the safety of trust funds in the hands of its trust companies does not affect this case. The power given by the Act of Congress purports to be general and independent of that circumstance and the Act provides its own safeguards. The authority of Congress is equally independent, as otherwise the State could make it nugatory. Since the decision in *First National Bank of Bay City* v. *Fellows*, it generally has been recognized that the law is now as the relator contends. . . .

Judgment reversed.

[Mr. Justice Sutherland (joined by Mr. Justice McReynolds) felt that the authority of the *Fellows Case* was pressed too far; the matter was in the State's exclusive control; the Federal Government had no right to meddle with it. "The probate courts of a State have only such powers as the State Legislature gives them. They are wholly beyond the jurisdiction of Congress." The dissenting justices felt that this precedent would go far toward reducing the States of the Union "to the status of mere geographical subdivisions."]

State of Missouri, ex rel. Burnes National Bank of St. Joseph v. *Duncan, Judge of the Probate Court of Buchanan County, Missouri*
265 U. S. 17

Inconveniences of Daylight Saving

(*Mass. State Grange* v. *Benton*, 1926)

THIS is a bill brought by different parties having different and unconnected interests seeking a declaration that the Daylight Saving Acts of Massachusetts, Acts of 1920, c. 280, Acts of 1921, c. 145, are inconsistent with the Act of Congress of March 19, 1918, c. 24; 40 Stat. 450; (see Act of August 20, 1919, c. 51; 41 Stat. 280), and unconstitutional, and asking an injunction to prevent the several defendants from doing their respective official parts to carry out the Massachusetts law. It was heard by three judges in the District Court, and upon motion it was dismissed. . . .

The Act of Congress, § 2, fixes the standard time and provides that "In all statutes, orders, rules, and regulations relating to the time of performance of any act by any officer or department of the United States, whether in the legislative, executive, or judicial branches of the Government, or relating to the time within which any rights shall accrue or determine, or within which any act shall or shall not be performed by any person subject to the jurisdiction of the United States, it shall be understood and intended that the time shall be the United States standard time of the zone within which the act is to be performed." The Massachusetts statute advances the standard time thus fixed by one hour; and provides that the time shall be the United States standard eastern time so advanced, in all laws, regulations, &c., relating to the time of performance of any act by any officer or department of the Commonwealth or of any county, city, &c.,

thereof, or relating to the time in which any rights shall accrue or determine, or within which any act shall or shall not be performed by any person subject to the jurisdiction of the Commonwealth, and in all the public schools and institutions of the Commonwealth, &c., and in all contracts or choses in action made or to be performed in the Commonwealth.

The court below found no inconsistency between the two Acts and we have seen no sufficient reason for differing from it upon that point. But it also went on the important rule, which we desire to emphasize, that no injunction ought to issue against officers of a State clothed with authority to enforce the law in question, unless in a case reasonably free from doubt and when necessary to prevent great and irreparable injury. . . . No such necessity is shown here. The corporations other than the Town of Hadley do not even allege any direct interest. The Town of Hadley makes a case that concerns none of the other plaintiffs, and complains only that by failure to comply with the Massachusetts statute it will be held to have lost its claim to certain State aid for its schools. It is said that in fact Hadley has received its share and has no further interest in the case, but in any event it is plain that a court of the United States would not intervene between a State and a town of the State's creation to determine how far the town should share in the State's benevolence. Of the individual plaintiffs, Mann alleges that the statute makes it more costly for him to employ labor at the first hours of the day, that he owns land on both sides of the New Hampshire line and has to travel to and fro between them, that New Hampshire and the railroad keep to the standard eastern time, and that to adjust himself to the two standards causes him worry and pecuniary loss. The plaintiff Snow alleges that her children have to get up an hour earlier to go to school and so lose an hour's sleep, and that women who have husbands employed by the railroads as well as children have to keep two standards of time in their heads, and other matters that do not concern her. The plaintiff Clarke alleges nothing that needs mention. Evidently this is not a case for an exception to the general rule.

Courts sometimes say that there is no jurisdiction in equity when they mean only that equity ought not to give the relief asked. In a strict sense the court in this case had jurisdiction. It had power to grant an injunction, and if it had granted one its decree, although wrong, would not have been void. But upon the merits we think it too plain to need argument that to grant an injunction upon the allegations of this bill would be to fly in the face of the rule which, as we have said, we think should be very strictly observed.

Decree affirmed.

[Justice McReynolds wrote a separate opinion, expressing the view that the suit against Massachusetts was "beyond the possible jurisdiction of Federal courts, as expressly declared by the Eleventh Amendment."]

Massachusetts State Grange v. *Benton, Attorney General*
272 U. S. 525

Abusing the Commerce Clause

(*Superior Oil Co.* v. *Mississippi*, 1930)

This is a suit by the State of Mississippi to collect a tax on distributors of gasoline of three and four cents respectively per gallon sold, according to the statute in force at the time of the sales. The defense was that the sales were in interstate commerce. The Supreme Court of the State upheld the tax, 119 So. Rep. 360, and the defendant, the Superior Oil Company, appealed to this Court on the ground that the statutes as applied violated the commerce clause of the Constitution of the United States. Article I, Section 8.

The facts are as follows: The Superior Oil Company, a corporation created and doing business in Mississippi, sold gasoline to packers in Biloxi in that State and delivered it at the packers' wharves. The latter loaded the oil upon their own fishing boats and sent it out to the neighborhood of Grants Pass, Louisiana, where they delivered it to shrimp fishermen for use in fishing. The fishermen brought their catch back to Biloxi, sold it to the packers and were charged with the cost of the oil on account. The appellant received in each case from the purchaser what is called a bill of lading, signed by the master of the boat on which the oil was loaded and reading in part: "Consigned to Gussie Fontaine Pkg. Co. [or other purchasers]. Destination: Grants Pass, La. By boat Frank Louis, owned or operated by Gussie Fontaine Pkg. Co." The instrument then provided that "the property consigned herein remains the property of said Superior Oil Company until it shall be delivered to consignee or consignee's agent at point of destination," with provisions throwing all risks upon the purchasers. The seller of course paid no freight. The document seems to have had no other use than, as the Supreme Court of Mississippi said, to try to convert a domestic transaction into one of interstate commerce. There was no consignee at the point of destination. The goods were delivered to the so-called consignee before they started, and were in its hand throughout. There was no point of destination for delivering of the oil but merely a neighborhood in which the packers that had bought it and already held it expected to sell it again. The document hardly can affect the case, because it is "not within the power of the parties by the form of their contract to convert what was exclusively a local business, subject to state control, into an interstate commerce protected by the commerce clause"; *Browning v. Waycross*, 233 U. S. 16, 23; at least when the contract achieves nothing else.

The importance of the commerce clause to the Union of course is very great. But it also is important to prevent that clause being used to deprive the States of their lifeblood by a strained interpretation of facts. We may admit that this case is near the line. There was a regular course of business known to the appellant, that took the gasoline into another State, and if by mutual agreement the oil had been put into the hands of a third person, a common carrier, for transportation to Louisiana the mere possibility that the vendor might be able to induce the carrier to forego his rights might not have been enough to keep the transaction out of interstate commerce. *A. G. Spalding & Bros. v. Edwards*, 262 U. S. 66, (a case of foreign export, see *Sonneborn Brothers v. Cureton*, 262 U. S. 506, 520, 521). But here the gasoline was in the hands of the purchaser to do with as it liked, and there was nothing that in any way committed it to sending the oil to Louisiana except its own wishes. If it had bought bait for fishing that it intended to do itself, the purchase would not have been in interstate commerce because the fishing grounds were known by both parties to be beyond the State line. A distinction has been taken between sales made with a view to a certain result and those made simply with indifferent knowledge that the buyer contemplates that result. . . . The only purpose of the vendor here was to escape taxation. It was not taxed in Louisiana and hoped not to be in Mississippi. The fact that it desired to evade the law, as it is called, is immaterial, because the very meaning of a line in the law is that you intentionally may go as close to it as you can if you do not pass it. . . . But on the other hand the desire to make its act an act in commerce among the States was equally unimportant when it was apparent that the buyer's journey to Louisiana was accidental so far as the appellant was concerned. It is a matter of proximity and degree as to which minds will differ, but it seems to us that the connection of the seller with the steps taken by the buyer after the sale was too remote to save the seller from the tax. Dramatic circumstances, such as a great universal stream of grain from the State of purchase to a market elsewhere, may affect the legal conclusion by showing the manifest certainty of the destination and exhibiting grounds of policy that are absent here.

Judgment affirmed.

[Justices Van Devanter and Butler dissented without opinion.]

Superior Oil Co. v. State of Mississippi
ex rel. Knox, Attorney General
280 U. S. 390

III. ON TRADE COMBINATIONS AND BOYCOTTS

A Combination to Monopolize Meat

(*Swift & Co.* v. *United States*, 1905)

This is an appeal from a decree of the Circuit Court, on demurrer, granting an injunction against the appellants' commission of alleged violations of the Act of July 2, 1890, c. 647, 26 Stat. 209, "to protect trade and commerce against unlawful restraints and monopolies."

It will be necessary to consider both the bill and the decree. The bill is brought against a number of corporations, firms and individuals of different States and makes the following allegations: 1. The defendants (appellants) are engaged in the business of buying live stock at the stock yards in Chicago, Omaha, St. Joseph, Kansas City, East St. Louis and St. Paul, and slaughtering such live stock at their respective plants in places named, in different States, and converting the live stock into fresh meat for human consumption. 2. The defendants "are also engaged in the business of selling such fresh meats, at the several places where they are so prepared, to dealers and consumers in divers States and Territories of the said United States other than those wherein the said meats are so prepared and sold as aforesaid, and in the District of Columbia, and in foreign countries, and shipping the same meats, when so sold from the said places of their preparation over the several lines of transportation of the several railroad companies serving the same as common carriers, to such dealers and consumers pursuant to such sales." 3. The defendants also are engaged in the business of shipping such fresh meats to their respective agents at the principal markets in other States, etc., for sale by those agents in those markets to dealers and consumers. 4. The defendants together control about six-tenths of the whole trade and commerce in fresh meats among the States, Territories and District of Columbia, and, 5, but for the acts charged would be in free competition with one another.

6. In order to restrain competition among themselves as to the purchase of live stock, defendants have engaged in, and intend to continue, a combination for requiring and do and will require their respective purchasing agents at the stock yards mentioned, where defendants buy their live stock (the same being stock produced and owned principally in other States and shipped to the yards for sale), to refrain from bidding against each other, "except perfunctorily and without good faith," and by this means compelling the owners of such stock to sell at less prices than they would receive if the bidding really was competitive.

7. For the same purposes the defendants combine to bid up, through their agents, the prices of live stock for a few days at a time, "so that the market reports will show prices much higher than the state of the trade will warrant," thereby inducing stock owners in other States to make large shipments to the stock yards to their disadvantage.

8. For the same purposes, and to monopolize the commerce protected by the statute, the defendants combine "to arbitrarily, from time to time raise, lower, and fix prices, and to maintain uniform prices at which they will sell" to dealers throughout the States. This is effected by secret periodical meetings, where are fixed prices to be enforced until changed at a subsequent meeting. The prices are maintained directly, and by collusively restricting the meat shipped by the defendants, whenever conducive to the result, by imposing penalties for deviations, by establishing a uniform rule for the giving of credit to dealers, etc., and by notifying one another of the delinquencies of such dealers and

keeping a black list of delinquents, and refusing to sell meats to them.

9. The defendants also combine to make uniform charges for cartage for the delivery of meats sold to dealers and consumers in the markets throughout the States, &c., shipped to them by the defendants through the defendants' agents at the markets, when no charges would have been made but for the combination.

10. Intending to monopolize the said commerce and to prevent competition therein, the defendants "have all and each engaged in and will continue" arrangements with the railroads whereby the defendants received, by means of rebates and other devices, rates less than the lawful rates for transportation, and were exclusively to enjoy and share this unlawful advantage to the exclusion of competition and the public. By force of the consequent inability of competitors to engage or continue in such commerce, the defendants are attempting to monopolize, have monopolized, and will monopolize the commerce in live stock and fresh meats among the States and Territories, and with foreign countries, and, 11, the defendants are and have been in conspiracy with each other, with the railroad companies and others unknown, to obtain a monopoly of the supply and distribution of fresh meats throughout the United States, etc. And to that end defendants artificially restrain the commerce and put arbitrary regulations in force affecting the same from the shipment of the live stock from the plains to the final distribution of the meats to the consumer. There is a prayer for an injunction of the most comprehensive sort, against all the foregoing proceedings and others, for discovery of books and papers relating directly or indirectly to the purchase or shipment of live stock, and the sale or shipment of fresh meat, and for an answer under oath. The injunction issued is appended in a note [in the margin].

To sum up the bill more shortly, it charges a combination of a dominant proportion of the dealers in fresh meat throughout the United States not to bid against each other in the live stock markets of the different States, to bid up prices for a few days in order to induce the cattle men to send their stock to the stock yards, to fix prices at which they will sell, and to that end to restrict shipments of meat when necessary, to establish a uniform rule of credit to dealers and to keep a black list, to make uniform and improper charges for cartage, and finally, to get less than lawful rates from the railroads to the exclusion of competitors. It is true that the last charge is not clearly stated to be a part of the combination. But as it is alleged that the defendants have each and all made arrangements with the railroads, that they were exclusively to enjoy the unlawful advantage, and that their intent in what they did was to monopolize the commerce and to prevent competition, and in view of the general allegation to which we shall refer, we think that we have stated correctly the purport of the bill. It will be noticed that the intent to monopolize is alleged for the first time in the eighth section of the bill as to raising, lowering and fixing prices. In the earlier sections the intent alleged is to restrain competition among themselves. But after all the specific charges there is a general allegation that the defendants are conspiring with one another, the railroads and others, to monopolize the supply and distribution of fresh meats throughout the United States, &c., as has been stated above, and it seems to us that this general allegation of intent colors and applies to all the specific charges of the bill. Whatever may be thought concerning the proper construction of the statute, a bill in equity is not to be read and construed as an indictment would have been read and construed a hundred years ago, but it is to be taken to mean what it fairly conveys to a dispassionate reader by a fairly exact use of English speech. Thus read this bill seems to us intended to allege successive elements of a single connected scheme.

We read the demurrer with the same liberality. Therefore we take it as applying to the bill generally for multifariousness and want of equity, and also to each section of it which makes a charge and to the discovery. The demurrer to the discovery will not need discussion in the view which we take concerning the relief, and therefore we turn at once to that.

The general objection is urged that the bill does not set forth sufficient definite or specific facts. This objection is serious, but it seems to us inherent in the nature of the case. The scheme alleged is so vast that it presents a new problem in pleading. If, as we must assume, the scheme is entertained, it is, of course, contrary to the very words of the statute. Its size makes the violation of the law more conspicuous, and yet the same thing makes it impossible to fasten the principal fact to a certain time and place. The elements, too, are so numerous and shifting, even the constituent parts alleged are and from their nature must be so extensive in time and space, that something of the same impossibility applies to them. The law has been upheld, and therefore we are bound to enforce it notwithstanding these difficulties. On the other hand, we equally are bound by the first principles of justice not to sanction a decree so vague as to put the whole conduct of the defendants' business at the peril of a summons for contempt. We cannot issue a general injunction against all possible breaches of the law. We must steer between these opposite difficulties as best we can.

The scheme as a whole seems to us to be within reach of the law. The constituent elements, as we have stated them, are enough to give to the scheme a body and, for all that we can say, to accomplish it. Moreover, whatever we may think of them separately when we take them up as distinct charges, they are alleged sufficiently as elements of the scheme. It is suggested that the several acts charged are lawful and that intent can make no difference. But they are bound together as the parts of a single plan. The plan may make the parts unlawful. . . . The statute gives this proceeding against combinations in restraint of commerce among the States and against attempts to monopolize the same. Intent is almost essential to such a combination and is essential to such an attempt. Where acts are not sufficient in themselves to produce a result which the law seeks to prevent—for instance, the monopoly—but require further acts in addition to the mere forces of nature to bring that result to pass, an intent to bring it to pass is necessary in order to produce a dangerous probability that it will happen. . . . But when that intent and the consequent dangerous probability exist, this statute, like many others and like the common law in some cases, directs itself against that dangerous probability as well as against the completed result. What we have said disposes incidentally of the objection to the bill as multifarious. The unity of the plan embraces all the parts.

One further observation should be made. Although the combination alleged embraces restraint and monopoly of trade within a single State, its effect upon commerce among the States is not accidental, secondary, remote or merely probable. On the allegations of the bill the latter commerce no less, perhaps even more, than commerce within a single State is an object of attack. . . . Moreover, it is a direct object, it is that for the sake of which the several specific acts and courses of conduct are done and adopted. Therefore the case is not like *United States* v. *E. C. Knight Co.*, 156 U. S. 1, where the subject-matter of the combination was manufacture and the direct object monopoly of manufacture within a State. However likely monopoly of commerce among the States in the article manufactured was to follow the agreement it was not a necessary consequary nor a primary end. Here the subject-matter is sales and the very point of the combination is to restrain and monopolize commerce among the States in respect to such sales. The two cases are near to each other, as sooner or later always must happen where lines are to be drawn, but the line between them is distinct. . . .

So, again, the line is distinct between this case and *Hopkins* v. *United States*, 171 U. S. 578. All that was decided there was that the local business of commission brokers was not commerce among the States, even if what the brokers were employed to sell was an object of such commerce. The brokers were not like the defendants before us, themselves the buyers and sellers. They only furnished certain facilities for the sales. Therefore, there again the effects of the combination of brokers upon the commerce was only indirect and not within the Act. Whether the case would have been different if the combination had resulted in exorbitant charges, was left often. In *Anderson* v. *United States,* 171 U. S. 604, the defendants were buyers and sellers at the stock yards, but their agreement was merely not to employ brokers, or to recognize yard-traders, who were not members of their association. Any yard-trader could become a member of the association on complying with the conditions, and there was said to be no feature of monopoly in the case. It was held that the combination did not directly regulate commerce between the States, and, being formed with a different intent, was not within the Act. The present case is more like *Montague & Co.* v. *Lowry,* 193 U. S. 38.

For the foregoing reasons we are of opinion that the carrying out of the scheme alleged, by the means set forth, properly may be enjoined, and that the bill cannot be dismissed.

So far it has not been necessary to consider whether the facts charged in any single paragraph constitute commerce among the States or show an interference with it. There can be no doubt, we apprehend, as to the collective effect of all the facts, if true, and if the defendants entertain the intent alleged. We pass now to the particulars, and will consider the corresponding parts of the injunction at the same time. The first question arises on the sixth section. That charges a combination of independent dealers to restrict the competition of their agents when purchasing stock for them in the stock yards. The purchasers and their slaughtering establishments are largely in different States from those of the stock yards, and the sellers of the cattle, perhaps it is not too much to assume, largely in different States from either. The intent of the combination is not merely to restrict competition among the parties, but, as we have said, by force of the general allegation at the end of the bill, to aid in an attempt to monopolize commerce among the States.

It is said that this charge is too vague and that it does not set forth a case of commerce among the States. Taking up the latter objection first, commerce among the States is not a technical legal conception, but a practical one, drawn from the course of business. When cattle are sent for sale from a place in one State, with the expectation that they will end their transit, after purchase, in another, and when in effect they do so, with only the interruption necessary to find a purchaser at the stock yards, and when this is a typical, constantly recurring course, the current thus existing is a current of commerce among the States, and the purchase of the cattle is a part and incident of such commerce. What we say is true at least of such a purchase by residents in another State from that of the seller and of the cattle. And we need not trouble ourselves at this time as to whether the statute could be escaped by any arrangement as to the place where the sale in point of law was consummated. See *Norfolk & Western Ry.* v. *Sims,* 191 U. S. 441. But the sixth section of the bill charges an interference with such sales, a restraint of the parties by mutual contract and a combination not to compete in order to monopolize. It is immaterial if the section also embraces domestic transactions.

It should be added that the cattle in the stock yard are not at rest even to the extent that was held sufficient to warrant taxation in *American Steel & Wire Co.* v. *Speed,* 192 U. S. 500. But it may be that the question of taxation does not depend upon whether the article taxed may or may not be said to be in the course of commerce between the States, but depends upon whether the tax so far affects that commerce as to amount to a regulation of it. The injunction against taking part in a combination, the effect of which will be a restraint of trade among the States by directing the defendants' agents to refrain from bidding against one another at the sales of live stock, is justified so far as the subject-matter is concerned.

The injunction, however, refers not to trade among the States in cattle, concerning which there can be no question of original packages, but to trade in fresh meats, as the trade forbidden to be restrained, and it is objected that the trade in fresh meats described in the second and third sections of the bill is not commerce among the States, because the meat is sold at the slaughtering places, or when sold elsewhere may be sold in less than the original packages. But the allegations of the second section, even if they import a technical passing of title at the slaughtering places, also import that the sales are to persons in other States, and that the shipments to other States are part of the transaction— "pursuant to such sales"—and the third section imports that the same things which are sent to agents are sold by them, and sufficiently indicates that some at least of the sales are of the original packages. Moreover, the sales are by persons in one State to persons in another. But we do not mean to imply that the rule which marks the point at which State taxation or regulation becomes permissible necessarily is beyond the scope of interference by Congress in cases where such interference is deemed necessary for the protection of commerce among the States. Nor do we mean to intimate that the statute under consideration is limited to that point. Beyond what we have said above, we leave those questions as we find them. They were touched upon in the *Northern Securities Company Case,* 193 U. S. 197.

We are of opinion, further, that the charge in the sixth section is not too vague. The charge is not of a single agreement but of a course of conduct intended to be continued. Under the Act it is the duty of the Court, when applied to, to stop the conduct. The thing done and intended to be done is perfectly definite: with the purpose mentioned, directing the defendants' agents and inducing each other to refrain from competition in bids. The defendants cannot be ordered to compete, but they properly can be forbidden to give directions or to make agreements not to compete. See *Addyston Pipe & Steel Co.* v. *United States,* 175 U. S. 211. The injunction follows the charge. No objection was made on the ground that it is not confined to the places specified in the bill. It seems to us, however, that it ought to set forth more exactly the transactions in which such directions and agreements are forbidden. The trade in fresh meat referred to should be defined somewhat as it is in the bill, and the sales of stock should be confined to sales of stock at the stock yards named, which stock is sent from other States to the stock yards for sale or is bought at those yards for transport to another State.

After what we have said, the seventh, eighth and ninth sections need no special remark, except that the cartage referred to in section nine is not an independent matter, such as was dealt with in *Pennsylvania R. R. Co.* v. *Knight,* 192 U. S. 21, but a part of the contemplated transit—cartage for delivery of the goods. The general words of the injunction "or by any other method or device, the purpose and effect of which is to restrain commerce as aforesaid," should be stricken out. The defendants ought to be informed as accurately as the case permits what they are forbidden to do. Specific devices are mentioned in the bill, and they stand prohibited. The words quoted are a sweeping injunction to obey the law, and are open to the objection which we stated at the beginning that it was our duty to avoid. To the same end of definiteness so far as attainable, the words "as charged in the bill," should be inserted between "dealers in such meats," and "the effect of which rules," and two lines lower, as to charges for cartage, the same words should be inserted between "dealers and consumers" and "the effect of which."

The acts charged in the tenth section, apart from the combination and the intent, may, perhaps, not necessarily be unlawful, except for the adjective which proclaims them so. At least we may assume, for purposes of decision, that they are not unlawful. The defendants, severally, lawfully may obtain less than the regular rates for transportation if the circumstances are not substantially similar to those for which the regular rates are fixed. Act of Feb. 4, 1887, c. 104, § 2, 24 Stat. 379. It may be that the regular rates are fixed for carriage in cars furnished by the railroad companies, and that the defendants furnish their own cars and other necessities of transportation. We see nothing to hinder them from combining to that end. We agree, as we already have said, that such a combination may be unlawful as part of the general scheme set forth in the bill, and that this scheme as a whole might be enjoined. Whether this particular combination can be enjoined, as it is, apart from its connection with the other elements, if entered into with the intent to monopolize, as alleged, is a more delicate question. The question is how it would stand if the tenth section were the whole bill. Not every act that may be done with intent to produce an unlawful result is unlawful, or constitutes an attempt. It is a question of proximity and degree. The distinction between mere preparation and attempt is well known in the criminal law. . . . The same distinction is recognized in cases like the present. . . . We are of opinion, however, that such a combination is within the meaning of the statute. It is obvious that no more powerful instrument of monopoly could be used than an advantage in the cost of transportation. And even if the advantage is one which the Act of 1887 permits, which is denied, perhaps inadequately, by the adjective "unlawful," still a combination to use it for the purpose prohibited by the Act of 1890 justifies the adjective and takes the permission away.

It only remains to add that the foregoing question does not apply to the earlier sections, which charge direct restraint of trade within the decisions of the Court, and that the criticism of the decree, as if it ran generally against combinations in restraint of trade or to monopolize trade, ceases to have any force when the clause against "any other method or device" is stricken out. So modified it restrains such combinations only to the extent of certain specified devices, which the defendants are alleged to have used and intend to continue to use.

Decree modified and affirmed.

Swift & Co. v. *United States*
196 U. S. 375

Conspiracy in Restraint of Trade

(*United States* v. *Kissel,* 1910)

This is a writ of error brought by the United States to reverse a judgment of the Circuit Court sustaining pleas in bar pleaded to an indictment by the defendants in error. . . . The first count of the indictment alleges that the defendants in error and others named, on December 30, 1903, and from that day until the day of presenting the indictment (July 1, 1909), have engaged in an unlawful conspiracy in restraint of trade in refined sugar among the several States of the Union, that is to say, to eliminate free competition and prevent all competition with the American Sugar Refining Company, one of the defendants, by a would-be competitor, the Pennsylvania Sugar Refining Company. It then sets forth, at length, the means by which the alleged purpose was to be accomplished, and what are put forward as overt acts done in pursuance of the plan. In other counts, referring to the first, the defendants are alleged to have conspired to monopolize the trade in refined sugar among the States. There are similar counts as to the trade in raw sugar and molasses, and as to trade with foreign nations. The offenses aimed at, of course, are the conspiracies punished by the Act of July 2, 1890, c. 647, 26 Stat. 209, commonly known as the Sherman Act.

There are other counts in the indictment, but the argument was devoted mainly to these. The defendants severally pleaded to all of them the limitation of three years fixed by Rev. Stat. § 1044, alleging that for more than three years before the finding of the indictment on July 1, 1909, they did not engage in, or do any act in aid of, such conspiracies. The defendant Kissel added averments that all the overt acts alleged to have been done within three years before July 1, 1909, were done without his participation, consent or knowledge. He also pleaded that since October 6, 1906, the Pennsylvania Sugar Refining Company had been in the hands of a duly appointed receiver.

We deem it unnecessary to state the pleadings with more particularity, because the only question before us under the Act of March 2, 1907, c. 2564, 34 Stat. 1246, is whether the plea in bar can be sustained. That this Court is confined to a consideration of the grounds of decision mentioned in the statute when an indictment is quashed was decided in *United States* v. *Keitel*, 211 U. S. 370, 399. We think that there is a similar limit when the case comes up under the other clause of the Act, from a "judgment sustaining a special plea in bar, when the defendant has not been put in jeopardy." This being so, we are not concerned with the technical efficiency or redundancy of the indictment, or even, in the view that we presently shall express, with any consideration of the nature of the overt acts alleged. The indictment charges a conspiracy beginning in 1903, but continuing down to the date of filing. It pretty nearly was conceded that if a conspiracy of this kind can be continuous, then the pleas in bar are bad. Therefore we first will consider whether a conspiracy can have continuance in time.

The defendants argue that a conspiracy is a completed crime as soon as formed, that it is simply a case of unlawful agreement, and that therefore the *continuando* may be disregarded and a plea is proper to show that the statute of limitations has run. Subsequent acts in pursuance of the agreement may renew the conspiracy or be evidence of a renewal, but do not change the nature of the original offense. So also, it is said, the fact that an unlawful contract contemplates future acts or that the results of a successful conspiracy endure to a much later date does not affect the character of the crime.

The argument, so far as the premises are true, does not suffice to prove that a conspiracy, although it exists as soon as the agreement is made, may not continue beyond the moment of making it. It is true that the unlawful agreement satisfies the definition of the crime, but it does not exhaust it. It also is true, of course that the mere continuance of the result of a crime does not continue the crime. . . . But when the plot contemplates bringing to pass a continuous result that will not continue without the continuous cooperation of the conspirators to keep it up, and there is such a continuous cooperation, it is a perversion of natural thought and of natural language to call such continuous cooperation a cinematographic series of distinct conspiracies rather than to call it a single one. Take the present case. A conspiracy to restrain or monopolize trade by improperly excluding a competitor from business contemplates that the conspirators will remain in business and will continue their combined efforts to drive the competitor out until they succeed. If they do continue such efforts in pursuance of the plan the conspiracy continues up to the time of abandonment or success. A conspiracy in restraint of trade is different from and more than a contract in restraint of trade. A conspiracy is constituted by an agreement, it is true, but it is the result of the agreement, rather than the agreement itself, just as a partnership, although constituted by a contract, is not the contract but the result of it. The contract is instantaneous, the partnership may endure as one and the same partnership for years. A conspiracy is a partnership in criminal purposes. That as such it may have continuation in time is shown by the rule that an overt act of one partner may be the act of all without any new agreement specifically directed to that act.

The means contemplated for the exclusion of the Pennsylvania Sugar Refining Company were the making of a large loan by the American Sugar Refining Company through Kissel to one Segal and the receiving from him of more than half the stock of the Pennsylvania Company with a power of attorney to vote upon it, Segal not knowing that the American Company was behind Kissel. The loan was to be for a year, but the American Company was to use the power of voting to prevent the Pennsylvania Company from going on with its business, and, as Segal was dependent largely upon the returns from that company for means of repaying the loan, he was to be prevented from repaying it and the control of the Pennsylvania Company retained until it should be ruined and finally driven from business. It is alleged that the loan was made and that a vote was passed that the Pennsylvania Company refrain from business until further order of the board of directors. Now of course it well may be that the object was so far accomplished by this vote that the conspiracy was at an end; but a vote upon pledged stock that might be redeemed was not necessarily lasting, and further action might be necessary to reach the desired result. The allegation that the conspiracy continued down to the date of the indictment is not contradicted by the vote. Furthermore, as we have said, the only question here is whether the plea of the statute of limitations is good.

Taking it that the conspiracies made criminal by the Act of July 2, 1890, may have continuance, we are of opinion that the pleas are bad. To be sure, it still might be argued that the general rule that time need not be proved as laid applies to continuing offenses, that therefore the allegation in the indictment, so far as it specifies the time in which the conspiracy was maintained, is immaterial, and that a plea traversing only that is, in substance, a plea in confession and avoidance and good. Whether in a charge of a continuing offense even such specific earmarks of time as this in this indictment make it enter into the essence of the offense we shall not discuss. Time is held to be of the essence in Massachusetts and some other States; *Commonwealth* v. *Pray*, 13 Pick. 359, 364; *Commonwealth* v. *Briggs*, 11 Met. 573; *State* v. *Small*, 80 Maine, 452; *Fleming* v. *State*, 28 Tex. App. 234; while this has been thought to be a local peculiarity, and the contrary has been decided elsewhere . . . Bishop, *New Criminal Procedure*, §§ 397, 402. However this may be, if the plea of the statute of limitations is good where it confesses and avoids all that the indictment avers, still, as was pointed out in an able brief by the late lamented Solicitor General, it is open to too many objections and difficulties to be encouraged or allowed except in clear cases. Apart from technical rules the averments of time in the indictment are expected and intended to be proved as laid. The overt acts relied upon coming down to within three years of the indictment are alleged to have been done in pursuance of the conspiracy, and the pleas must be taken to deny that allegation, unless they rely upon the supposed impossibility of the acts having the character alleged. It is only by an artificial rule, if at all, that the plea can be treated as not traversing the indictment, and we are not prepared to give that supposed rule such an effect.

The discussion at the bar took a wider range than is open at this stage. It hardly is necessary to explain that we have nothing to say as to what evidence would be sufficient to prove the continuation of the conspiracy, or where the burden of pleading or proof as to abandonment would be. We deal only with a naked and highly technical question, when once the possibility of continuation is established, and as to that we cannot bring ourselves to doubt.

To sum up and repeat: The indictment charges a continuing conspiracy. Whether it does so with technical sufficiency is not before us. All that we decide is that a conspiracy may have continuance in time, and that where, as here, the indictment, consistently with the other facts, alleges that it did so continue to the date of filing, that allegation must be denied under the general issue and not by a special plea. Under the general issue all defenses, including the defense that the conspiracy was ended by success, abandonment, or otherwise more than three years before July 1, 1909, will be open and unaffected by what we now decide.

Judgment reversed.

United States v. *Kissel and Harned*
218 U. S. 601

"Mistaken Notions" on Price-Fixing

(Dr. Miles Medical Co. v. Park & Sons Co., 1911)

[A SYSTEM OF CONTRACTS BETWEEN MANUFACTURERS AND DISTRIBUtors fixing the re-sale price of the manufacturers' products was held by the Court to be an unlawful restraint of trade invalid (at common law and under the Sherman Law). Agreements or combinations between dealers for the purpose of destroying competition and fixing prices are injurious to the public interest, Mr. Justice Hughes said in his opinion. Mr. Justice Holmes dissented:]

THIS IS a bill to restrain the defendant from inducing, by corruption and fraud, agents of the plaintiff and purchasers from it to break their contracts not to sell its goods below a certain price. There are two contracts concerned. The first is that of the jobber or wholesale agent to whom the plaintiff consigns its goods, and I will say a few words about that, although it is not this branch of the case that induces me to speak. That they are agents and not buyers I understand to be conceded, and I do not see how it can be denied. We have nothing before us but the form and the alleged effect of the written instrument, and they both are express that the title to the goods is to remain in the plaintiff until actual sale as permitted by the contract. So far as this contract limits the authority of the agents as agents I do not understand its validity to be disputed. But it is construed also to permit the purchase of medicine by consignees from other consignees, and to make the specification of prices applicable to goods so purchased as well as to goods consigned. Hence when the bill alleges that the defendant has obtained medicine from these agents by inducing them to break their contracts, the allegation does not require proof of breach of trust by an agent, but would be satisfied by proving a breach of promise in respect of goods that the consignee had bought and owned. This reasoning would have been conclusive in the days of Saunders if the construction of the contract is right, as I suppose that it is. But the contract as to goods purchased is at least in the background and obscure; it is not the main undertaking that the instrument is intended to express. I should have thought that the bill ought to be read as charging the defendant with inducing a breach of the ordinary duty of consignees as such (*Swift* v. *United States*, 196 U. S. 375, 395), [see page 125] and, therefore, as entitling the plaintiff to relief. . . .

The second contract is that of the retail agents, so called, being really the first purchasers, fixing the price below which they will not sell to the public. There is no attempt to attach a contract or condition to the goods, as in *Bobbs-Merrill Co.* v. *Straus*, 210 U. S. 330, or in any way to restrict dealings with them after they leave the hands of the retail men. The sale to the retailers is made by the plaintiff, and the only question is whether the law forbids a purchaser to contract with his vendor that he will not sell below a certain price. This is the important question in this case. I suppose that in the case of a single object such as a painting or a statue the right of the artist to make such a stipulation hardly would be denied. In other words, I suppose that the reason why the contract is held bad is that it is part of a scheme embracing other similar contracts each of which applies to a number of similar things, with the object of fixing a general market price. This reason seems to me inadequate in the case before the Court. In the first place by a slight change in the form of the contract the plaintiff can accomplish the result in a way that would be beyond successful attack. If it should make the retail dealers also agents in law as well as in name and retain the title until the goods left their hands I cannot conceive that even the present enthusiasm for regulating the prices to be charged by other people would deny that the owner was acting within his rights. It seems to me that this consideration by itself ought to give us pause.

But I go farther. There is no statute covering the case; there is no body of precedent that by ineluctable logic requires the conclusion to which the Court has come. The conclusion is reached by extending a certain conception of public policy to a new sphere. On such matters we are in perilous country. I think that, at least, it is safe to say that the most enlightened judicial policy is to let people manage their own business in their own way, unless the ground for interference is very clear. What then is the ground upon which we interfere in the present case? Of course, it is not the interest of the producer. No one, I judge, cares for that. It hardly can be the interest of subordinate vendors, as there seems to be no particular reason for preferring them to the originator and first vendor of the product. Perhaps it may be assumed to be the interest of the consumers and the public. On that point I confess that I am in a minority as to larger issues than are concerned here. I think that we greatly exaggerate the value and importance to the public of competition in the production or distribution of an article (here it is only distribution), as fixing a fair price. What really fixes that is the competition of conflicting desires. We, none of us, can have as much as we want of all the things that we want. Therefore, we have to choose. As soon as the price of something that we want goes above the point at which we are willing to give up other things to have that, we cease to buy it and buy something else. Of course, I am speaking of things that we can get along without. There may be necessaries that sooner or later must be dealt with like short rations in a shipwreck, but they are not Dr. Miles' medicines. With regard to things like the latter it seems to me that the point of most profitable returns marks the equilibrium of social desires and determines the fair price in the only sense in which I can find meaning in those words. The Dr. Miles Medical Company knows better than we do what will enable it to do the best business. We must assume its retail price to be reasonable, for it is so alleged and the case is here on demurrer; so I see nothing to warrant my assuming that the public will not be served best by the company being allowed to carry out its plan. I cannot believe that in the long run the public will profit by this Court permitting knaves to cut reasonable prices for some ulterior purpose of their own and thus to impair, if not to destroy, the production and sale of articles which it is assumed to be desirable that the public should be able to get.

The conduct of the defendant falls within a general prohibition of the law. It is fraudulent and has no merits of its own to recommend it to the favor of the Court. An injunction against the defendant's dealing in non-transferable round-trip reduced rate tickets has been granted to a railroad company upon the general principles of the law protecting contracts, and the demoralization of rates has been referred to as a special circumstance in addition to the general grounds. . . . The general and special considerations equally apply here, and we ought not to disregard them, unless the evil effect of the contract is very plain. The analogy relied upon to establish that evil effect is that of combinations in restraint of trade. I believe that we have some superstitions on that head, as I have said; but those combinations are entered into with intent to exclude others from a business naturally open to them, and we unhappily have become familiar with the methods by which they are carried out. I venture to say that there is no likeness between them and this case. *Jayne* v. *Loder*, 149 Fed. Rep. 21, 27; and I think that my view prevails in England. . . . I think also that the importance of the question and the popularity of what I deem mistaken notions make it my duty to express my view in this dissent.

Dr. Miles Medical Co. v. *John D. Park & Sons Co.*
220 U. S. 373, 409

Criminal Prosecution Under the Sherman Act

(*Nash v. United States*, 1913)

This is an indictment in two counts—the first for a conspiracy in restraint of trade, the second for a conspiracy to monopolize trade, contrary to the Act of July 2, 1890, c. 647, 26 Stat. 209, commonly known as the Sherman Act. Originally there was a third count for monopolizing, but it was held bad on demurrer and was struck out.

The allegations of fact in the two counts are alike. Summed up in narrative form they are as follows: The American Naval Stores Company, a West Virginia corporation having its principal office in Savannah and branch offices in New York, Philadelphia, Chicago, etc., was engaged in buying, selling, shipping and exporting spirits of turpentine in and from Southern States to other States and abroad. Nash was the president; Shotter, chairman of the board of directors; Myers, vice-president; Boardman, treasurer; DeLoach, secretary, and Moller, manager of the Jacksonville, Florida, branch. The National Transportation and Terminal Company, a New Jersey corporation, had warehouses and terminals for handling spirits of turpentine and naval stores in Fernandina, and other places named, in Florida, Alabama, Mississippi, etc., and was engaged in storing such turpentine and rosin and issuing warehouse receipts for the same. Myers was the president; DeLoach the secretary and Moller manager of the Jacksonville branch. On May 1, 1907, it is alleged, these corporations and individuals conspired to restrain commerce in the articles named, among the States and with foreign nations—the restraint

[147]

to be effected in the following ways among others: (1) by bidding down turpentine and rosin so that competitors could sell them only at ruinous prices; (2) by causing naval stores receipts that naturally would go to one port to go to another; (3) by purchasing thereafter a large part of "its" supplies at ports known as closed ports and, with intent to depress the market, refraining from purchasing any appreciable part at Savannah, the primary market in the United States for naval stores, where purchases would tend to strengthen prices, the defendants taking the receipts at the closed ports named on a basis of the market at Savannah; (4) by coercing factors and brokers into contracts with the defendants for the storage and purchase of their receipts and refusing to purchase from such factors and brokers unless such contracts were entered into; (5) by circulating false statements as to naval stores production and stocks on hand; (6) by issuing fraudulent warehouse receipts; (7) by fraudulently grading, regrading and raising grades of rosins and falsely gauging spirits of turpentine; (8) by attempting to bribe employees of competitors so as to obtain information concerning their business and stocks; (9) by inducing consumers, by payments and threats of boycotts, to postpone dates of delivery of contract supplies and thus enabling defendants to postpone purchasing when to purchase would tend to strengthen the market; (10) by making tentative offers of large amounts of naval stores to depress the market, accepting contracts only for small amounts and purchasing when the market had been depressed by the offers; (11) by selling far below cost in order to compel competitors to meet prices ruinous to everybody; (12) by fixing the price of turpentine below the cost of production—all the foregoing being for the purpose of driving competitors out of business and restraining foreign trade or, in the second count, of doing the same and monopolizing the trade.

The two counts before us were demurred to on the grounds that the statute was so vague as to be inoperative on its criminal side; that neither of the counts alleged any overt act; that the contemplated acts and things would not have constituted an offense if they had been done, and that the same acts, etc., were too vaguely charged. The demurrer was overruled and this action of the court raised the important questions of the case. We will deal with them before passing to matters of detail.

The objection to the criminal operation of the statute is thought to be warranted by *The Standard Oil Co.* v. *United States*, 221 U. S. 1, and *United States* v. *American Tobacco Co.*, 221 U. S. 106. Those cases may be taken to have established that only such contracts and combinations are within the Act as, by reason of intent or the inherent nature of the contemplated acts, prejudice the public interest by unduly restricting competition or unduly obstructing the course of trade. 221 U. S. 179. And thereupon it is said that the crime thus defined by the statute contains in its definition an element of degree as to which estimates may differ, with the result that a man might find himself in prison because his honest judgment did not anticipate that of a jury of less competent men. The kindred proposition that "the criminality of an act cannot depend upon whether a jury may think it reasonable or unreasonable. There must be some definiteness and certainty," is cited from the late Mr. Justice Brewer sitting in the Circuit Court. *Tozer* v. *United States*, 52 Fed. Rep., 917, 919.

But apart from the common law as to restraint of trade thus taken up by the statute, the law is full of instances where a man's fate depends on his estimating rightly, that is, as the jury subsequently estimates it, some matter of degree. If his judgment is wrong, not only may he incur a fine or a short imprisonment, as here; he may incur the penalty of death. "An act causing death may be murder, manslaughter, or misadventure according to the degree of danger attending it" by common experience in the circumstances known to the actor. "The very meaning of the fiction of implied malice in such cases at common law was, that a man might have to answer with his life for consequences which he neither intended nor foresaw." *Commonwealth* v. *Pierce*, 138 Massachusetts, 165, 178. *Commonwealth* v. *Chance*, 174 Massachusetts, 245, 252. "The criterion in such cases is to examine whether common social duty would, under the circumstances, have suggested a more circumspect conduct." 1 East P. C. 262. If a man should kill another by driving an automobile furiously into a crowd he might be convicted of murder however little he expected the result. See *Reg.* v. *Desmond*, and other illustrations in Stephen, Dig. Crim. Law, art. 223, 1st ed., p. 146. If he did no more than drive negligently through a street he might get off with manslaughter or less. *Reg.* v. *Swindall*, 2 C. & K. 230; *Rex* v. *Burton*, 1 Strange, 481. And in the last case he might be held although he himself thought he was acting as a prudent man should. See *The Germanic*, 196 U. S. 589, 596. But without further argument, the case is very nearly disposed of by *Waters-Pierce Oil Co.* v. *Texas* (No. 1), 212 U. S. 86, 109, where Mr. Justice Brewer's decision and other similar ones were cited in vain. We are of opinion that there is no constitutional difficulty in the way of enforcing the criminal part of the Act.

Coming next to the objection that no overt act is laid, the answer is that the Sherman Act punishes the conspiracies at which it is aimed on the common-law footing—that is to say, it does not make the doing of any act other than the act of conspiring a condition of liability. The decisions as to the relations of a subsequent overt act to crimes under Rev. Stat., § 5440, in *Hyde* v. *United States*, 225 U. S. 347, and *Brown* v. *Elliott*, 225 U. S. 392, have no bearing upon a statute that does not contain the requirement found in that section. As we can see no reason for reading into the Sherman Act more than we find there, we think it unnecessary to offer arguments against doing so.

As to the suggestion that the matters alleged to have been contemplated would not have constituted an offense if they had been done, it is enough to say that some of them conceivably might have been adequate to accomplish the result, and that the intent alleged would convert what on their face might be no more than ordinary acts of competition or the small dishonesties of trade into a conspiracy of wider scope, as has been explained more than once. . . . Of course this fact calls for conscience and circumspection in prosecuting officers, lest by the unfounded charge of a wider purpose than the acts necessarily import they convert what at most would be small local offenses into crimes under the statutes of the United States. But we cannot say, as was the case in *United States* v. *Winslow*, 227 U. S. 202, 218, that no intent could convert the proposed conduct into such a crime.

Finally, we cannot pronounce the counts before us bad for uncertainty. On demand of the defendants a bill of particulars was furnished, and there is no reason to fear that injustice was done in that respect.—There was no need to allege or prove that the conspirators themselves were all traders. . . . The first count, at least, was well enough.

After the demurrer was overruled the defendants pleaded not guilty and there was a trial and a verdict finding that Nash, Shotter, Myers, Moller and Boardman were guilty and DeLoach not guilty, but saying nothing as to the corporations. Numerous exceptions were taken, but as writs of certiorari are not granted to bring up the ordinary incidents of a criminal trial we shall say little more than is necessary to dispose of the case. It was argued with a good deal of force that the only evidence of the alleged conspiracy was certain acts done on behalf of the corporations; that the only ground for charging the defendants who were found guilty was their relation to the companies and their being presumably cognizant of and more or less responsible for the corporate acts; that if those acts tended to prove a conspiracy they proved that the corporations more clearly than any one else were parties to it, and therefore that a verdict that was silent as to them ought to be set aside. We need not consider the effect of Rev. Stat., § 1036, or whether on the evidence it was possible to find the defendants guilty by reason of an intent not shown to be shared by the corporations, as the judgment must be reversed for another reason.

The reason is this. The court in its instructions told the jury to "consider the evidence of the means which it is insisted by the prosecution tends to show a conspiracy" and said: "You will consider carefully all the means which the indictment charges" and "It is sufficient if it be shown beyond a reasonable doubt that some of these means charged were a part of the common scheme, design or understanding or conspiracy by two or more of the defendants, and that these same means were of themselves sufficient to cause an essential obstruction and restraint of the free and untrammelled flow of trade and commerce between the States and foreign nations." Thus while it may be admitted that not all the means alleged need be proved, the charge invited the jury to consider all and permitted a verdict upon any one of them. The fifth, sixth and eighth statements of means to be employed were withdrawn from the jury, but the jury's attention seems not to have been called to the fact that some of the charges were abandoned, in the connection in which it was important. Furthermore one of the means alleged was the false raising of grades and false gauging. Taken with other evidence, if it was shown to be systematic it would have had a tendency to show the scheme alleged. But taken by itself, as the jury might have taken it under the instructions, it showed only cheating and could not warrant a finding of the conspiracy with which the defendants were charged. It is unnecessary to consider whether there was any evidence sufficient to warrant a conviction upon some of the other means alleged, for instance the first, as the absence of such evidence only would add another reason for holding the instructions wrong upon a vital point.

Judgment reversed.

[Mr. Justice Pitney dissented without opinion.]

Nash v. *United States*
229 U. S. 373

Control of Price in a Complex World

(*International Harvester Co.* v. *Kentucky*, 1914)

THE plaintiff in error was prosecuted, convicted and fined in three different counties for having entered into an agreement with other named companies for the purpose of controlling the price of harvesters, &c., manufactured by them and of enhancing it above their real value; and for having so fixed and enhanced the price, and for having sold their harvesters, &c., at a price in excess of their real value, in pursuance of the agreement alleged. The judgments were affirmed by the Court of Appeals. . . . The plaintiff in error saved its rights under the Fourteenth Amendment and brought the cases here.

The law of Kentucky in its present form is the result of the construction of several statutes somewhat far apart in time and of seemingly contradictory import. It was argued that the construction could not take the place of express language in a statute and *Louisville & Nashville R. R. Co.* v. *Central Stock Yards Co.*, 212 U. S. 132, 144, was cited for the proposition. But the case gives no sanction to it. The point there was that a defect in a law could not be cured by precautions in a judgment, not that what seemed a defect could not be cured by the construction given to the words by the court having final authority to declare their intent. We follow the Kentucky Court of Appeals in taking what they derive from the legislation of the State as if it were embodied in a single act.

The history in brief is this: By an Act of May 20, 1890, agreements for the purpose of fixing or limiting the amount or quantity of any article of merchandise to be produced or manufactured, mined, bought or sold; as also combinations by corporations with others to put the business of the combination under control with intent to limit, fix or change the price of articles of commerce or in any way to diminish the output of such articles, were made punishable by fine, imprisonment, or both. Carroll's Kentucky Statutes, §§ 3915, 3916, 3917. In 1891 a new constitution was adopted by the State, by § 198 of which it was made the duty of the General Assembly "from time to time, as necessity may require, to enact such laws as may be necessary to prevent all trusts . . . from combining to depreciate below its real value any article, or to enhance the cost of any article above its real value." (This was held not to repeal the earlier statute. . . .) But Kentucky grows tobacco and the farmers were dissatisfied with the prices that they were able to get, being oppressed as they alleged by a combination of buyers. So, on March 21, 1906, a statute was enacted that made it lawful for any number of persons to combine the crops of wheat, tobacco, corn, oats, hay, or any other farm products raised by them, for the purpose of obtaining a higher price than they could get by selling them separately. Session Laws, 1906, c. 117, p. 429. And later, by an Act of March 13, 1908 (Session Laws, 1908, c. 8, p. 38), not only was the legality of these last-mentioned combinations reaffirmed, but they were protected by injunction, and the sale by or purchase from the owner contrary to his agreement was punished by a fine.

When the Court of Appeals came to deal with the Act of 1890, the Constitution of 1891, and the Act of 1906, it reached the conclusion, which now may be regarded as the established construction of the three taken together, that by interaction and to avoid questions of constitutionality, they were to be taken to make any combination for the purpose of controlling prices lawful unless for the purpose or with the effect of fixing a price that was greater or less than the real value of the article. . . . The result seems to be that combinations of tobacco growers are held to do no more than restore an equilibrium that has been disturbed by a combination of buyers, *Owen County Burley Tobacco Society* v. *Brumback*, 128 Kentucky, 137, 152; *Collins* v. *Commonwealth*, 141 Kentucky, 564, whereas if prices rise after a combination of manufacturers it ·very nearly is presumed that the advance is above the real value and that there is a crime. . . .

The plaintiff in error contends that the law as construed offers no standard of conduct that it is possible to know. To meet this, in the present and earlier cases the real value is declared to be "the market value under fair competition, and under normal market conditions." 147 Kentucky, 566. . . . We have to consider whether in application this is more than an illusory form of words, when nine years after it was incorporated, a combination invited by the law is required to guess at its peril what its product would have sold for if the combination had not existed and nothing else violently affecting values had occurred. It seems that since 1902 the price of the machinery sold by the plaintiff in error has risen from ten to fifteen percent. The testimony on its behalf showed that meantime the cost of materials used had increased from 20 to 25 percent and labor 27½ percent. Whatever doubt there may be about the exact figures we hardly suppose the fact of a rise to be denied. But in order to reach what is called the real value, a price from which all effects of the combination are to be eliminated, the plaintiff in error is told that it cannot avail itself of the rise in materials because it was able to get them cheaper through one of the subsidiary companies of the combination, and that the saving through the combination more than offsets all the rise in cost.

This perhaps more plainly concerns the justice of the law in its bearing upon the plaintiff in error, when compared with its operation upon tobacco raisers who are said to have doubled or trebled their prices, than on the constitutional question proposed.

But it also concerns that, for it shows how impossible it is to think away the principal facts of the case as it exists and say what would have been the price in an imaginary world. Value is the effect in exchange of the relative social desire for compared objects expressed in terms of a common denominator. It is a fact and generally is more or less easy to ascertain. But what it would be with such increase of a never extinguished competition as it might be guessed would have existed had the combination not been made, with exclusion of the actual effect of other abnormal influences, and, it would seem with exclusion also of any increased efficiency in the machines but with inclusion of the effect of the combination so far as it was economically beneficial to itself and the community, is a problem that no human ingenuity could solve. The reason is not the general uncertainties of a jury trial but that the elements necessary to determine the imaginary ideal are uncertain both in nature and degree of effect to the acutest commercial mind. The very community, the intensity of whose wish relatively to its other competing desires determines the price that it would give, has to be supposed differently organized and subject to other influences than those under which it acts. It is easy to put simple cases; but the one before us is at least as complex as we have supposed, and the law must be judged by it. In our opinion it cannot stand.

We regard this decision as consistent with *Nash* v. *United States*, 229 U. S. 373, 377, in which it was held that a criminal law is not unconstitutional merely because it throws upon men the risk of rightly estimating a matter of degree—what is an undue restraint of trade. That deals with the actual, not with an imaginary condition other than the facts. It goes no further than to recognize that, as with negligence, between the two extremes of the obviously illegal and the plainly lawful there is a gradual approach and that the complexity of life makes it impossible to draw a line in advance without an artificial simplification that would be unjust. The conditions are as permanent as anything human, and a great body of precedents on the civil side coupled with familiar practice make it comparatively easy for common sense to keep to what is safe. But if business is to go on, men must unite to do it and must sell their wares. To compel them to guess on peril of indictment what the community would have given for them if the continually changing conditions were other than they are, to an uncertain extent; to divine prophetically what the reaction of only partially determinate facts would be upon the imaginations and desires of purchasers, is to exact gifts that mankind does not possess.

Judgments reversed.

[Justices McKenna and Pitney dissented without opinion.]

International Harvester Co. of America
v. Commonwealth of Kentucky
234 U. S. 216

Warfare Against Country Banks

(*Amer. Bank & Trust Co.* v. *Federal Reserve Bank*, 1921)

THIS is a bill in equity brought by country banks incorporated by the State of Georgia against the Federal Reserve Bank of Atlanta, incorporated under the laws of the United States, and its officers. It was brought in a State court but removed to the District Court of the United States on the petition of the defendants. A motion to remand was made by the plaintiffs but was overruled. The allegations of the bill may be summed up in comparatively few words. The plaintiffs are not members of the Federal Reserve System and many of them have too small a capital to permit their joining it—a capital that could not be increased to the required amount in the thinly populated sections of the country where they operate. An important part of the income of these small institutions is a charge for the services rendered by them in paying checks drawn upon them at a distance and forwarded, generally by other banks, through the mail. The charge covers the expense incurred by the paying bank and a small profit. The banks in the Federal Reserve System are forbidden to make such charges to other banks in the system. Federal Reserve Act of December 23, 1913, c. 6, § 13, 38 Stat. 263; amended March 3, 1915, c. 93, 38 Stat. 958; September 7, 1916, c. 461, 39 Stat. 752; and June 21, 1917, c. 32 §§ 4, 5, 40 Stat. 234, 235. It is alleged that in pursuance of a policy accepted by the Federal Reserve Board the defendant bank has determined to use its power to compel the plaintiffs and others in like situation to become members of the defendant, or at least to open a non-member clearing account with defendant, and thereby, under the defendant's requirements, to make it necessary for the plaintiffs to maintain a much larger reserve than in their present condition they need. This diminution of their lending power coupled with the loss of the profit caused by the above-mentioned clearing of bank checks and drafts at par will drive some of the plaintiffs out of business and diminish the income of all. To accomplish the defendants' wish they intend to accumulate checks upon the country banks until they reach a large amount and then to cause them to be presented for payment over the counter or by other devices detailed to require payment in cash and in such wise as to compel the plaintiffs to maintain so much cash in their vaults as to drive them out of business or force them, if able, to submit to the defendants' scheme. It is alleged that the proposed conduct will deprive the plaintiffs of their property without due process of law contrary to the Fifth Amendment of the Constitution and that it is *ultra vires*. The bill seeks an injunction against the defendants' collecting checks except in the usual way. The District Court dismissed the bill for want of equity and its decree was affirmed by the Circuit Court of Appeals. . . . The plaintiffs appealed, setting up want of jurisdiction in the District Court and error in the final decree.

We agree with the court below that the removal was proper. The principal defendant was incorporated under the laws of the United States and that has been established as a ground of jurisdiction since *Osborn* v. *Bank of the United States*, 9 Wheat. 738. . . . We shall say but a word in answer to the appellants' argument that a suit against such a corporation is not a suit arising under those laws within § 24 of the Judicial Code of March 3, 1911, c. 231, 36 Stat. 1087. The contrary is established, and the accepted doctrine is intelligible at least since it is part of the plaintiffs' case that the defendant bank existed and exists as an entity capable of committing the wrong alleged and of being sued. These facts depend upon the laws of the United States. . . . A more plausible objection is that by the Judicial Code, § 24, sixteenth, except as therein excepted, national banking associations for the purpose of suits against them are to be deemed citizens of the States in which they are respectively located. But we agree with the court below that the reasons for localizing ordinary commercial banks do not apply to the Federal Reserve Banks created after the Judicial Code was enacted and that the phrase "national banking associations" does not reach forward and include them. That phrase is used to describe the ordinary commercial banks whereas the others are systematically called "Federal Reserve Banks." We see no sufficient ground for supposing that Congress meant to open the questions that the other construction would raise.

On the merits we are of opinion that the courts below went too far. The question at this stage is not what the plaintiffs may be able to prove, or what may be the reasonable interpretation of the defendants' acts, but whether the plaintiffs have shown a ground for relief if they can prove what they allege. We lay on one side as not necessary to our decision the question of the defendants' powers, and assuming that they act within them consider only whether the use that according to the bill they intend to make of them will infringe the plaintiffs' rights. The defendants say that the holder of a check has a right to present it to the bank upon which it was drawn for payment over the counter, and that however many checks he may hold he has the same right as to all of them and may present them all at once, whatever his motive or intent. They ask whether a mortgagee would be prevented from foreclosing because he acted from disinterested malevolence and not from a desire to get his money. But the word "right" is one of the most deceptive of pitfalls; it is so easy to slip from a qualified meaning in the premise to an unqualified one in the conclusion. Most rights are qualified. A man has at least as absolute a right to give his own money as to demand money from a party that has made no promise to him; yet if he gives it to induce another to steal or murder the purpose of the act makes it a crime.

A bank that receives deposits to be drawn upon by check of course authorizes its depositors to draw checks against their accounts and holders of such checks to present them for payment. When we think of the ordinary case the right of the holder is so unimpeded that it seems to us absolute. But looked at from either side it cannot be so. The interests of business also are recognized as rights, protected against injury to a greater or less extent, and in case of conflict between the claims of business on the one side and of third persons on the other, lines have to be drawn to limit both. A man has a right to give advice, but advice given for the sole purpose of injuring another's business and effective on a large scale, might create a cause of action. Banks as we know them could not exist if they could not rely upon averages and lend a large part of the money that they receive from their depositors on the assumption that not more than a certain fraction of it will be demanded on any one day. If without a word of falsehood but acting from what we have called disinterested malevolence a man by persuasion should organize and carry into effect a run upon a bank and ruin it, we cannot doubt that an action would lie. A similar result even if less complete in its effect is to be expected from the course that the defendants are alleged to intend, and to determine whether they are authorized to follow that course it is not enough to refer to the general right of a holder of checks to present them but it is necessary to consider whether the collection of checks and presenting them in a body for the purpose of breaking down the plaintiffs' business as now conducted is justified by the ulterior purpose in view.

If this were a case of competition in private business it would be hard to admit the justification of self-interest considering the now current opinion as to public policy expressed in statutes and decisions. But this is not private business. The policy of the Federal Reserve Banks is governed by the policy of the United States with regard to them and to these relatively feeble competitors. We do not need aid from the debates upon the statute under which the Reserve Banks exist to assume that the United States did not intend by that statute to sanction this sort of warfare upon legitimate creations of the States.

Decree reversed.

American Bank & Trust Co., et al.
v. *Federal Reserve Bank of Atlanta, Georgia, et al.*
256 U. S. 350

A Combination of Labor

(*National Association of Window Glass Mfrs.* v. *U. S.*, 1923)

THIS is a proceeding brought by the United States under the Act of July 2, 1890, c. 647, § 4; 26 Stat. 209, to prevent an alleged violation of § 1, which forbids combinations in restraint of trade among the States. The defendants are all the manufacturers of handblown window glass, with certain of their officers, and the National Window Glass Workers, a voluntary association, its officers and members, embracing all the labor to be had for this work in the United States. The defendants established a wage scale to be in effect from September 25, 1922, to January 27, 1923, and from January 29, 1923, to June 11, 1923; and the feature that is the object of the present attack is that this scale would be issued to one set of factories for the first period and to another for the second, but that no factory could get it for both, and without it they could not get labor and therefore must stop work. After a hearing a final decree was entered enjoining the defendants from carrying out the above or any similar agreements so far as they might limit and prescribe the time during which the defendant manufacturers should operate their factories for handblown window glass. . . .

This agreement does not concern sales or distribution, it is directed only to the way in which union labor, the only labor obtainable it is true, shall be employed in production. If such an agreement can be within the Sherman Act at least it is not necessarily so.... To determine its legality requires a consideration of the particular facts....

The dominant fact in this case is that in the last quarter of a century machines have been brought into use that dispense with the employment of the highly trained blowers and the trained gatherers needed for the handmade glass, and in that and other ways have enabled the factories using machines to produce window glass at half the cost of the handmade. The price for the two kinds is the same. It has followed of course that the companies using machines fix the price, that they make much the greater part of the glass in the market, and probably, as was testified for the defendants, that the handmakers are able to keep on only by the sufferance of the others and by working longer hours. The defendants say, and it is altogether likely, that the conditions thus brought about and the nature of the work have driven many laborers away and made it impossible to get new ones. For the work is very trying, requires considerable training, and is always liable to a reduction of wages if the machine industry lowers the price. The only chance for the handworkers has been when and where they could get cheap fuel and therefore their tendency has been to follow the discoveries of natural gas. The defendants contend with a good deal of force that it is absurd to speak of their arrangements as possibly having any effect upon commerce among the States, when manufacturers of this kind obviously are not able to do more than struggle to survive a little longer before they disappear, as human effort always disappears when it is not needed to direct the force that can be got more cheaply from water or coal.

But that is not all of the defendants' case. There are not twenty-five hundred men at present in the industry. The Government says that this is the fault of the union; the defendants with much greater probability that it is the inevitable coming to pass. But wherever the fault, if there is any, that is the fact with which the defendants had to deal. There were not men enough to enable the factories to run continuously during the working season, leaving out the two or three summer months in which the heat makes it impossible to go on. To work undermanned costs the same in fuel and overhead expense as to work fully manned, and therefore means a serious loss. On the other hand the men are less well off with the uncertainties that such a situation brings. The purpose of the arrangement is to secure employment for all the men during the whole of the two seasons, thus to give all the labor available to the factories, and to divide it equally among them. From the view that we take we think it unnecessary to explain how the present system sprang from experience during the war when the Government restricted production to one-half of what it had been and an accident was found to work well, or to do more than advert to the defendants' contention that with the means available the production is increased. It is enough that we see no combination in unreasonable restraint of trade in the arrangements made to meet the short supply of men.

Decree reversed. Petition dismissed.

National Association of Window Glass Manufacturers, et al.
v. United States
263 U. S. 403

Boycotting a Producers' Cooperative

(*U. S.* v. *American Livestock Co.*, 1929)

This is a proceeding under the Packers & Stockyards Act, 1921, Act of August 15, 1921, c. 64, § 316, 42 Stat. 159, 168. U. S. Code, Title 7, § 217. The American Livestock Association and others seek an injunction against the carrying out of an order of the Secretary of Agriculture requiring them to discontinue a boycott by which they refused dealings with the Producers Commission Association at the Oklahoma National Stock Yards. A District Court of three judges granted the injunction. . . . The United States appealed.

The Secretary found the existence of the boycott, the persistent refusal to buy or sell livestock from or to the Producers Commission Association, and that the American Livestock Association and its fellow conspirators thereby restrained commerce and discriminated unfairly against the Producers Commission Association contrary to the statute. The appellees urged that there is nothing to prevent their dealing or refusing to deal with whom they choose. But we think that it does not need argument to show that a boycott of a dealer in a stockyard may be an unfair practice under the Act as it is found to have been in this case. . . . We pass at once to the only real question in debate.

The Producers Commission Association is a cooperative association for mutual help under the laws of Oklahoma and is forbidden to "handle the agricultural or horticultural product of any non-member except for storage." It is agreed that "the record contains no evidence as to whether the live stock which the Producers Commission Association bought or sold or attempted to buy or sell upon the Oklahoma City Stockyards was or was not the live stock of its members." It is said so far as appears all the sales were *ultra vires* and that the appellees should not be enjoined from refusing to cooperate in an illegal act. But apart from the presumption that the corporation was acting only within its powers and from the burden resting on the doer of a *prima facie* illegal act, the boycott, to justify it, we agree with the Government that it would be absurd to suppose that a cooperative society organized for the special purpose of aiding its members should confine its business to the illegal sale of the products of nonmembers. If not all, we must assume that some at least of its business was legitimate and that to some extent it might sell live stock that its members produced. But the boycott was general, intended, it would seem, to drive the Producers Commission Association out of business. That association was a competitor of the appellees and the suggestion that it was acting *ultra vires* sounds like an afterthought and cannot be supposed to have been the motive for the act. It is said that motive does not matter, but motive may be very material when it is sought to justify what until justified is a wrong. But, whatever the motive, nothing is shown or suggested by the evidence to justify the general boycott that the Secretary's order forbade. The Secretary's order should be enforced, but without prejudice to the right of the appellees to refuse to deal with the Producers Commission Association in matters beyond its power.

A suggestion was made that the last named association was not within the protection of the Act of Congress. We see nothing in the limitation of its powers to prevent it, the statute seems to recognize it, § 306 (f), and the corporation was found by the Secretary to be a market agency duly registered as such.

Decree reversed.

United States v. *American Livestock Commission Co., et al.*
279 U. S. 435

IV. ON INTERPRETING STATUTES

Soliciting Political Funds

(*United States* v. *Thayer*, 1908)

This is an indictment for soliciting a contribution of money for political purposes from an employee of the United States in a post office building of the United States occupied by the employee in the discharge of his duties. By the Civil Service Act of January 16, 1883, c. 27, § 12, 22 Stat. 403, 407, "No person shall, in any room or building occupied in the discharge of official duties by any officer or employee of the United States mentioned in this act, or in any navy-yard, fort, or arsenal, solicit in any manner whatever, or receive any contribution of money or any other thing of value for any political purpose whatever." By § 15 a penalty is imposed for fine, imprisonment, or both. The indictment is in eleven counts, and charges the sending of letters to employees, which were intended to be received and read by them in the building and were so received and read by them in fact. It is admitted that the defendant was not in the building. There was a demurrer, which was sustained by the District Court on the ground that the case was not within the Act. 154 Fed. Rep. 508. The only question argued or intended to be raised is whether the defendant's physical presence in the building was necessary to create the offense.

Of course it is possible to solicit by letter as well as in person. It is equally clear that the person who writes the letter and intentionally puts it in the way of delivery solicits, whether the delivery is accomplished by agents of the writer, by agents of the person addressed, or by independent middlemen, if it takes place in the intended way. It appears to us no more open to doubt that the statute prohibits solicitation by writing as well as by spoken words. It forbids all persons to solicit "in any manner whatever." The purpose is wider than that of a notice prohibiting book peddling in a building. It is not, even primarily, to save employees from interruption or annoyance in their business. It is to check a political abuse, which is not different in kind, whether practised by letter or by word of mouth. The limits of the Act, presumably, were due to what was considered the reasonable and possibly the constitutional freedom of citizens, whether officeholders or not when in private life, and it may be conjectured that it was upon this ground that an amendment of broader scope was rejected. If the writer of the letter in person had handed it to the man addressed, in the building without a word, and the latter had read it then and there, we suppose that no one would deny that the writer fell within the statute. We can see no distinction between personally delivering the letter and sending it by a servant of the writer. If the solicitation is in the building the statute does not require personal presence, so that the question is narrowed to whether the solicitation alleged took place in the building or outside.

The solicitation was made at some time, somewhere. The time determines the place. It was not complete when the letter was dropped into the post. If the letter had miscarried or had been burned, the defendant would not have accomplished a solicitation. The court below was misled by cases in which, upon an indictment for obtaining money by false pretenses, the crime was held to have been committed at the place where drafts were put into the post by the defrauded person. . . . But these stand on the analogy of the acceptance by mail of an offer and throw no light. A relation already existed between the parties, and it is because of that relation that posting the letter made the transaction complete. See *Brauer* v. *Shaw,* 168 Massachusetts, 198, 200.

Here a relation was to be established, just as there is at the first stage of a contract when an offer is to be made. Whether or not, as Mr. Langdell thinks, nothing less than bringing the offer to the actual consciousness of the person addressed would do, Contr. § 151, certainly putting a letter into a post office is neither an offer nor a solicitation. "An offer is nothing until it is communicated to the party to whom it is made." *Thomson* v. *James*, 18 Ct. of Sess. Cas. (2d Series), 1, 10, 15. Therefore, we repeat, until after the letter had entered the building the offense was not complete, but, when it had been read, the case was not affected by the nature of the intended means by which it was put into the hands of the person addressed. Neither can the case be affected by speculations as to what the position would have been if the receiver had put the letter in his pocket and had read it later at home. Offenses usually depend for their completion upon events that are not wholly within the offender's control and that may turn out in different ways.

No difficulty is raised by the coupling of solicitation and receipt in the statute. If receipt required personal presence, it still would be obvious that "solicit in any manner whatever" was a broader term. But the cases that have been relied upon to establish that solicitation did not happen in the building, although inadequate for that, do sufficiently show that the money might be received there without the personal presence of the defendant. If, in answer to the defendant's letter, the parties addressed had posted money to him in the building where they were employed, the money undoubtedly would have been received there. To sum up, the defendant solicited money for campaign purposes, he did not solicit until his letter actually was received in the building; he did solicit when it was received and read there, and the solicitation was in the place where the letter was received. We observe that this is the opinion expressed by the Civil Service Commission in a note upon this section, and the principle of our decision is similar to that recognized in several cases in this

Court. . . . We do not cite them more at length, as the only dispute possible is on the meaning of the particular words that Congress has used.

We may add that this case does not raise the question presented by an act done in one jurisdiction and producing effects in another which threatens the actor with punishment if it can catch him. Decisions in that class of cases, however, illustrate the indisputable general proposition that a man sometimes may be punished where he has brought consequences to pass, although he was not there in person. They are cited in *In re Palliser*, 136 U. S. 257. Here the defendant was within and subject to the jurisdiction of the United States to the extent of its constitutional power, and the power is not in dispute. . . .

Judgment reversed.

United States v. *Thayer*
209 U. S. 39

A Music Roll Not a "Copy"

(*White-Smith Music Co.* v. *Apollo Co.*, 1908)

[THE COURT HELD THAT A PERFORATED MUSIC ROLL WAS NOT A COPY of a composition within the meaning of the Copyright Act. The opinion was written by Mr. Justice Day. Concurring specially, Mr. Justice Holmes said:]

IN VIEW of the facts and opinions in this country and abroad to which my brother Day has called attention I do not feel justified in dissenting from the judgment of the Court, but the result is to give to copyright less scope than its rational significance and the ground on which it is granted seem to me to demand. Therefore I desire to add a few words to what he has said.

The notion of property starts, I suppose, from confirmed possession of a tangible object and consists in the right to exclude others from interference with the more or less free doing with it as one wills. But in copyright property has reached a more abstract expression. The right to exclude is not directed to an object in possession or owned, but is *in vacuo*, so to speak. It restrains the spontaneity of men where but for it there would be nothing of any kind to hinder their doing as they saw fit. It is a prohibition of conduct remote from the persons or tangibles of the party having the right. It may be infringed a thousand miles from the owner and without his ever becoming aware of the wrong. It is a right which could not be recognized or endured for more than a limited time, and therefore, I may remark in passing, it is one which hardly can be conceived except as a product of statute, as the authorities now agree.

The ground of this extraordinary right is that the person to whom it is given has invented some new collocation of visible or audible points,—of lines, colors, sounds, or words. The restraint is directed against reproducing this collocation, although but for the invention and the statute anyone would be free to combine the contents of the dictionary, the elements of the spectrum, or the notes of the gamut in any way that he had the wit to devise. The restriction is confined to the specific form, to the collocation devised, of course, but one would expect that, if it was to be protected at all, that collocation would be protected according to what was its essence. One would expect the protection to be coextensive not only with the invention, which, though free to all, only one had the ability to achieve, but with the possibility of reproducing the result which gives to the invention its meaning and worth. A musical composition is a rational collocation of sounds apart from concepts, reduced to a tangible expression from which the collocation can be reproduced either with or without continuous human intervention. On principle anything that mechanically reproduces that collocation of sounds ought to be held a copy, or if the statute is too narrow ought to be made so by a further act, except so far as some extraneous consideration of policy may oppose. What license may be implied from a sale of the copyrighted article is a different and harder question, but I leave it untouched, as license is not relied upon as a ground for the judgment of the Court.

White-Smith Music Publishing Co. v. *Apollo Co.*
209 U. S. 1, 18

Union Leader Punished for Contempt

(*Gompers* v. *United States*, 1914)

THESE are proceedings for alleged criminal contempts in the matter that was before this Court in *Gompers* v. *Bucks Stove & Range Co.*, 221 U. S. 418. In that case the proceedings instituted by the Bucks Stove & Range Company to punish the petitioners were ordered to be dismissed, but without prejudice to the power of the Supreme Court of the District to punish contempt, if any, committed against it. The decision was rendered on May 15, 1911, and the next day the Supreme Court of the District appointed a committee to inquire whether there was reasonable cause to believe the plaintiffs in error guilty, in wilfully violating an injunction issued by that court on December 18, 1907, and, if yea, to present and prosecute charges to that effect. The inquiry was directed solely with a view to punishment for past acts, not to secure obedience for the future; and to avoid repetition it will be understood that all that we have to say concerns proceedings of this sort only, and further, only proceedings for such contempt not committed in the presence of the court.

The committee, on June 26, 1911, reported and charged that the parties severally were guilty of specified acts in violation of the injunction, being the same acts of which they had been found guilty by the Supreme Court in the former case. Rules to show cause were issued on the same day. The defendants pleaded the Statute of Limitations, Rev. Stat., § 1044, as to most of the charges, and not guilty. There was a trial, the Statute of Limitations was held inapplicable and the defendants were found guilty and sentenced to imprisonment for terms of different lengths, subject to exceptions which by agreement were embodied in a single bill. The Court of Appeals reduced the sentences to imprisonment for thirty days in the case of Gompers and fines of $500 for each of the other two. 40 App. D. C. 293. The defendants brought a writ of error and an appeal to this Court and also petitioned for a writ of certiorari. Of course an appeal does not lie, nor does a writ of error, but the writ of certiorari is granted. The judges of the Supreme Court also petitioned for a writ of certiorari, but as the case will be disposed of on the first mentioned petition, the other will be denied.

The injunction, subsequently held too broad, not only forbade the defendants to combine to obstruct the business of the Bucks Stove & Range Company, or to declare or threaten any boycott against it (such a boycott already having been declared), but also to publish any statement calling attention of any body to any such boycott, or any statement of like effect, tending to any injury of the Company's business. This decree, although made on December 18, did not become operative until December 23, 1907. Before going to the Court of Appeals the injunction in substantially the same form was made permanent on March 23, 1908. It may be assumed for the purposes of our decision that the evidence not only warranted but required a finding that the defendants were guilty of some at least of the violations of this decree that were charged against them, and so we come at once to consider the Statute of Limitations, which is their only real defense. A preliminary objection was urged, to be sure, that the question of the validity of that defense was not reserved, but there is nothing in it. The bar was pleaded, there was a motion to dismiss on that ground for want of a replication, there was a decision that the statute did not apply to contempts, and the counsel for the plaintiffs in error stated at the trial that there was one general exception presented on their behalf with regard to that. We cannot doubt that it was perfectly understood, or that the record shows, that the plaintiffs in error preserved all their rights.

The statute provides that "no person shall be prosecuted, tried, or punished for any offense, not capital, except. . . , unless the indictment is found, or the information is instituted within three years next after such offense shall have been committed." Rev. Stat., § 1044. Act of April 13, 1876, c. 56, 19 Stat. 32. The plaintiffs in error treat these proceedings as having begun on May 16, 1911, when the Supreme Court directed an inquiry. They certainly did not begin before that date; so that, if the statute applies, contempts prior to May 16, 1908, would be barred. It is argued with force that the inquiry was directed only to breaches of the preliminary injunction, which expired by its own terms upon the making of the final decree on March 23, 1908, and that therefore everything legitimately before the court, happened more than three years before. But as the report mentioned the final decree and charged a few acts later than March 23, though mostly rather unimportant, and as the order to show cause referred to a violation of the injunctions, in the plural, it perhaps would savor of a technicality that we should be loath to apply on either side, if we did not deal with all that is charged.

The charges against Gompers are: 1. hurrying the publication of the January number of the *American Federationist* and distributing many copies after the injunction was known and before it went into effect, in which number the Bucks Stove & Range Company was included in the "We don't patronize" list; 2, circulating other copies in January, 1908; 3, on and after December 23, 1907, circulating another document to the like effect with comments, some of which were lawful criticism but others of which suggested that the injunction left the members of labor organizations free to continue their boycott; 4, publishing in February, 1908, a copy of the decree with the suggestion that those who violated the injunction outside of the District of Columbia could not be punished unless they came within it; 5, in January and February, 1908, publishing in conjunction with the other defendants a paper appealing for financial aid, commenting on the injunction as invading the liberty of the press and free speech and reprinting the before-mentioned comments and suggestions; 6, in March, 1908, again suggesting that no law compelled the purchase of a Buck stove; 7, in April, 1908, after the final decree, reiterating the same suggestion in the *American Federationist;* 8, in April, 1908, repeating similar suggestions by transparent innuendo in a public address; 9, again repeating them in another address, on or about May 1; 10, and again in the July issue of the *American Federationist;* 11, publishing in the September *Federationist* an editorial characterizing the injunction as an invasion of constitutional freedom, (which hardly seems to exceed lawful comment unless on the ground that the case was not finished, although mistaken in its law); 12, in a report published after September 9, 1908, saying that if the Executive Council of the Federation of Labor obeyed the injunction they could not report the state of the case to the Denver Convention, and that they did not see how they could refuse to give an account of their doings; 13, on September 29, 1908, saying in a public address that the injunction forbade him to discuss the case, but that he must, (seemingly not going beyond that declaration); 14, on October 26, 1908, recurring in a single phrase in an address, to his old suggestion that no law compelled his hearers to buy a Buck stove; 15, in November, 1908, in an address which he caused to be published in the *Federationist* in January, 1909, again referring to the injunction, mentioning his past advice and suggestions and that he had been called on to show cause why he should not be adjudged guilty of contempt, (in the former proceeding), and asking how he could have done otherwise; and finally, 16, in a report made in November, 1909, referring to the Judge as so far having transcended his authority that even judges of the Court of Appeals have felt called upon to criticize his action, and saying that in such circumstances it is the duty of the citizens to refuse obedience and to take whatever consequences may ensue. The charges against Mitchell and Morrison are mainly for having taken part in some of the above mentioned publications, but need not be stated particularly, as all the acts of any substance in Mitchell's case and all in that of Morrison were more than three years old when these proceedings began.

The boycott against the Company was not called off until July 19 to 29, 1910, and it is argued that even if the statute applies the conspiracy was continuing until that date, *United States v. Kissel*, [see page 137 of this volume], and therefore that the statute did not begin to run until then. But this is not an indictment for conspiracy, it is a charge of specific acts in disobedience of an injunction. The acts are not charged as evidence but as substantive offenses; each of them, so far as it was a contempt, was punishable as such, and was charged as such, and therefore each must be judged by itself; and so we come to what, as we already have intimated, is the real question in the case.

It is urged in the first place that contempts cannot be crimes, because, although punishable by imprisonment and therefore, if crimes, infamous, they are not within the protection of the Constitution and the amendments giving a right to trial by jury &c. to persons charged with such crimes. But the provisions of the Constitution are not mathematical formulas having their essence in their form; they are organic living institutions transplanted from English soil. Their significance is vital not formal; it is to be gathered not simply by taking the words and a dictionary, but by considering their origin and the line of their growth. *Robertson v. Baldwin*, 165 U. S. 275, 281, 282. It does not follow that contempts of the class under consideration are not crimes, or rather, in the language of the statute, offenses, because trial by jury as it has been gradually worked out and fought out has been thought not to extend to them as a matter of constitutional right. These contempts are infractions of the law, visited with punishment as such. If such acts are not criminal, we are in error as to the most fundamental characteristic of crimes as that word has been understood in English speech. So truly are they crimes that it seems to be proved that in the early law they were punished only by the usual criminal procedure, 3 *Transactions of the Royal Historical Society*, N. S. p. 147 (1885), and that at least in England it seems that they still may be and preferably are tried in that way....

We come then to the construction of the statute. It has been assumed that the concluding words "unless the indictment is found or the information is instituted within three years" limit the offenses given the benefit of the Act to those usually prosecuted in that way, and the counsel for the petitioners were at some pains to argue that the charges of the committee amounted to an information; a matter that opens vistas of antiquarian speculation. But this question is not one to be answered by refinements and curious inquiries.—In our opinion the proper interpretation of the statute begins with the substantive not with the adjective part. The substantive portion of the section is that no person shall be tried for any offense not capital except within a certain time. Those words are of universal scope. What follows is a natural way of expressing that the proceedings must be begun within three years; indictment and information being the usual modes by which they are begun and very likely no other having occurred to those who drew the law. But it seems to us plain that the dominant words of the Act are "no person shall be prosecuted, tried or punished for any offense not capital" unless.——

No reason has been suggested to us for not giving to the statute its natural scope. The English courts seem to think it wise, even when there is much seeming reason for the exercise of a summary power, to leave the punishment of this class of contempts to the regular and formal criminal process. *Matter of Macleod*, 6 Jur. 461. Maintenance of their authority does not often make it really necessary for courts to exert their own power to punish, as is shown by the English practice in more violent days than these, and there is no more reason for prolonging the period of liability when they see fit to do so than in the case where the same offense is proceeded against in the common way. Indeed the punishment of these offenses peculiarly needs to be speedy if it is to occur. The argument loses little of its force if it should be determined hereafter, a matter on which we express no opinion, that in the present state of the law an indictment would not lie for a contempt of a court of the United States.

Even if the statute does not cover the case by its express words, as we think it does, still, in dealing with the punishment of crime a rule should be laid down, if not by Congress by this Court. The power to punish for contempt must have some limit in time, and in defining that limit we should have regard to what has been the policy of the law from the foundation of the Government. By analogy if not by enactment the limit is three years. The case cannot be concluded otherwise so well as in the language of Chief Justice Marshall in a case where the statute was held applicable to an action of debt for a penalty. *Adams* v. *Woods*, 2 Cranch, 336, 340, 341, 342: "It is contended that the prosecutions limited by this law, are those only which are carried on in the form of an indictment or information, and not those where the penalty is demanded by an action of debt.—But if the words of the act be examined they will be found to apply, not to any particular mode of proceeding, but generally to any prosecution, trial or punishment for the offence. It is not declared that no indictment shall be found . . . But it is declared that 'No person shall be prosecuted, tried or punished' . . . . In expounding this law, it deserves some consideration, that if it does not limit actions of debt for penalties, those actions might, in many cases, be brought at any distance of time. This would be utterly repugnant to the genius of our laws. In a country where not even treason can be prosecuted after a lapse of three years, it could scarcely be supposed that an individual would remain forever liable to a pecuniary forfeiture." The result is that the judgments, based as they are mainly upon offenses that could not be taken into consideration, must be reversed.

Judgments reversed.

[Justices Van Devanter and Pitney dissented without opinion.]

Gompers v. *United States*
233 U. S. 604

Taxing the Transfer of Estates

(N. Y. Trust Co. v. Eisner, 1921)

This is a suit brought by the executors of one Purdy to recover an estate tax levied under the Act of Congress of September 8, 1916, c. 463, Title II, § 201, 39 Stat. 756, 777, and paid under duress on December 14, 1917. According to the complaint Purdy died leaving a will and codicil directing that all succession, inheritance and transfer taxes should be paid out of the residuary estate, which was bequeathed to the descendants of his brother. The value of the residuary estate was $427,414.96, subject to some administration expenses. The executors had been required to pay and had paid inheritance and succession taxes to New York ($32,988.97) and other States ($4,780.91) amounting in all to $37,769.88. The gross estate as defined in § 202 of the Act of Congress was $769,799.39; funeral expenses and expenses of administration, except the above taxes, $61,322.08; leaving a net value for the payment of legacies, except as reduced by the taxes of the United States, of $670,707.43. The plaintiffs were compelled to pay $23,910.77 to the United States, no deduction of any part of the above-mentioned $37,769.88 being allowed. They allege that the Act of Congress is unconstitutional, and also that it was misconstrued in not allowing a deduction of State inheritance and succession taxes as charges within the meaning of § 203. On demurrer the District Court dismissed the suit.

By § 201 of the Act, "a tax . . . equal to the following percentage, of the value of the net estate, to be determined as provided in section two hundred and three, is hereby imposed upon the transfer of the net estate of every decedent dying after the passage of this Act," with percentages rising from one per centum of the amount of the net estate not in excess of $50,000 to ten per centum of the amount in excess of $5,000,000. Section 202 gives the mode of determining the value of the gross estate. Then, by § 203 it is enacted "That for the purpose of the tax the value of the net estate shall be determined—(a) In the case of a resident, by deducting from the value of the gross estate— (1) Such amounts for funeral expenses, administration expenses, claims against the estate, unpaid mortgages, losses incurred during the settlement of the estate arising from fires, storms, shipwreck, or other casualty, and from theft, when such losses are not compensated for by insurance or otherwise, support during the settlement of the estate of those dependent upon the decedent, and such other charges against the estate, as are allowed by the laws of the jurisdiction, whether within or without the United States, under which the estate is being administered; and (2) an exemption of $50,000." The tax is to be due in one year after the decedent's death. § 204. Within thirty days after qualifying the executor is to give written notice to the collector and later to make return of the gross estate, deductions allowed, net estate and the tax payable thereon. § 205. The executor is to pay the tax. § 207. The tax is a lien for ten years on the gross estate except such part as is paid out for allowed charges, § 209, and if not paid within sixty days after it is due is to be collected by a suit to subject the decedent's property to be sold. § 208. In case of collection from some person other than the executor, the same section provides for contribution from or marshaling of persons subject to equal or prior liability "it being the purpose and intent of this title that so far as is practicable and unless otherwise directed by the will of the decedent the tax shall be paid out of the estate before its distribution." These provisions are assailed by the plaintiffs in error as an unconstitutional interference with the rights of the States to regulate descent and distribution, as unequal and as a direct tax not apportioned as the Constitution requires.

The statement of the constitutional objections urged imports on its face a distinction that, if correct, evidently hitherto has escaped this Court. See *United States* v. *Field,* 255 U. S. 257. It is admitted, as since *Knowlton* v. *Moore,* 178 U. S. 41, it has to be, that the United States has power to tax legacies, but it is said that this tax is cast upon a transfer while it is being effectuated by the State itself and therefore is an intrusion upon its processes, whereas a legacy tax is not imposed until the process is complete. An analogy is sought in the difference between the attempt of a State to tax commerce among the States and its right after the goods have become mingled with the general stock in the State. A consideration of the parallel is enough to detect the fallacy. A tax that was directed solely against goods imported into the State and that was determined by the fact of importation would be no better after the goods were at rest in the State than before. It would be as much an interference with commerce in one case as in the other. . . . Conversely if a tax on the property distributed by the laws of a State, determined by the fact that distribution has been accomplished, is valid, a tax determined by the fact that distribution is about to begin is no greater interference and is equally good.

Knowlton v. *Moore,* 178 U. S. 41, dealt, it is true, with a legacy tax. But the tax was met with the same objection; that it usurped or interfered with the exercise of State powers, and the answer to the objection was based upon general considerations and treated the "power to transmit or the transmission or receipt of property by death" as all standing on the same footing. 178 U. S. 57, 59. After the elaborate discussion that the subject received in that case we think it unnecessary to dwell upon matters that in principle were disposed of there. The same may be said of the argument that the tax is direct and therefore is void for want of apportionment. It is argued that when the tax is on the privilege of receiving, the tax is indirect because it may be avoided, whereas here the tax is inevitable and therefore direct. But that matter also is disposed of by *Knowlton* v. *Moore*, not by an attempt to make some scientific distinction, which would be at least difficult, but on an interpretation of language by its traditional use—on the practical and historical ground that this kind of tax always has been regarded as the antithesis of a direct tax—"has ever been treated as a duty or excise, because of the particular occasion which gives rise to its levy." 178 U. S. 81-83. Upon this point a page of history is worth a volume of logic.

The inequalities charged upon the statute, if there is an intestacy, are all inequalities in the amounts that beneficiaries might receive in case of estates of different values, of different proportions between real and personal estate, and of different numbers of recipients; or if there is a will affect legatees. As to the inequalities in case of a will they must be taken to be contemplated by the testator. He knows the law and the consequences of the disposition that he makes. As to intestate successors the tax is not imposed upon them but precedes them and the fact that they may receive less or different sums because of the statute does not concern the United States.

There remains only the construction of the Act. The argument against its constitutionality is based upon a premise that is unfavorable to the contention of the plaintiffs in error upon this point. For if the tax attaches to the estate before distribution—if it is a tax on the right to transmit or on the transmission at its beginning, obviously it attaches to the whole estate except so far as the statute sets a limit. "Charges against the estate" as pointed out by the court below are only charges that affect the estate as a whole, and therefore do not include taxes on the right of individual beneficiaries. This reasoning excludes not only the New

York succession tax but those paid to other States, which can stand no better than that paid in New York. What amount New York may take as the basis of taxation and questions of priority between the United States and the State are not open in this case.

Decree affirmed.

New York Trust Co., et al., as Executors of Purdy, v. *Eisner*
256 U. S. 345

Avoiding the Constitutional Question

(*Blodgett* v. *Holden,* 1928, Separate Opinion)

[THE CIRCUIT COURT OF APPEALS CERTIFIED TO THE SUPREME COURT the question whether the provisions of the Revenue Act of 1924 were unconstitutional in so far as they imposed a tax on gifts made prior to June 2 1924, when the Act was approved. The eight justices who considered the case agreed that the tax imposed on gifts made by Blodgett in January of that year could not be sustained; they were equally divided as to the ground on which the decision should be placed. Chief Justice Taft and Justices Van Devanter and Butler concurred in the opinion of Mr. Justice McReynolds, that the enforcement of the tax was arbitrary and violated the due process clause of the Fifth Amendment. Justices Brandeis, Sanford and Stone concurred in Mr. Justice Holmes' opinion:]

ALTHOUGH research has shown and practice has established the futility of the charge that it was a usurpation when this Court undertook to declare an Act of Congress unconstitutional, I suppose that we all agree that to do so is the gravest and most delicate duty that this Court is called on to perform. Upon this among other considerations the rule is settled that as between two possible interpretations of a statute, by one of which it would be unconstitutional and by the other valid, our plain duty is to adopt that which will save the Act. Even to avoid a serious doubt the rule is the same. . . . Words have been strained more than they need to be strained here in order to avoid that doubt. . . . In a different sphere but embodying the same general attitude as to construction, see *United States* v. *Goelet,* 232 U. S. 293, 297.

ON INTERPRETING STATUTES

By § 319 of the Revenue Act of 1924 (June 2, 1924, c. 234; 43 Stat. 253, 313) a tax is laid on gifts "For the calendar year 1924 and each calendar year thereafter." In the Code the words are "during any calendar year." Title 26, § 1131. The latter phrase brings out what I should think was obvious without its aid, that the purpose is a general one to indicate the periods to be regarded, as distinguished from fiscal years not necessarily to run counter to the usual understanding that statutes direct themselves to future not to past transactions. . . . If when the statute was passed it had been well recognized that Congress had no power to tax past gifts I think that we should have no trouble in reading the Act as meant to operate only from its date and only to tax gifts thereafter made. If I am right, we should read it in that way now. By § 324 (a) of the Revenue Act of 1926 (February 26, 1926, c. 27; 44 Stat. 9, 86,) § 319 of the Act of 1924 is amended and the rates of taxation are reduced, and then by (b) it is provided that "subdivision (a) of this section shall take effect as of June 2, 1924," the date when the earlier Act was passed. A reasonable interpretation is that the reduction and the tax operate alike on gifts after that date. Taking both statutes into account, and the principles of construction to which I have referred, I think it tolerably plain that the Act should be read as referring only to transactions taking place after it was passed, when to disregard the rule "would be to impose an unexpected liability that if known might have induced those concerned to avoid it and to use their money in other ways," *Lewellyn* v. *Frick,* 268 U. S. 238, 251, 252.

On the general question whether there is power to tax gifts I express no opinion now. I agree with the result that the plaintiff is entitled to recover the taxes paid in respect of gifts made before the statute went into effect.

Blodgett v. *Holden, Collector*
275 U. S. 142, 147

V. ON CONSTITUTIONAL GUARANTIES

Excluding Chinese Without a Court Hearing

(*United States* v. *Ju Toy*, 1905)

THIS case comes here on a certificate from the Circuit Court of Appeals presenting certain questions of law. It appears that the appellee, being detained by the matter of the Steamship *Doric* for return to China, presented a petition for *habeas corpus* to the District Court, alleging that he was a native-born citizen of the United States, returning after a temporary departure, and was denied permission to land by the collector of the port of San Francisco. It also appears from the petition that he took an appeal from the denial, and that the decision was affirmed by the Secretary of Commerce and Labor. No further grounds are stated. The writ issued and the United States made return, and answered showing all the proceedings before the Department, which are not denied to have been in regular form, and setting forth all of the evidence and the orders made. The answer also denied the allegations of the petition. Motions to dismiss the writ were made on the grounds that the decision of the Secretary was conclusive and that no abuse of authority was shown. These were denied, and the District Court decided seemingly on new evidence, subject to exceptions, that Ju Toy was a native-born citizen of the United States. An appeal was taken to the Circuit Court of Appeals alleging errors the nature of which has been indicated. Thereupon the latter court certified the following questions:

"*First.* Should a District Court of the United States grant a writ of *habeas corpus* in behalf of a person of Chinese descent being held for return to China by the steamship company which brought him therefrom, who having recently arrived at a port of the United States made application to land as a native-born citizen thereof and who, after examination by the duly authorized immigration officers, was found by them not to have been born in the United States, was denied admission and ordered deported, which finding and action upon appeal was affirmed by the Secretary of Commerce and Labor, when the foregoing facts appear to the court and the petition for the writ alleges unlawful detention on the sole ground that the petitioner does not come within the restrictions of the Chinese exclusions acts, because born in and a citizen of the United States and does not allege or show in any other way unlawful action or abuse of their discretion or powers by the immigration officers who excluded him?

"*Second.* In a *habeas corpus* proceeding should a District Court of the United States dismiss the writ or should it direct a new or further hearing upon evidence to be presented where the writ had been granted in behalf of a person of Chinese descent being held by the steamship company for return to China from whence it brought him, who recently arrived from that country and asked permission to land upon the ground that he was born in and was a citizen of the United States, when the uncontradicted return and answer show that such person was granted a hearing by the proper immigration officers who found he was not born in the United States, that his application for admission was considered and denied by such officers, and that the denial was affirmed upon appeal to the Secretary of Commerce and Labor, and where nothing more appears to show that such executive officers failed to grant a proper hearing, abused their discretion, or acted in any unlawful or improper way upon the case presented to them for determination?

"*Third.* In a *habeas corpus* proceeding in a District Court of the United States instituted in behalf of a person of Chinese descent being held for return to China by the steamship company which recently brought him therefrom to a port of the United States and who applied for admission therein upon the ground that he was a native-born citizen thereof but who, after a hearing, the lawfully designated immigration officers found was not born therein and to whom they denied admission which finding and denial, upon appeal to the Secretary of Commerce and Labor, was affirmed—should the court treat the finding and action of such executive officers upon the question of citizenship and other questions of fact as having been made by a tribunal authorized to decide the same and as final and conclusive unless it be made affirmatively to appear that such officers, in the case submitted to them, abused the discretion vested in them or in some other way in hearing and determining the same committed prejudicial error?"

We assume in what we have to say, as the questions assume, that no abuse of authority of any kind is alleged. That being out of the case, the first of them is answered by the case of *United States* v. *Sing Tuck*, 194 U. S. 161, 170 [opinion by Holmes]: "A petition for *habeas corpus* ought not to be entertained, unless the court is satisfied that the petitioner can make out at least a *prima facie* case." This petition should have been denied on this ground, irrespective of what more we have to say, because it alleged nothing except citizenship. It disclosed neither abuse of authority nor the existence of evidence not laid before the Secretary. It did not even set forth that evidence or allege its effect. But as it was entertained and the District Court found for the petitioner it would be a severe measure to order the petition to be dismissed on that ground now, and we pass on to further considerations.

The broad question is presented whether or not the decision of the Secretary of Commerce and Labor is conclusive. It was held in *United States* v. *Sing Tuck*, 194 U. S. 161, 167, that the Act of August 18, 1894, c. 301, § 1, 28 Stat. 372, 390, purported to make it so, but whether the statute could have that effect constitutionally was left untouched, except by a reference to cases where an opinion already had been expressed. To quote the latest first, in *The Japanese Immigrant Case (Yamataya v. Fisher)*, 189 U. S. 86, 97, it was said: "That Congress may exclude aliens of a particular race from the United States; prescribe the terms and conditions upon which certain classes of aliens may come to this country; establish regulations for sending out of the country such aliens as come here in violation of law; and commit the enforcement of such provisions, conditions and regulations exclusively to executive officers, without judicial intervention, are principles firmly established by the decisions of this court." See also *Turner* v. *Williams*, 194 U. S. 279, 290, 291; *Chin Bak Kan* v. *United States*, 186 U. S. 193, 200. In *Fok Young Yo* v. *United States*, 185 U. S. 296, 304, 305, it was held that the decision of the collector of customs on the right of transit across the territory of the United States was conclusive, and, still more to the point, in *Lem Moon Sing* v. *United States*, 158 U. S. 538, where the petitioner for *habeas corpus* alleged facts which, if true, gave him a right to enter and remain in the country, it was held that the decision of the collector was final as to whether or not he belonged to the privileged class.

It is true that it may be argued that these cases are not directly conclusive of the point now under decision. It may be said that the parties concerned were aliens, and that although they alleged absolute rights, and facts which it was contended went to the jurisdiction of the officer making the decision, still their rights were only treaty or statutory rights, and therefore were subject to the implied qualification imposed by the later statute, which made the decision of the collector with regard to them final. The meaning of the cases and the language which we have quoted is not satisfied by so narrow an interpretation, but we do not delay upon them. They can be read.

It is established, as we have said, that the Act purports to make the decision of the Department final, whatever the ground on which the right to enter the country is claimed, as well when it is citizenship as when it is domicil and the belonging to a class excepted from the Exclusion Acts. . . . It also is established by the former case and others which it cites that the relevant portion of the Act of August 18, 1894, c. 301, is not void as a whole. The statute has been upheld and enforced. But the relevant portion being a single section, accomplishing all its results by the same general words, must be valid as to all that it embraces, or altogether void. An exception of a class constitutionally exempted cannot be read into those general words merely for the purpose of saving what remains. That has been decided over and over again. . . . It necessarily follows that when such words are sustained, they are sustained to their full extent.

In view of the cases which we have cited it seems no longer open to discuss the question propounded as a new one. Therefore we do not analyze the nature of the right of a person presenting himself at the frontier for admission. . . . But it is not improper to add a few words. The petitioner, although physically within our boundaries, is to be regarded as if he had been stopped at the limit of our jurisdiction and kept there while his right to enter was under debate. If, for the purpose of argument, we assume that the Fifth Amendment applied to him and that to deny entrance to a citizen is to deprive him of liberty, we nevertheless are of opinion that with regard to him due process of law does not require a judicial trial. That is the result of the cases which we have cited and the almost necessary result of the power of Congress to pass exclusion laws. That the decision may be entrusted to an executive officer and that his decision is due process of law was affirmed and explained in *Nishimura Ekiu* v. *United States,* 142 U. S. 651, 660, and in *Fong Yue Ting* v. *United States,* 149 U. S. 698, 713, before the authorities to which we already have referred. It is unnecessary to repeat the often quoted remarks of Mr. Justice Curtis, speaking for the whole court in *Murray's Lessee* v. *Hoboken Land & Improvement Co.,* 18 How. 272, 280, to show that the requirement of a judicial trial does not prevail in every case. . . .

We are of opinion that the first question should be answered, no; that the third question should be answered, yes, with the result that the second question should be answered that the writ should be dismissed, as it should have been dismissed in this case.

It will be so certified.

[Mr. Justice Brewer dissented. He said that the rules for examining Chinese constituted a "star chamber proceeding of the most stringent sort. . . . I do not see how any one can read those rules and hold that they constitute due process of law for the arrest and deportation of a citizen of the United States." The decision was to his mind "appalling," and Mr. Justice Peckham agreed. Mr. Justice Day dissented without opinion.]

United States v. *Ju Toy*
198 U. S. 253

Using Illegally Seized Papers

(Silverthorne Lumber Co. v. United States, 1920)

THIS is a writ of error brought to reverse a judgment of the District Court fining the Silverthorne Lumber Company two hundred and fifty dollars for contempt of court and ordering Frederick W. Silverthorne to be imprisoned until he should purge himself of a similar contempt. The contempt in question was a refusal to obey subpoenas and an order of court to produce books and documents of the company before the grand jury to be used in regard to alleged violation of the statutes of the United States by the said Silverthorne and his father. One ground of the refusal was that the order of the court infringed the rights of the parties under the Fourth Amendment of the Constitution of the United States.

The facts are simple. An indictment upon a single specific charge having been brought against the two Silverthornes mentioned, they both were arrested at their homes early in the morning of February 25, 1919, and were detained in custody a number of hours. While they were thus detained representatives of the Department of Justice and the United States marshal without a shadow of authority went to the office of their company and made a clean sweep of all the books, papers and documents found there. All the employees were taken or directed to go to the office of the District Attorney of the United States to which also the books, &c., were taken at once. An application was made as soon as might be to the District Court for a return of what had thus been taken unlawfully. It was opposed by the District Attorney so far as he had found evidence against the plaintiffs in error, and it was stated that the evidence so obtained was before the grand jury. Color had been given by the District Attorney to the approach of those concerned in the act by an invalid subpoena for certain documents relating to the charge in the indictment then on file. Thus the case is not that of knowledge acquired through the wrongful act of a stranger, but it must be assumed that the Government planned or at all events ratified the whole performance. Photographs and copies of material papers were made and a new indictment was framed based upon the knowledge thus obtained. The District Court ordered a return of the originals but impounded the photographs and copies. Subpoenas to produce the originals then were served and on the refusal of the plaintiffs in error to produce them the court made an order that the subpoenas should be complied with, although it had been found that all the papers had been seized in violation of the parties' constitutional rights. The refusal to obey this order is the contempt alleged. The Government now, while in form repudiating and condemning the illegal seizure, seeks to maintain its right to avail itself of the knowledge obtained by that means which otherwise it would not have had.

The proposition could not be presented more nakedly. It is that although of course its seizure was an outrage which the Government now regrets, it may study the papers before it returns them, copy them, and then may use the knowledge that it has gained to call upon the owners in a more regular form to produce them; that the protection of the Constitution covers the physical possession but not any advantages which the Government can gain over the object of its pursuit by doing the forbidden act. *Weeks* v. *United States*, 232 U. S. 383, to be sure had established that laying the papers directly before the grand jury was unwarranted, but it is taken to mean only that two steps are required instead of one. In our opinion such is not the law. It reduces the Fourth Amendment to a form of words. 232 U. S. 393. The essence of a provision forbidding the acquisition of evidence in a certain way is that not merely evidence so acquired shall not be used before the court but that it shall not be used at all. Of course this does not mean that the facts thus obtained become sacred and inaccessible. If knowledge of them is gained from an independent source they may be proved like any others, but the knowledge gained by the Government's own wrong cannot be used by it in the way proposed. The numerous decisions, like *Adams* v. *New York,* 192 U. S. 585, holding that a collateral inquiry into the mode in which evidence has been got will not be allowed when the question is raised for the first time at the trial, are no authority in the present proceeding, as is explained in *Weeks* v. *United States,* 232 U. S. 383, 394, 395. Whether some of those decisions have gone too far or have given wrong reasons it is unnecessary to inquire; the principle applicable to the present case seems to us plain. It is stated satisfactorily in *Flagg* v. *United States,* 233 Fed. Rep. 481, 483. In *Linn* v. *United States,* 251 Fed. Rep. 476, 480, it was thought that a different rule applied to a corporation, on the ground that it was not privileged from producing its books and papers. But the rights of a corporation against unlawful search and seizure are to be protected even if the same result might have been achieved in a lawful way.

Judgment reversed.

[Chief Justice White and Justice Pitney dissented without opinion.]

Silverthorne Lumber Co., Inc., et al. v. *United States*
251 U. S. 385

Mob Domination of a Court

(*Moore* v. *Dempsey*, 1923)

This is an appeal from an order of the District Court for the Eastern District of Arkansas dismissing a writ of *habeas corpus* upon demurrer, the presiding judge certifying that there was probable cause for allowing the appeal. There were two cases originally, but by agreement they were consolidated into one. The appellants are five Negroes who were convicted of murder in the first degree and sentenced to death by the court of the State of Arkansas. The ground of the petition for the writ is that the proceedings in the State court, although a trial in form, were only a form, and that the appellants were hurried to conviction under the pressure of a mob without any regard for their rights and without according to them due process of law.

The case stated by the petition is as follows, and it will be understood that while we put it in narrative form, we are not affirming the facts to be as stated but only what we must take them to be, as they are admitted by the demurrer: On the night of September 30, 1919, a number of colored people assembled in their church were attacked and fired upon by a body of white men, and in the disturbance that followed a white man was killed. The report of the killing caused great excitement and was followed by the hunting down and shooting of many Negroes and also by the killing on October 1 of one Clinton Lee, a white man, for whose murder the petitioners were indicted. They seem to have been arrested with many others on the same day. The petitioners say

ON CONSTITUTIONAL GUARANTIES

that Lee must have been killed by other whites, but that we leave on one side as what we have to deal with is not the petitioners' innocence or guilt but solely the question whether their constitutional rights have been preserved. They say that their meeting was to employ counsel for protection against extortions practiced upon them by the landowners and that the landowners tried to prevent their effort, but that again we pass by as not directly bearing upon the trial. It should be mentioned however that O. S. Bratton, a son of the counsel who is said to have been contemplated and who took part in the argument here, arriving for consultation on October 1, is said to have barely escaped being mobbed; that he was arrested and confined during the month on a charge of murder and on October 31 was indicted for barratry, but later in the day was told that he would be discharged but that he must leave secretly by a closed automobile to take the train at West Helena, four miles away, to avoid being mobbed. It is alleged that the judge of the court in which the petitioners were tried facilitated the departure and went with Bratton to see him safely off.

A Committee of Seven was appointed by the Governor in regard to what the Committee called the "insurrection" in the county. The newspapers daily published inflammatory articles. On the 7th a statement by one of the Committee was made public to the effect that the present trouble was "a deliberately planned insurrection of the Negroes against the whites, directed by an organization known as the 'Progressive Farmers' and Household Union of America' established for the purpose of banding Negroes together for the killing of white people." According to the statement the organization was started by a swindler to get money from the banks.

Shortly after the arrest of the petitioners a mob marched to the jail for the purpose of lynching them but were prevented by the presence of United States troops and the promise of some of the Committee of Seven and other leading officials that if the mob would refrain, as the petition puts it, they would execute those found guilty in the form of law. The Committee's own statement was that the reason that the people refrained from mob violence was "that this Committee gave our citizens their solemn promise that the law would be carried out." According to affidavits of two white men and the colored witnesses on whose testimony the petitioners were convicted, produced by the petitioners since the last decision of the Supreme Court hereafter mentioned, the Committee made good their promise by calling colored witnesses and having them whipped and tortured until they would say what was wanted, among them being the two relied on to prove the petitioners' guilt. However this may be, a grand jury of white men was organized on October 27 with one of the Committee of Seven and, it is alleged, with many of a posse organized to fight the blacks, upon it, and on the morning of the 29th the indictment was returned. On November 3 the petitioners were brought into court, informed that a certain lawyer was appointed their counsel and were placed on trial before a white jury—blacks being systematically excluded from both grand and petit juries. The court and neighborhood were thronged with an adverse crowd that threatened the most dangerous consequences to anyone interfering with the desired result. The counsel did not venture to demand delay or a change of venue, to challenge a juryman or to ask for separate trials. He had had no preliminary consultation with the accused, called no witnesses for the defense although they could have been produced, and did not put the defendants on the stand. The trial lasted about three-quarters of an hour and in less than five minutes the jury brought in a verdict of guilty of murder in the first degree. According to the allegations and affidavits there never was a chance for the petitioners to be acquitted; no juryman could have voted for an acquittal and continued to live in Phillips County and if any prisoner by any chance had been acquitted by a jury he could not have escaped the mob.

The averments as to the prejudice by which the trial was environed have some corroboration in appeals to the Governor, about a year later, earnestly urging him not to interfere with the execution of the petitioners. One came from five members of the Committee of Seven, and stated in addition to what has been quoted heretofore that "all our citizens are of the opinion that the law should take its course." Another from a part of the American Legion protests against a contemplated commutation of the sentence of four of the petitioners and repeats that a "solemn promise was given by the leading citizens of the community that if the guilty parties were not lynched, and let the law take its course, that justice would be done and the majesty of the law upheld." A meeting of the Helena Rotary Club attended by members representing, as it said, seventy-five of the leading industrial and commercial enterprises of Helena, passed a resolution approving and supporting the action of the American Legion post. The Lions Club of Helena at a meeting attended by members said to represent sixty of the leading industrial and commercial enterprises of the city passed a resolution to the same effect. In May of the same year, a trial of six other Negroes was coming on and it was represented to the Governor by the white citizens and officials of Phillips County that in all probability those Negroes would be lynched. It is alleged that in order to appease the mob spirit and in a measure secure the safety of the six the Governor fixed the date for the execution of the petitioners at June 10, 1921, but that the execution was stayed by proceedings in court—we presume, the proceedings before the Chancellor to which we shall advert.

In *Frank* v. *Mangum*, 237 U. S. 309, 335, it was recognized, of course, that if in fact a trial is dominated by a mob so that there is an actual interference with the course of justice, there is a departure from due process of law; and that "if the State, supplying no corrective process, carries into execution a judgment of death or imprisonment based upon a verdict thus produced by mob domination, the State deprives the accused of his life or liberty without due process of law." We presume in accordance with that case that the corrective process supplied by the State may be so adequate that interference by *habeas corpus* ought not to be allowed. It certainly is true that mere mistakes of law in the course of a trial are not to be corrected in that way. But if the case is that the whole proceeding is a mask—that counsel, jury and judge were swept to the fatal end by an irresistible wave of public passion, and that the State courts failed to correct the wrong, neither perfection in the machinery for correction nor the possibility that the trial court and counsel saw no other way of avoiding an immediate outbreak of the mob can prevent this Court from securing to the petitioners their constitutional rights.

In this case a motion for a new trial on the ground alleged in this petition was overruled and upon exceptions and appeal to the Supreme Court the judgment was affirmed. The Supreme Court said that the complaint of discrimination against petitioners by the exclusion of colored men from the jury came too late and by way of answer to the objection that no fair trial could be had in the circumstances, stated that it could not say "that this must necessarily have been the case"; that eminent counsel was appointed to defend the petitioners, that the trial was had according to law, the jury correctly charged, and the testimony legally sufficient. On June 8, 1921, two days before the date fixed for their execution, a petition for *habeas corpus* was presented to the Chancellor and he issued the writ and an injunction against the execution of the petitioners; but the Supreme Court of the State held that the Chancellor had no jurisdiction under the State law whatever might be the law of the United States. The present petition perhaps was suggested by the language of the court: "What the result would be of an application to a Federal Court we need not inquire." It was presented to the District Court on September 21. We shall not say more concerning the corrective process afforded to the petitioners, than that it does not seem to us sufficient to allow a judge of the United States to escape the duty of examining the facts for himself when if true as alleged they make the trial absolutely void. We have confined the statement to facts admitted by the demurrer. We will not say that they cannot be met, but it appears to us unavoidable that the District Judge should find whether the facts alleged are true and whether they can be explained so far as to leave the State proceedings undisturbed.

Order reversed. The case to stand for hearing before the District Court.

[Mr. Justice McReynolds dissented, quoting the opinion in the *Frank Case* to show that the petitioners had been afforded due process: "I cannot agree now to put it aside and substitute the views expressed by the minority of the Court in that cause." * Justice Sutherland agreed with him.]

Moore et al. v. Dempsey, Keeper of the Arkansas State Penitentiary
261 U. S. 86

---

* See page 58, *The Dissenting Opinions of Mr. Justice Holmes.*

Barring Negroes from Primaries

(*Nixon* v. *Herndon*, 1927)

THIS is an action against the judges of elections for refusing to permit the plaintiff to vote at a primary election in Texas. It lays the damages at five thousand dollars. The petition alleges that the plaintiff is a Negro, a citizen of the United States and of Texas and a resident of El Paso, and in every way qualified to vote, as set forth in detail, except that the statute to be mentioned interferes with his right; that on July 26, 1924, a primary election was held at El Paso for the nomination of candidates for a senator and representatives in Congress and State and other offices, upon the Democratic ticket; that the plaintiff, being a member of the Democratic party, sought to vote but was denied the right by the defendants; that the denial was based upon a statute of Texas enacted in May, 1923, and designated Article 3093*a*, by the words of which "in no event shall a negro be eligible to participate in a Democratic party primary election held in the State of Texas," &c., and that this statute is contrary to the Fourteenth and Fifteenth Amendments to the Constitution of the United States. The defendants moved to dismiss upon the ground that the subject-matter of the suit was political and not within the jurisdiction of the court and that no violation of the Amendments was shown. The suit was dismissed and a writ of error was taken directly to this Court. Here no argument was made on behalf of the defendants but a brief was allowed to be filed by the Attorney General of the State.

The objection that the subject-matter of the suit is political is little more than a play upon words. Of course the petition concerns political action but it alleges and seeks to recover for private damage. That private damage may be caused by such political action and may be recovered for in a suit at law hardly has been doubted for over two hundred years, since *Ashby* v. *White*, 2 Ld. Raym. 938, 3 *id*. 320, and has been recognized by this Court. . . . (See also Judicial Code, § 24 (11), (12), (14). Act of March 3, 1911, c. 231; 36 Stat. 1087, 1092.) If the defendants' conduct was a wrong to the plaintiff the same reasons that allow a recovery for denying the plaintiff a vote at a final election allow it for denying a vote at the primary election that may determine the final result.

The important question is whether the statute can be sustained. But although we state it as a question the answer does not seem to us open to a doubt. We find it unnecessary to consider the Fifteenth Amendment, because it seems to us hard to imagine a more direct and obvious infringement of the Fourteenth. That Amendment, while it applies to all, was passed, as we know, with a special intent to protect the blacks from discrimination against them. . . . That Amendment "not only gave citizenship and the privileges of citizenship to persons of color, but it denied to any State the power to withhold from them the equal protection of the laws. . . . What is this but declaring that the law in the States shall be the same for the black as for the white; that all persons whether colored or white, shall stand equal before the laws of the States, and, in regard to the colored race, for whose protection the Amendment was primarily designed, that no discrimination shall be made against them by law because of their color?" Quoted from [*Strauder* v. *West Virginia*, 100 U. S. 303] in *Buchanan* v. *Warley*, 245 U. S. 60, 77. See *Yick Wo* v. *Hopkins*, 118 U. S. 356, 374. The statute of Texas in the teeth of the prohibitions referred to assumes to forbid Negroes to take part in a primary election the importance of which we have indicated, discriminating against them by the distinction of color alone. States may do a good deal of classifying that it is difficult to believe rational, but there are limits, and it is too clear for extended argument that color cannot be made the basis of a statutory classification affecting the right set up in this case.

Judgment reversed.

Nixon v. *Herndon et al.*
273 U. S. 536

A Self-Incriminating Tax Return

(*United States* v. *Sullivan,* 1927)

THE defendant in error was convicted of wilfully refusing to make a return of his net income as required by the Revenue Act of 1921; November 23, 1921, c. 136, §§ 223 (a), 253; 42 Stat. 227, 250, 268. The judgment was reversed by the Circuit Court of Appeals. 15 F. (2d) 809. A writ of certiorari was granted by this Court.

We may take it that the defendant had sufficient gross income to require a return under the statute unless he was exonerated by the fact that the whole or a large part of it was derived from business in violation of the National Prohibition Act. The Circuit Court of Appeals held that gains from illicit traffic in liquor were subject to the income tax, but that the Fifth Amendment to the Constitution protected the defendant from the requirement of a return.

The Court below was right in holding that the defendant's gains were subject to the tax. By § 213(a) gross income includes "gains, profits, and income derived from . . . the transaction of any business carried on for gain or profit, or gains or profits and income derived from any source whatever." These words are also those of the earlier Act of October 3, 1913, c. 16, § II, B; 38 Stat. 114, 167, except that the word "lawful" is omitted before "business" in the passage just quoted. By § 600 (42 Stat. 285), and by another Act approved on the same day Congress applied other tax laws to this forbidden traffic. Act of November

23, 1921, c. 134, § 5; 42 Stat. 222, 223. . . . We see no reason to doubt the interpretation of the Act, or any reason why the fact that a business is unlawful should exempt it from paying the taxes that if lawful it would have to pay.

As the defendant's income was taxed, the statute of course required a return. See *United States* v. *Sischo*, 262 U. S. 165. In the decision that this was contrary to the Constitution we are of opinion that the protection of the Fifth Amendment was pressed too far. If the form of return provided called for answers that the defendant was privileged from making he could have raised the objection in the return, but could not on that account refuse to make any return at all. We are not called on to decide what, if anything, he might have withheld. Most of the items warranted no complaint. It would be an extreme if not an extravagant application of the Fifth Amendment to say that it authorized a man to refuse to state the amount of his income because it had been made in crime. But if the defendant desired to test that or any other point he should have tested it in the return so that it could be passed upon. He could not draw a conjurer's circle around the whole matter by his own declaration that to write any word upon the government blank would bring him into danger of the law. . . . In this case the defendant did not even make a declaration, he simply abstained from making a return. See further the decision of the Privy Council, *Minister of Finance* v. *Smith*, [1927] A. C. 193.

It is urged that if a return were made the defendant would be entitled to deduct illegal expenses such as bribery. This by no means follows, but it will be time enough to consider the question when a taxpayer has the temerity to raise it.

Judgment reversed.

United States v. *Sullivan*
274 U. S. 259

VI. On Torts and Criminal Law

Libel by Photograph

(*Peck* v. *Tribune Co.*, 1909)

This is an action on the case for a libel. The libel alleged is found in an advertisement printed in the defendant's newspaper *The Chicago Sunday Tribune,* and so far as is material is as follows: "Nurse and Patients Praise Duffy's—Mrs. A. Schuman, One of Chicago's Most Capable and Experienced Nurses, Pays an Eloquent Tribute to the Great Invigorating Life-Giving and Curative Properties of Duffy's Pure Malt Whiskey. . . ." Then followed a portrait of the plaintiff, with the words "Mrs. A. Schuman" under it. Then, in quotation marks, "After years of constant use of your Pure Malt Whiskey, both by myself and as given to patients in my capacity as nurse, I have no hesitation in recommending it as the very best tonic and stimulant for all weak and run-down conditions," &c., &c., with the words "Mrs. A. Schuman, 1576 Mozart St., Chicago, Ill.," at the end, not in quotation marks, but conveying the notion of a signature, or at least that the words were hers. The declaration alleged that the plaintiff was not Mrs. Schuman, was not a nurse, and was a total abstainer from whiskey and all spirituous liquors. There was also a count for publishing the plaintiff's likeness without leave. The defendant pleaded not guilty. At the trial, subject to exceptions, the judge excluded the plaintiff's testimony in support of her allegations just stated, and directed a verdict for the defendant. His action was sustained by the Circuit Court of Appeals. . . .

Of course the insertion of the plaintiff's picture in the place and with the concomitants that we have described imported that she was the nurse and made the statements set forth, as rightly was decided in *Wandt* v. *Hearst's Chicago American,* 129 Wisconsin, 419, 421. *Morrison* v. *Smith,* 177 N. Y. 366. Therefore the publication was of and concerning the plaintiff, notwithstanding the presence of another fact, the name of the real signer of the certificate, if that was Mrs. Schuman, that was inconsistent, when all the facts were known, with the plaintiff's having signed or adopted it. Many might recognize the plaintiff's face without knowing her name, and those who did know it might be led to infer that she had sanctioned the publication under an alias. There was some suggestion that the defendant published the portrait by mistake, and without knowledge that it was the plaintiff's portrait or was not what it purported to be. But the fact, if it was one, was no excuse. If the publication was libellous the defendant took the risk. As was said of such matters by Lord Mansfield, "Whenever a man publishes, he publishes at his peril." *The King* v. *Woodfall,* Lofft, 776, 781. See further *Hearne* v. *Stowell,* 12 A. & E. 719, 726; *Shepheard* v. *Whitaker,* L. R. 10 C. P. 502; *Clark* v. *North American Co.,* 203 Pa. St. 346, 351, 352. The reason is plain. A libel is harmful on its face. If a man sees fit to publish manifestly hurtful statements concerning an individual, without other justification than exists for an advertisement or a piece of news, the usual principles of tort will make him liable, if the statements are false or are true only of some one else. See *Morasse* v. *Brochu,* 151 Massachusetts, 567, 575.

The question, then, is whether the publication was a libel. It was held by the Circuit Court of Appeals not to be, or at most to entitle the plaintiff only to nominal damages, no special damage being alleged. It was pointed out that there was no general consensus of opinion that to drink whiskey is wrong or that to be a nurse is discreditable. It might have been added that very possibly giving a certificate and the use of one's portrait in aid of an advertisement would be regarded with irony, or a stronger feeling, only by a few. But it appears to us that such inquiries are beside the point. It may be that the action for libel is of little use, but while it is maintained it should be governed by the general principles of tort. If the advertisement obviously would hurt the plaintiff in the estimation of an important and respectable part of the community, liability is not a question of a majority vote.

We know of no decision in which this matter is discussed upon principle. But obviously an unprivileged falsehood need not entail universal hatred to constitute a cause of action. No falsehood is thought about or even known by all the world. No conduct is hated by all. That it will be known by a large number and will lead an appreciable fraction of that number to regard the plaintiff with contempt is enough to do her practical harm. Thus if a doctor were represented as advertising, the fact that it would affect his standing with others of his profession might make the representation actionable, although advertising is not reputed dishonest and even seems to be regarded by many with pride. See *Martin* v. *The Picayune,* 115 Louisiana, 979. It seems to us impossible to say that the obvious tendency of what is imputed to the plaintiff by this advertisement is not seriously to hurt her standing with a considerable and respectable class in the community. Therefore it was the plaintiff's right to prove her case and go to the jury, and the defendant would have got all that it could ask if it had been permitted to persuade them, if it could, to take a contrary view. . . .

It is unnecessary to consider the question whether the publication of the plaintiff's likeness was a tort *per se*. It is enough for the present case that the law should at least be prompt to recognize the injuries that may arise from an unauthorized use in connection with other facts, even if more subtlety is needed to state the wrong than is needed here. In this instance we feel no doubt.

Judgment reversed.

Peck, Petitioner, v. *Tribune Co.*
214 U. S. 185

Presumption of Good Character

(*Greer* v. *United States,* 1918)

THE petitioner was tried for introducing whiskey from without the State into that part of Oklahoma that formerly was within the Indian Territory. He was convicted and sentenced to fine and imprisonment. Material error at the trial is alleged because the court refused to instruct the jury that the defendant was presumed to be a person of good character, and that the supposed presumption should be considered as evidence in favor of the accused, with some further amplifications not necessary to be repeated. The court did instruct the jury that the defendant was presumed to be innocent of the charge until his guilt was established beyond a reasonable doubt, and that the presumption followed him throughout the trial until so overcome. The Circuit Court of Appeals sustained the court below. . . . This judgment was in accordance with a carefully reasoned earlier decision in the same circuit, *Price* v. *United States,* 218 Fed. Rep. 149; 132 C. C. A. 1, with an acute statement in *United States* v. *Smith,* 217 Fed. Rep. 839, and with numerous State cases and text books. But as other Circuit Courts of Appeals had taken a different view, *Mullen* v. *United States,* 106 Fed. Rep. 892; 46 C. C. A. 22; *Garst* v. *United States,* 180 Fed. Rep. 339, 344, 345; 103 C. C. A. 469, also taken by other cases and text books, it becomes necessary for this Court to settle the doubt.

Obviously the character of the defendant was a matter of fact, which if investigated, might turn out either way. It is not established as matter of law that all persons indicted are men of good character. If it were a fact regarded as necessarily material to the main issues it would be itself issuable, and the Government would be entitled to put in evidence whether the prisoner did so or not. As the Government cannot put in evidence except to answer evidence introduced by the defense the natural inference is that the prisoner is allowed to try to prove a good character for what it may be worth, but that the choice whether to raise that issue rests with him. The rule that if he prefers not to go into the matter the Government cannot argue from it would be meaningless if there were a presumption in his favor that could not be attacked. For the failure to put on witnesses, instead of suggesting unfavorable comment, would only show the astuteness of the prisoner's counsel. The meaning must be that character is not an issue in the case unless the prisoner chooses to make it one; otherwise he would be foolish to open the door to contradiction by going into evidence when without it good character would be incontrovertibly presumed. . . .

Our reasoning is confirmed by the fact that the right to introduce evidence of good character seems formerly to have been regarded as a favor to prisoners, McNally, *Evidence*, 320, which sufficiently implies that good character was not presumed. In reason it should not be. A presumption upon a matter of fact, when it is not merely a disguise for some other principle, means that common experience shows the fact to be so generally true that courts may notice the truth. Whatever the scope of the presumption that a man is innocent of the specific crime charged, it cannot be said that by common experience the character of most people indicted by a grand jury is good.

It is argued that the court was bound by the rules of evidence as they stood in 1789. That those rules would not be conclusive is sufficiently shown by *Rosen* v. *United States*, 245 U. S. 467. But it is safe to believe that the supposed presumption is of later date, of American origin, and comes from overlooking the distinction between this and the presumption of innocence and from other causes not necessary to detail.

Judgment affirmed.

[Mr. Justice McKenna dissented without opinion.]

Greer v. United States
245 U. S. 559

A Judge Influencing a Jury

(*Horning* v. *District of Columbia*, 1920)

THIS case comes here upon a writ of certiorari granted to review a judgment of the Court of Appeals, that affirmed a conviction of the petitioner doing business as a pawnbroker and charging more than six percent interest, without a license, which is forbidden by the Act of Congress of February 4, 1913, c. 26, 37 Stat. 657. . . .

The external facts are not disputed. The defendant had been in business as a pawnbroker in Washington but anticipating the enactment of the present law removed his headquarters to a place in Virginia at the other end of a bridge leading from the city. He continued to use his former building as a storehouse for his pledges but posted notices on his office there that no applications for loans would be received or examination of pledges made there. He did, however, maintain a free automobile service from there to Virginia and offered to intending borrowers the choice of calling upon him in person or sending their application and security by a dime messenger service not belonging to him but established in his Washington building. If the loan was made, in the latter case the money and pawn ticket were brought back and handed to the borrower in Washington. When a loan was paid off the borrower received a redemption certificate, presented it in Washington, and got back his pledge. The defendant estimated the number of persons applying to the Washington office for loans or redemption at fifty to seventy-five a day. His Washington clerk, a witness in his behalf, put it at from seventy-five to one hundred. We may take it that there was a fairly steady stream of callers, as is implied by the automobile service being maintained. It is said with reference to the charge of the judge to which we shall advert that there was a question for the jury as to the defendant's intent. But we perceive none. There is no question that the defendant intentionally maintained his storehouse and managed his business in the way described. It may be assumed that he intended not to break the law but only to get as near to the line as he could, which he had a right to do, but if the conduct described crossed the line, the fact that he desired to keep within it will not help him. It means only that he misconceived the law.

As to whether the conduct described did contravene the law, it is urged that a pledgee has a right to keep the pledged property where he likes and as he likes provided he returns it in proper condition when redeemed. But that hardly helps the defendant. To keep for return, whatever latitude there may be as to place and mode, is part of the duty of a pledgee, and in the case of one who makes a business of lending on pledges is as much a part of his business as making the loan. As we read the statute its prohibition is not confined to cases where the whole business is done in Washington. If an essential part of it is done there and a Washington office is used as a collecting centre, it does not matter that care is taken to complete every legal transaction on the other side of the Potomac. We cannot suppose that it was intended to allow benefits so similar to those coming from business done wholly in the city to be derived from acts done there and yet go free. We are of opinion that upon the undisputed evidence the defendant was guilty of a breach of the law and turn at once to the question which seemed to warrant allowing the case to be brought to this Court.

The question relates to the charge of the judge. The judge said to the jury that the only question for them to determine was whether they believed the concurrent testimony of the witnesses for the Government and the defendant describing the course of business that we have stated and as to which there was no dispute. Those facts, he correctly instructed them, constituted an engaging in business in the District of Columbia. This was excepted to and the jury retired. The next day they were recalled to court and were told that there really was no issue of fact for them to decide; that they were not warranted in capriciously saying that the witness for the Government and the defendant were not telling the truth; that the course of dealing constituted a breach of the law; that it was their duty to accept this exposition of the law; that in a criminal case the court could not peremptorily instruct them to find the defendant guilty but that if the law permitted he would. The court added that a failure to bring in a verdict could only arise from a flagrant disregard of the evidence, the law, and their obligation as jurors. On an exception being taken the judge repeated that he could not tell them in so many words to find the defendant guilty but that what he said amounted to that; that the facts proved were in accord with the information and that the Court of Appeals had said that that showed a violation of law.

This was not a case of the judge's expressing an opinion upon the evidence, as he would have had a right to do. . . . The facts were not in dispute, and what he did was to say so and to lay down the law applicable to them. In such a case obviously the function of the jury if they do their duty is little more than formal. The judge cannot direct a verdict, it is true, and the jury has the power to bring in a verdict in the teeth of both law and facts. But the judge always has the right and duty to tell them what the law is upon this or that state of facts that may be found, and he can do the same none the less when the facts are agreed. If the facts are agreed the judge may state that fact also, and when there is no dispute he may say so although there has been no formal agreement. Perhaps there was a regrettable peremptoriness of tone—but the jury were allowed the technical right,

if it can be called so, to decide against the law and the facts—
and that is all there was left for them after the defendant and
his witness took the stand. If the defendant suffered any wrong
it was purely formal since, as we have said, on the facts admitted
there was no doubt of his guilt. Act of February 26, 1919, c. 48,
40 Stat. 1181, amending § 269 of the Judicial Code; Act of
March 3, 1911, c. 231, 36 Stat. 1087.

Judgment affirmed.

[Mr. Justice McReynolds dissented without opinion. Mr. Justice
Brandeis, also dissenting, said that the judge had exceeded his power in
directing the verdict: "He does coerce when without convincing the
judgment he overcomes the will by the weight of his authority." Quoting
a paragraph of the charge, Justice Brandeis termed it "a moral command."
He claimed that the judge had usurped the province of the jury. Chief
Justice White and Mr. Justice Day agreed with Justice Brandeis.]

Horning v. *District of Columbia*
254 U. S. 135

The Obligation to Retreat

(*Brown* v. *United States*, 1921)

THE petitioner was convicted of murder in the second degree committed upon one Hermes at a place in Texas within the exclusive jurisdiction of the United States, and the judgment was affirmed by the Circuit Court of Appeals. . . . A writ of certiorari was granted by this Court. . . . Two questions are raised. The first is whether the indictment is sufficient, inasmuch as it does not allege that the place of the homicide was acquired by the United States "for the erection of a fort, magazine, arsenal, dockyard, or other needful building," although it does allege that it was acquired from the State of Texas by the United States for the exclusive use of the United States for its public purposes and was under the exclusive jurisdiction of the same. Penal Code of March 4, 1909, c. 321, § 272, Third, 35 Stat. 1088. Constitution, Art. I, § 8. In view of our opinion upon the second point we think it unnecessary to do more than to refer to the discussion in the court below upon this.

The other question concerns the instructions at the trial. There had been trouble between Hermes and the defendant for a long time. There was evidence that Hermes had twice assaulted the defendant with a knife and had made threats communicated to the defendant that the next time one of them would go off in a black box. On the day in question the defendant was at the time above-mentioned superintending excavation work for a postoffice. In view of Hermes' threats he had taken a pistol with him and had laid it in his coat upon a dump. Hermes was driven up by a witness, in a cart to be loaded, and the defendant said that certain earth was not to be removed, whereupon Hermes came toward him, the defendant says, with a knife. The defendant retreated some twenty or twenty-five feet to where his coat was and got his pistol. Hermes was striking at him and the defendant fired four shots and killed him. The judge instructed the jury among other things that "it is necessary to remember, in considering the question of self-defense, that the party assaulted is always under the obligation to retreat, so long as retreat is open to him, provided he can do so without subjecting himself to the danger of death or great bodily harm." The instruction was reinforced by the further intimation that unless "retreat would have appeared to a man of reasonable prudence, in the position of the defendant, as involving the danger of death or serious bodily harm" the defendant was not entitled to stand his ground. An instruction to the effect that if the defendant had reasonable grounds of apprehension that he was in danger of losing his life or of suffering serious bodily harm from Hermes he was not bound to retreat was refused. So the question is brought out with sufficient clearness whether the formula laid down by the court and often repeated by the ancient law is adequate to the protection of the defendant's rights.

It is useless to go into the developments of the law from the time when a man who had killed another no matter how innocently had to get his pardon, whether of grace or of course. Concrete cases or illustrations stated in the early law in conditions very different from the present, like the reference to retreat in Coke, *Third Inst.* 55, and elsewhere, have had a tendency to ossify into specific rules without much regard for reason. Other examples may be found in the law as to trespass *ab initio, Commonwealth* v. *Rubin,* 165 Massachusetts, 453, and as to fresh complaint after rape. . . . Rationally the failure to retreat is a circumstance to be considered with all the others in order to determine whether the defendant went farther than he was justified in doing; not a categorical proof of guilt. The law has grown, and even if historical mistakes have contributed to its growth it has tended in the direction of rules consistent with human nature. Many respectable writers agree that if a man reasonably believes that he is in immediate danger or grievous bodily harm from his assailant he may stand his ground and that if he kills him he has not exceeded the bounds of lawful self-defense. That has been the decision of this Court. *Beard* v. *United States,* 158 U. S. 550, 559. Detached reflection cannot be demanded in the presence of an uplifted knife. Therefore in this Court, at least, it is not a condition of immunity that one in that situation should pause to consider whether a reasonable man might not think it possible to fly with safety or to disable his assailant rather than kill him. *Rowe* v. *United States,* 164 U. S. 546, 558. The law of Texas very strongly adopts these views as is shown by many cases, of which it is enough to cite two. . . .

It is true that in the case of Beard he was upon his own land (not in his house), and in that of Rowe he was in the room of a hotel, but those facts, although mentioned by the Court, would not have bettered the defense by the old common law and were not appreciably more favorable than that the defendant here was at a place where he was called to be, in the discharge of his duty. There was evidence that the last shot was fired after Hermes was down. The jury might not believe the defendant's testimony that it was an accidental discharge, but the suggestion of the Government that this Court may disregard the considerable body of evidence that the shooting was in self-defense is based upon a misunderstanding of what was meant by some language in *Battle* v. *United States,* 209 U. S. 36, 38. Moreover if the last shot was intentional and may seem to have been unnecessary when considered in cold blood, the defendant would not necessarily lose his immunity if it followed close upon the others while the heat of the conflict was on, and if the defendant believed that he was fighting for his life.

The Government presents a different case. It denies that Hermes had a knife and even that Brown was acting in self-defense. Notwithstanding the reputed threats of Hermes and intimations that one of the two would die at the next encounter, which seem hardly to be denied, of course it was possible for the jury to find that Brown had not sufficient reason to think that his life was in danger at that time, that he exceeded the limits of reasonable self-defense or even that he was the attacking party. But upon the hypothesis to which the evidence gave much color, that Hermes began the attack, the instruction that we have stated was wrong.

Judgment reversed.

[Justices Pitney and Clarke dissented without opinion.]

Brown v. *United States*
256 U. S. 335

Children as Trespassers

(*United Zinc Co.* v. *Britt*, 1922)

THIS is a suit brought by the respondents against the petitioner to recover for the death of two children, sons of the respondents. The facts that for the purposes of decision we shall assume to have been proved are these: The petitioner owned a tract of about twenty acres in the outskirts of the town of Iola, Kansas. Formerly it had there a plant for the making of sulphuric acid and zinc spelter. In 1910 it tore the buildings down but left a basement and cellar in which in July, 1916, water was accumulated, clear in appearance but in fact dangerously poisoned by sulphuric acid and zinc sulphate that had come in one way or another from the petitioner's works, as the petitioner knew. The respondents had been travelling and had encamped at some distance from this place. A travelled way passed within 120 or 100 feet of it. On July 27, 1916, the children, who were eight and eleven years old, came upon the petitioner's land, went into the water, were poisoned and died. The petitioner saved the question whether it could be held liable. At the trial the judge instructed the jury that if the water looked clear but in fact was poisonous and thus the children were allured to it the petitioner was liable. The respondents got a verdict and judgment, which was affirmed by the Circuit Court of Appeals. . . .

Union Pacific Ry. v. *McDonald*, 152 U. S. 262, and kindred cases were relied upon as leading to the result, and perhaps there is language in that and in *Railroad Co.* v. *Stout*, 17 Wall.

657, that might seem to justify it; but the doctrine needs very careful statement not to make an unjust and impracticable requirement. If the children had been adults they would have had no case. They would have been trespassers and the owner of the land would have owed no duty to remove even hidden danger; it would have been entitled to assume that they would obey the law and not trespass. The liability for spring guns and mantraps arises from the fact that the defendant has not rested on that assumption, but on the contrary has expected the trespasser and prepared an injury that is no more justified than if he had held the gun and fired it. ... Infants have no greater right to go upon other peoples' land than adults, and the mere fact that they are infants imposes no duty upon the landowners to expect them and to prepare for their safety. On the other hand the duty of one who invites another upon his land not to lead him into a trap is well settled, and while it is very plain that temptation is not invitation, it may be held that knowingly to establish and expose, unfenced, to children of an age when they follow a bait as mechanically as a fish, something that is certain to attract them, has the legal effect of an invitation to them although not to an adult. But the principle if accepted must be very cautiously applied.

In *Railroad Co.* v. *Stout*, 17 Wall. 657, the well-known case of a boy injured on a turntable, it appeared that children had played there before to the knowledge of employees of the railroad, and in view of that fact and the situation of the turntable near a road without visible separation, it seems to have been assumed without much discussion that the railroad owed a duty to the boy. Perhaps this was as strong a case as would be likely to occur of maintaining a known temptation, where temptation takes the place of invitation. A license was implied and liability for a danger not manifest to a child was declared in the very similar case of *Cooke* v. *Midland Great Western Ry. of Ireland* [1909], A. C. 229.

In the case at bar it is at least doubtful whether the water could be seen from any place where the children lawfully were and there is no evidence that it was what led them to enter the land. But that is necessary to start the supposed duty. There can be no general duty on the part of a landowner to keep his land safe for children, or even free from hidden dangers, if he has not directly or by implication invited or licensed them to come there. The difficulties in the way of implying a license are adverted to in *Chenery* v. *Fitchburg R. R. Co.*, 160 Mass. 211, 212, but need not be considered here. It does not appear that children were in the habit of going to the place; so that foundation also fails.

Union Pacific Ry. Co. v. *McDonald*, 152 U. S. 262, is less in point. There a boy was burned by falling into burning coal slack close by the side of a path on which he was running homeward from other boys who had frightened him. It hardly appears that he was a trespasser and the path suggests an invitation; at all events boys habitually resorted to the place where he was. Also the defendant was under a statutory duty to fence the place sufficiently to keep out cattle. The decision is very far from establishing that the petitioner is liable for poisoned water not bordering a road, not shown to have been the inducement that led the children to trespass, if in any event the law would deem it sufficient to excuse their going there, and not shown to have been the indirect inducement because known to the children to be frequented by others. It is suggested that the roads across the place were invitations. A road is not an invitation to leave it elsewhere than at its end.

Judgment reversed.

[Mr. Justice Clarke opposed the substitution of the "Hard" or "Draconian Doctrine" applied in the Massachusetts courts to "attractive nuisance" cases for the "Humane Doctrine" of the United States Supreme Court, which made allowance for the instincts and impulses of childhood. He approved the charge of the trial court, giving to the jury the question whether the defendant knew or in the exercise of ordinary care should have known that the water was poisoned and that children were likely to go to its vicinity and be attracted by it. The doctrine of the earlier cases, he contended, "is a sound doctrine, calculated to make men more reasonably considerable of the safety of the children of their neighbors, than will the harsh rule which makes trespassers of little children which the Court is now substituting for it." Chief Justice Taft and Mr. Justice Day concurred in his dissent.]

United Zinc & Chemical Co. v. *Britt, et al.*
258 U. S. 268

Without Consent of Convict

(Biddle v. Perovich, 1927)

THE Circuit Court of Appeals for the eighth circuit has certified questions of law to this Court upon facts of which we give an abridged statement. Perovich was convicted in Alaska of murder; the verdict being that he was "guilty of murder in the first degree and that he suffer death." On September 15, 1905, he was sentenced to be hanged; and the judgment was affirmed by this Court. . . . Respites were granted from time to time, and on June 5, 1909, President Taft executed a document by which he purported to "commute the sentence of the said Vuco Perovich . . . to imprisonment for life in a penitentiary to be designated by the Attorney General of the United States." Thereupon Perovich was transferred from jail in Alaska to a penitentiary in Washington, and, some years later, to one in Leavenworth, Kansas. In November, 1918, Perovich, reciting that his sentence had been commuted to life imprisonment, applied for a pardon—and did the same thing again on December 10, 1921. On February 20, 1925, he filed in the District Court for the District of Kansas an application for a writ of *habeas corpus*, on the ground that his removal from jail to a penitentiary, and the order of the President, were without his consent and without legal authority. The District Judge adopted this view and thereupon ordered the prisoner to be set at large. We pass over the difficulties in the way of this conclusion and confine ourselves to the questions proposed. The first is: "Did the President have authority to commute the sentence of Perovich from death to life imprisonment?"

Both sides agree that the act of the President was properly styled a commutation of sentence, but the counsel of Perovich urge that when the attempt is to commute a punishment to one of a different sort it cannot be done without the convict's consent. The Solicitor General presented a very persuasive argument that in no case is such consent necessary to an unconditional pardon and that it never had been adjudged necessary before *Burdick* v. *United States*, 236 U. S. 79. He argued that the earlier cases here and in England turned on the necessity that the pardon should be pleaded, but that when it was brought to the judicial knowledge of the Court "and yet the felon pleads not guilty and waives the pardon, he shall not be hanged." Jenkins, 129, Third Century, case 62.

We will not go into history, but we will say a word about the principles of pardons in the law of the United States. A pardon in our days is not a private act of grace from an individual happening to possess power. It is a part of the Constitutional scheme. When granted it is the determination of the ultimate authority that the public welfare will be better served by inflicting less than what the judgment fixed. See *Ex parte Grossman*, 267 U. S. 87, 120, 121. Just as the original punishment would be imposed without regard to the prisoner's consent and in the teeth of his will, whether he liked it or not, the public welfare, not his consent, determines what shall be done. So far as a pardon legitimately cuts down a penalty, it affects the judgment imposing it. No one doubts that a reduction of the term of an imprisonment or the amount of a fine would limit the sentence effectively on the one side and on the other would leave the reduced term or fine valid and to be enforced, and that the convict's consent is not required.

When we come to the commutation of death to imprisonment for life it is hard to see how consent has any more to do with it than it has in the cases first put. Supposing that Perovich did not accept the change, he could not have got himself hanged against the Executive order. Supposing that he did accept, he could not affect the judgment to be carried out. The considerations that led to the modification had nothing to do with his will. The only question is whether the substituted judgment was authorized by law—here, whether the change is within the scope of the words of the Constitution, Article II, §2: "The President ... shall have Power to grant Reprieves and Pardons for Offences against the United States, except in Cases of Impeachment." We cannot doubt that the power extends to this case. By common understanding imprisonment for life is a less penalty than death. It is treated so in the statute under which Perovich was tried, which provides that "the jury may qualify their verdict [guilty of murder] by adding thereto 'without capital punishment'; and whenever the jury shall return a verdict qualified as aforesaid the person convicted shall be sentenced to imprisonment at hard labor for life." Criminal Code of Alaska, Act of March 3, 1899, c. 429, § 4; 30 Stat. 1253. See *Ex parte Grossman*, 267 U. S. 87, 109. The opposite answer would permit the President to decide that justice requires the diminution of a term or a fine without consulting the convict, but would deprive him of the power in the most important cases and require him to permit an execution which he had decided ought not to take place unless the change is agreed to by one who on no sound principle ought to have any voice in what the law should do for the welfare of the whole. We are of opinion that the reasoning of *Burdick* v. *United States*, 236 U. S. 79, is not to be extended to the present case. The other questions certified become immaterial as we answer the first question: *Yes.*

Biddle, Warden, v. *Perovich*
274 U. S. 480

Trafficking in Narcotics

(*Casey* v. *United States*, 1928)

THE petitioner, Casey, was convicted upon two counts of an indictment, the first of which charged him with the purchase of three and four-tenths grains of morphine not in or from the original stamped package, at Seattle, within the jurisdiction of the court. The conviction was sustained by the Circuit Court of Appeals. . . . A writ of certiorari was granted by this Court.

Here the second count was admitted by the Government to be bad, so that the only matter to be considered is whether the conviction can be sustained upon the first. It is argued that the evidence is not enough.—Casey had practiced law in Seattle for many years, had been in the habit of visiting King County jail and had defended prisoners addicted to the use of narcotics. There was evidence tending to show that on different occasions he had promised to furnish them with opiates and that in pursuance of such promises and for pay received by him he had given or sent to them preparations of morphine, concealed, it was said, by soaking towels or the like in a solution of the drug. If this evidence was believed it showed that Casey was in possession or control of what he had sent and it safely may be inferred that he did not proclaim his illegal purpose by putting stamps upon the towels. But the charge is a purchase, not a sale. There was no testimony directly concerning the purchase and the Government relies in part at least upon the presumption of a violation of § 1 of the Act of December 17, 1914, c. 1, as amended by the Act of February 24, 1919, c. 18,

§ 1006; 40 Stat. 1057, 1130, 1131, that that section purports to create. U. S. C. Title 26, § 692.

The amended section makes the purchase, sale, &c., of opium and derivatives unlawful except in or from the original stamped package, and the absence of the required stamps from any of the said drugs "shall be *prima facie* evidence of a violation of this section by the person in whose possession same may be found." For the petitioner it was argued that the presumption thus created does not and, consistently with the Sixth Amendment to the Constitution, cannot extend so far as to show a purchase within the district and thus to bring the case within the jurisdiction of the trial court. The Circuit Court of Appeals answered that the objection to the venue was not raised specifically below. The court was asked to direct a verdict for the defendant on the ground that the evidence was not sufficient and elsewhere it has been held that such a request is enough to save the question, and that a presumption extended to the place of purchase could not be upheld. . . . But we are of opinion that upon the facts of this case the court was right. If the jury believed that the defendant, long established in Seattle, said that he had not the drug but would, and shortly thereafter did, furnish it, the inference that he bought it in Seattle is strong, and it is reasonable to suppose that if attention had been called to the point the inference could have been made stronger still. But the effort of the defense did not stop at this detail but was to show that Casey had nothing to do with the business and was wholly innocent of the offense charged.

With regard to the presumption of the purchase of a thing manifestly not produced by the possessor, there is a "rational connection between the fact proved and the ultimate fact presumed." *Luria* v. *United States*, 231 U. S. 9, 35; *Yee Hen* v. *United States*, 268 U. S. 178, 183. Furthermore there are presumptions that are not evidence in a proper sense but simply regulations of the burden of proof. . . . The statute here talks of *prima facie* evidence but it means only that the burden shall be upon the party found in possession to explain and justify it when accused of the crime that the statute creates. 4 Wigmore, *Evidence*, § 2494. It is consistent with all the constitutional protections of accused men to throw on them the burden of proving facts peculiarly within their knowledge and hidden from discovery by the Government. 4 Wigmore, *Evidence*, § 2486. In dealing with a poison not commonly used except upon a doctor's prescription easily proved, or for a debauch only possible by a breach of law, it seems reasonable to call on a person possessing it in a form that warrants suspicion to show that he obtained it in a mode permitted by the law.—The petitioner cannot complain of the statute except as it affects him.

We do not feel at liberty to accept the suggestion that the Government induced the crime. A court rarely can act with advantage of its own motion, and very rarely can be justified in giving judgment upon grounds that the record was not intended to present. Upon this record, it was testified and might easily have been found for the Government that after Casey's visits addicts were noticed by the jailers to be under the influence of narcotics and that on a previous occasion Casey for money had got morphine at the request of Cicero, the supposed stool pigeon. It does not appear expressly that this last was told to the jailer before the supposed plot to entrap Casey, but in view of the relation between the parties it was very likely—and had the matter been in issue very probably would have been proved. We do not think that we are entitled to assume the contrary. If known to the jailers there was very probable cause to believe Casey an habitual practitioner. His own language when he was on guard, admitting that he frequently had promised the drug to prisoners, the testimony as to what was said in his presence (to the effect that he was the man who supplied the boys with narcotics when they wanted it) and his language importing habit, (as, that he hadn't a thing with him today) all tend to the same conclusion. We hardly can assume that the jailers did not know the facts in order to convict them of a gross wrong, when we keep in mind that the case was tried and the record made up without this in mind. Furthermore Casey according to the story was in no way induced to commit the crime beyond the simple request of Cicero to which he seems to have acceded without hesitation and as a matter of course. According to the evidence he seems to have promised morphine to Nelson, who does not appear to have been in the supposed plot. We are not persuaded that the conduct of the officials was different from or worse than ordering a drink of a suspected bootlegger. Whatever doubts we may feel as to the truth of the testimony we are not at liberty to consider them on the only question before the Court. The grounds for uneasiness can be considered only by another power.

The statute is much more obviously a revenue measure now than when *United States* v. *Doremus*, 249 U. S. 86, was decided, and is said to produce a considerable return. . . . It is too late to attempt to overthrow the whole Act on *Child Labor Tax Case*, 259 U. S. 20. It is said also that no opium is produced in the United States, and at all events the statute has been so modified that now at least *United States* v. *Jim Fuey Moy*, 241 U. S. 394, does not apply to this case. . . . We pass as not needing discussion some minor points.

Judgment upon the first count affirmed.

[Mr. Justice McReynolds dissented on the ground that "the suggested rational connection between the fact proved" (possession of unstamped package) "and the ultimate fact presumed" (unlawful purchase) "is imaginary." Mr. Justice Butler also thought the connection "too remote" and found no evidence to support the conviction. Mr. Justice Brandeis felt that "the prosecution must fail because officers of the Government instigated the commission of the alleged crime." * Mr. Justice Sanford also dissented.]

Casey v. *United States*
276 U. S. 413

---

* See p. 269, *The Social and Economic Views of Mr. Justice Brandeis*.

VII. ON REGULATION OF PUBLIC UTILITIES

Rate-Making a Legislative Function

(*Prentis* v. *Atlantic Coast Line,* 1908)

THESE are bills in equity brought in the Circuit Court to enjoin the members and clerk of the Virginia State Corporation Commission from publishing or taking any other steps to enforce a certain order fixing passenger rates. The bills allege, with some elaboration of the facts, that the rates in question are confiscatory, and other matters not necessary to mention, and set up the Fourteenth Amendment, etc. The defendants appeared specially, and by demurrer and plea respectively put forward that the proceedings before the Commission are proceedings in a court of the State, which the courts of the United States are forbidden to enjoin, Rev. Stats. § 720, and that the decision of the Commission makes the legality of the rates *res judicata.* On these pleadings final decrees were entered for the plaintiffs, and the defendants appealed to this Court. Therefore, as the case is presented, it is to be assumed that the order confiscates the plaintiff's property and infringes the Fourteenth Amendment if the matter is open to inquiry. The question principally argued, and the main question to be discussed, is whether the order is one which, in spite of its constitutional invalidity, the courts of the United States are not at liberty to impugn.

The State Corporation Commission is established and its powers are defined at length by the constitution of the State. There is no need to rehearse the provisions that give it dignity and importance or that add judicial to its other functions, because we shall assume that for some purposes it is a court within the meaning of Rev. Stat. § 720, and in the commonly accepted sense of that word. Among its duties it exercises the authority of the State to supervise, regulate and control public service corporations, and to that end, as is said by the Supreme Court of Virginia and repeated by counsel at the bar, it has been clothed with legislative, judicial and executive powers. . . .

The State constitution provides that the Commission, in the performance of the duty just mentioned, shall from time to time prescribe and enforce such rates, charges, classification of traffic, and rules and regulations for transportation and transmission companies doing business in the State, and shall require them to establish and maintain all such public service facilities and conveniences, as may be reasonable and just. Before prescribing or fixing any rate or charge, etc., it is to give notice (in case of a general order not directed against any specific company by name, by four weeks' publication in a newspaper) of the substance of the contemplated action and of a time and place when the Commission will hear objections and evidence against it. If an order is passed, the order again is to be published as above before it shall go into effect. An appeal to the Supreme Court of Appeals is given of right to any party aggrieved, upon conditions not necessary to be stated, and that court, if it reverses what has been done, is to substitute such order as in its opinion the Commission should have made. The Commission is to certify the facts upon which its action was based and such evidence as may be required, but no new evidence is to be received, and how far the findings of the Commission can be revised perhaps is not quite plain. No other court of the State can review, reverse, correct or annul the action of the Commission, and in collateral proceedings the validity of the rates established by it cannot be called in doubt.

When a rate has been fixed, the Commission has power to enforce compliance with its order by adjudging and enforcing, by its own appropriate process, against the offending company the fines and penalties established by law. But a hearing is required, and the validity and reasonableness of the order may be attacked again in this proceeding, and all defenses seem to be open to the party charged with a breach.

On July 31, 1906, under the provisions outlined, the Commission published in a newspaper notice to the several steam railroad companies doing business in Virginia, and all persons interested, that at a certain time and place it would hear objections to an order prescribing the maximum rate of two cents a mile for the transportation of passengers, with details not needing to be stated. A hearing was had, and the complainants (appellees) severally appeared and urged objections similar to those set up in the bills. On April 27, 1907, the Commission passed an order prescribing the rates, but in more specific form. For certain railroads named, including all of the complainants except as we shall state, the rate was to be two cents; for certain excepted branches of the Southern Railway Company, two and a half; for others, including the Chesapeake Western Railway, three; and for others three and a half cents a mile, with a minimum charge of ten cents. Publication of the order was directed, and at that stage these bills were brought.

In order to decide the cases it is not necessary to discuss all the questions that were raised or touched upon in argument, and some we shall lay on one side. We shall assume that when, as here, a State constitution sees fit to unite legislative and judicial powers in a single hand, there is nothing to hinder so far as the Constitution of the United States is concerned. . . . We shall assume, as we have said, that some of the powers of the Commission are judicial, and we shall assume, without deciding, that, if it was proceeding against the appellees to enforce this order and to punish them for a breach, it then would be sitting as a court and would be protected from interference on the part of courts of the United States.

But we think it equally plain that the proceedings drawn in question here are legislative in their nature, and none the less so that they have taken place with a body which at another moment, or in its principal or dominant aspect, is a court such as is meant by § 720. A judicial inquiry investigates, declares and enforces liabilities as they stand on present or past facts and under laws supposed already to exist. That is its purpose and end. Legislation on the other hand looks to the future and changes existing conditions by making a new rule to be applied thereafter to all or some part of those subject to its power. The establishment of a rate is the making of a rule for the future, and therefore is an act legislative not judicial in kind, as seems to be fully recognized by the Supreme Court of Appeals, *Commonwealth* v. *Atlantic Coast Line Railway Co.*, 106 Virginia, 61, 64, and especially by its learned President in his pointed remarks in *Winchester and Strasburg R. R. Co. and others* v. *Commonwealth*, 106 Virginia, 264, 281. See further *Interstate Commerce Commission* v. *Cincinnati, New Orleans & Texas Pacific Ry. Co.*, 167 U. S. 479, 500, 505; *San Diego Land & Town Co.* v. *Jasper*, 189 U. S. 439, 440.

Proceedings legislative in nature are not proceedings in a court within the meaning of Rev. Stats. § 720, no matter what may be the general or dominant character of the body in which they may take place. . . . That question depends not upon the character of the body but upon the character of the proceedings. . . . They are not a suit in which a writ of error would lie under Rev. Stats. § 709, and Act of February 18, 1875, c. 80, 18 Stat. 318. See *Upshur County* v. *Rich*, 135 U. S. 467; *Wallace* v. *Adams*, 204 U. S. 415, 423. The decision upon them cannot be *res judicata* when a suit is brought. See *Reagan* v. *Farmers' Loan & Trust Co.*, 154 U. S. 362. And it does not matter what inquiries may have been made as a preliminary to the legislative act. Most legislation is preceded by hearings and investigations. But the effect of the inquiry, and of the decision upon it, is determined by the nature of the act to which the inquiry and decision lead up. A judge sitting with a jury is not competent to decide issues of fact; but matters of fact that are merely premises to a rule of law he may decide. He may find out for himself, in whatever way seems best, whether a supposed statute ever really was passed. In *Pickering* v. *Barkley*, Style, 132, merchants were asked by the court to state their understanding as an aid to the decision of a demurrer. The nature of the final act determines the nature of the previous inquiry. As the judge is bound to declare the law he must know or discover the facts that establish the law. So when the final act is legislative the decision which induces it cannot be judicial in the practical sense, although the questions considered might be the same that would arise in the trial of a case. If a State constitution should provide for a hearing before any law should be passed, and should declare that it should be a judicial proceeding *in rem* and the decision binding upon all the world, it hardly is to be supposed that the simple device could make the constitutionality of the law *res judicata*, if it subsequently should be drawn in question before a court of the United States. And all that we have said would be equally true if an appeal had been taken to the Supreme Court of Appeals and it had confined the rate. Its action in doing so would not have been judicial, although the questions debated by it might have been the same that might come before it as a court, and would have been discussed and passed upon it in the same way that it would deal with them if they arose afterwards in a case properly so called. We gather that these are the views of the Supreme Court of Appeals itself. . . . They are implied in many cases in this and other United States courts in which the enforcement of rates has been enjoined, notwithstanding notice and hearing, and what counsel in this case call litigation in advance. Legislation cannot bolster itself up in that way. Litigation cannot arise until the moment of legislation is past. See *Southern Ry. Co.* v. *Commonwealth*, 107 Virginia, 771, 772.

It appears to us that the most plausible objection to these bills is not the one most dwelt upon in argument, but that they were brought too soon. Our doubt is a narrow one and its limits should be understood. It seems to us clear that the appellees were not bound to wait for proceedings brought to enforce the rate and to punish them for departing from it. Those, we have assumed in favor of the appellants would be proceedings in court and could not be enjoined; while to confine the railroads to them for the assertion of their rights would be to deprive them of a part of those rights. If the railroads were required to take no active steps until they could bring a writ of error from this Court to the Supreme Court of Appeals after a final judgment, they would come here with the facts already found against them. But the determination as to their rights turns almost wholly upon the facts to be found. Whether their property was taken unconstitutionally depends upon the valuation of the property, the income to be derived from the proposed rate and the proportion between the two—pure matters of fact. When those are settled the law is tolerably plain. All their constitutional rights, we repeat, depend upon what the facts are found to be. They are not to be forbidden to try those facts before a court of their own choosing if otherwise competent. "A State cannot tie up a citizen of another State, having property within its territory invaded by unauthorized acts of its own officers, to suits for redress in its own courts." *Reagan* v. *Farmers' Loan & Trust Co.*, 154 U. S. 362, 391; *Smyth* v. *Ames,* 169 U. S. 466, 517. See *McNeill* v. *Southern Railway Co.*, 202 U. S. 543; *Ex parte Young,* 209 U. S. 123, 165. Other cases further illustrating this point are *Chicago & N. W. Ry. Co.* v. *Day,* 35 Fed. Rep. 866; *Northern Pacific Ry. Co.* v. *Keyes,* 91 Fed. Rep. 47; *Western Union Telegraph Co.* v. *Myatt,* 98 Fed. Rep. 335.

Our hesitation has been on the narrower question whether the railroads, before they resorted to the Circuit Court, should not have taken the appeal allowed to them by the Virginia constitution at the legislative stage, so as to make it absolutely certain that the officials of the State would try to establish and enforce an unconstitutional rule. Considerations of comity and convenience have

ON REGULATION OF PUBLIC UTILITIES

led this Court ordinarily to decline to interfere by *habeas corpus* where the petitioner had open to him a writ of error to a higher court of a State, in cases where there was no merely logical reason for refusing the writ. The question is whether somewhat similar considerations ought not to have some weight here.

We admit at once that they have not the same weight in this case. The question to be decided, we repeat, is legislative, whether a certain rule shall be made. Although the appeal is given as a right, it is not a remedy, properly so called. At that time no case exists. We should hesitate to say, as a general rule, that a right to resort to the courts could be made always to depend upon keeping a previous watch upon the bodies that make laws, and using every effort and all the machinery available to prevent unconstitutional laws from being passed. It might be said that a citizen has a right to assume that the constitution will be respected, and that the very meaning of our system in giving the last word upon constitutional questions to the courts is that he may rest upon that assumption and is not bound to be continually on the alert against covert or open attacks upon his rights in bodies that cannot finally take them away. It is a novel ground for denying a man a resort to the courts that he has not used due diligence to prevent a law from being passed.

But this case hardly can be disposed of on purely general principles. The question that we are considering may be termed a question of equitable fitness or propriety, and must be answered on the particular facts. The establishment of railroad rates is not like a law that affects private persons who may never have heard of it till it was passed. It is a matter of great interest, both to the railroads and to the public, and is watched by both with scrutinizing care. The railroads went into evidence before the Commission. They very well might have taken the matter before the Supreme Court of Appeals. No new evidence and no great additional expense would have been involved.

The State of Virginia has endeavored to impose the highest safeguards possible upon the exercise of the great power given to the State Corporation Commission, not only by the character of the members of that Commission, but by making its decisions dependent upon the assent of the same historic body that is entrusted with the preservation of the most valued constitutional rights, if the railroads see fit to appeal. It seems to us only a just recognition of the solicitude with which their rights have been guarded, that they should make sure that the State in its final legislative action would not respect what they think their rights to be, before resorting to the courts of the United States.

If the rate should be affirmed by the Supreme Court of Appeals and the railroads still should regard it as confiscatory, it will be understood from what we have said that they will be at liberty then to renew their application to the Circuit Court, without fear of being met by a plea of *res judicata*. It will not be necessary to wait for a prosecution by the Commission. We may add that when the rate is fixed a bill against the Commission to restrain the members from enforcing it will not be bad as an attempt to enjoin legislation or as a suit against a State, and will be the proper form of remedy....

It is proper before closing to mention one decision that was relied upon by the appellees, and one or two other matters peculiar to the cases before the Court. In *McNeill* v. *Southern Ry. Co.*, 202 U. S. 543, the same moment was selected for bringing suit as in these cases, while an examination of the laws of North Carolina discloses that there were statutory provisions for appeal somewhat similar to those in the Virginia constitution, to which we now are referring. But, apart from other differences, in that case the ground of the decree was that the State Commission was dealing with a subject-matter beyond its power; no regulation would have been valid, 202 U. S. 561, and the considerations to which we now are giving weight naturally were not urged. But this decision suggests that in three of the present cases an equally potent

ON REGULATION OF PUBLIC UTILITIES

constitutional bar is alleged against the proceedings of the Commission. The Chesapeake and Ohio, the Norfolk and Western and the Southern Railway Companies all set up general laws, alleged to be incorporated in their charters and to constitute contracts, providing that their tolls should not be diminished except under conditions of fact alleged not to exist.

If the State has bound itself by contract not to cut down the rates as contemplated, there would seem to be no reason why the suit should not be entertained now. See *Reagan* v. *Farmers' Loan & Trust Co.*, 154 U. S. 362, 393. But it would be premature and is unnecessary to decide whether the State has done so or not. No rate is irrevocably fixed by the State until the matter has been laid before the body having the last word. It may be that that body will adhere to the old rate or will establish one that will not be open to the charge of violating the contracts alleged. The contracts alleged do not prohibit a certain reduction if the profits heretofore realized have exceeded a certain amount. On the question of contract as on that of confiscation it is reasonable and proper that the evidence should be laid, in the first instance, before the body having the last legislative word.

There is yet another difficulty in applying to these cases the comity which it is desirable if possible to apply. The Virginia statute of April 15, 1903, enacted to carry into effect the provision of the constitution, requires, by § 34, certain, if not all, appeals to be taken and perfected within six months from the date of the order. 1 Pollard's Code of Virginia, c. 56a, 714. It may be that when an appeal is taken to the Supreme Court of Appeals this section will be held to apply and the appeal be declared too late. We express no opinion upon the matter, which is for the State tribunals to decide, but simply notice a possibility. If the present bills should be dismissed, and then that possible conclusion reached, injustice might be done. As our decision does not go upon a denial of power to entertain the bills at the present stage but upon our views as to what is the most proper and orderly course in cases of this sort when practicable, it seems to us that the bills should be retained for the present to await the result of the appeals if the companies see fit to take them. If the appeals are dismissed as brought too late the companies will be entitled to decrees. If they are entertained and the orders of the Commission affirmed, the bills may be dismissed without prejudice and filed again.

Decrees reversed.

[Mr. Justice Brewer believed that the decrees should be affirmed. Chief Justice Fuller concurred in the reversals but dissented from the opinion, saying that the appellees did not avail themselves of the right of appeal to the Virginia Court of Appeals and holding that the rule of comity obligated the Federal Government to abstain from interfering: "Power grows by what it feeds on, and to hold that State railroad companies can take their chances for the fixing of rates in accordance with their views in a tribunal provided for that purpose by State constitution and laws, and then, if dissatisfied with the result, decline to seek a review in the highest court of the State, though possessed of the absolute right to do so, and invoke the power of the Federal courts to put a stop to such proceedings, is, in my opinion, utterly inadmissible and of palpably dangerous tendency." Mr. Justice Harlan likewise concurred in reversing the decrees and dissented from the opinion of the Court, stating that he went further than the Chief Justice and maintaining that under § 720 of the Revised Statutes, the Circuit Court was entirely without authority, by injunction, to stay the proceedings of the State Corporation Commission. The Commission, he said, "is, in every substantial sense, a court" and the Circuit Court could not grant the injunction in face of the Act of Congress forbidding such action; the railroads' rights could be protected adequately by presenting the question to the United States Supreme Court upon writ of error to the highest State court.]

Prentis et al., constituting the State Corporation Commission of Virginia, v. Atlantic Coast Line Co.
211 U. S. 210

Fixing a Maximum Price for Gas

(*Cedar Rapids Gas Co.* v. *Cedar Rapids*, 1912)

This is a bill brought by the plaintiff in error to restrain the enforcement of an ordinance fixing ninety cents per thousand cubic feet as the highest price to be charged in Cedar Rapids for gas. As the ordinance was passed in 1906 and had not yet been enforced, the Supreme Court of the State dismissed the bill without prejudice to a later suit after it should have been given a fair test. . . . The plaintiff, having specially set up that the ordinance violated the contract clause of the Constitution (Art. I, § 10), and the Fourteenth Amendment, brings the case here. There is a motion to dismiss, but the constitutional questions appear upon the record and are not so frivolous as to warrant that summary course.

The supposed contract arises from a term in the ordinance under which the plaintiff was granted a renewal of its franchise in 1896. By § 3, "in consideration of the privileges herein granted to said company, it shall furnish to the inhabitants of the said city gas for lighting at a price not to exceed $1.80 per thousand feet and 20 cents per thousand cubic feet discount if consumers pay on or before the 10th of each month after consumption," &c. It is admitted that under the laws of Iowa the rate could be changed by the city, but it is argued that the quoted words import a contract that it shall not be changed to such an extent as to make impossible the offer of a discount for prompt payment; that being the cheapest and most efficient way of collecting the price of the gas. The

State court assumed that there was no contract in the case, and in discussing what it treated as the sole question, whether the plaintiff would be deprived of a fair compensation for its services, pointed out that the company could secure payment by requiring a deposit in advance or by making other reasonable rules.

We are of opinion that there was no contract on the part of the city that the price should be kept high enough to allow a discount for prompt payment. The general power reserved to regulate rates was limited only by the Fourteenth Amendment. The words relied upon by the plaintiff express its promise in consideration of the privileges granted, not a promise by the city. . . . It is true that the contract was in the form of an ordinance, but the ordinance was drawn as a contract to be accepted and it was accepted by the plaintiff; it contained reciprocal undertakings, the one in question being that of the plaintiff, as we have said; and it was subject to the power retained by the city to regulate rates. That power, it was expressly provided by Iowa statute, was not to be abridged by ordinance, resolution or contract. Code of 1897, § 725, 22 G. A. (1888) ch. 16.

Upon the issue under the Fourteenth Amendment, the plaintiff argues on the strength of Rev. Stat. § 709, that the facts are open to reexamination here. By that section it is provided that a writ of error to a State court "shall have the same effect as if the judgment or decree complained of had been rendered or passed in a court of the United States." It is argued that as the decree of a State court can be reviewed only by writ of error the foregoing words give to a writ of error in a chancery case the effect of an appeal and open the evidence to reexamination to the same extent as upon an appeal. A suggestion to that effect was made in *Republican River Bridge Co. v. Kansas Pacific Ry. Co.,* 92 U. S. 315, 317, but the practice and decisions from an early date have been the other way. . . .

But of course findings either at law or in equity may depend upon questions that are reexaminable here. The admissibility of

ON REGULATION OF PUBLIC UTILITIES

evidence or its sufficiency to warrant the conclusion reached may be denied; or the conclusion may be a composite of fact and law, such as ownership or contract; or in some way the record may disclose that the finding necessarily involved a ruling within the appellate jurisdiction of this Court. Such questions properly saved must be answered, and, so far as it is necessary to examine the evidence in order to answer them or to prevent an evasion of real issues, the evidence will be examined.... For instance, in this case the finding of the court that it was not prepared to say that a ninety cent rate was confiscatory may perhaps be taken to have been made subject to the admission that the rate was too low to permit a discount for prompt payment, and if so opens the question whether it was not confiscatory on that account, as matter of law. The plaintiff presents a number of such objections to the decision of the court below, although confused with arguments on pure matter of fact.

It would require a very clear case to warrant the reversal of the decree of a State court which though final in form merely postpones a decision upon the merits for further experience. The present one is far from being such a case. To refer in the first instance to the point just mentioned, we cannot say as matter of law that at ninety cents a thousand feet the company will be unable to collect payment without losses that will amount to a taking of its property. Then again, although it is argued that the court excluded going value, the court expressly took into account the fact that the plant was in successful operation. What it excluded was the good will or advantage incident to the possession of a monopoly, so far as that might be supposed to give the plaintiff the power to charge more than a reasonable price.... An adjustment of this sort under a power to regulate rates has to steer between Scylla and Charybdis. On the one side if the franchise is taken to mean that the most profitable return that could be got, free from competition, is protected by the Fourteenth Amendment, then the power to regulate is null. On the other hand if the power to regulate withdraws the protection of the Amendment altogether, then the property is nought. This is not a matter of economic theory, but of fair interpretation of a bargain. Neither extreme can have been meant. A midway between them must be hit.

In this case the court fixed a value on the plant that considerably exceeded its cost and estimated that under the ordinance the return would be over six percent. Its attitude was fair and we do not feel called upon to follow the plaintiff into a nice discussion of details. We perhaps should have adopted a rule as to depreciation somewhat more favorable to the plaintiff, or, it may be, might have allowed this or that item that the State court struck out, but there is nothing of which we can take notice in the case that could warrant us in changing the result or in saying that the plaintiff did not get as much as it could except when leave was reserved for it to try again.

Decree affirmed.

Cedar Rapids Gas Light Co. v. *City of Cedar Rapids*
223 U. S. 655

Rates Under Municipal Ownership

(*Springfield Gas Co.* v. *Springfield,* 1921)

This is a bill in equity brought by the plaintiff in error, a private gas and electric company, to restrain the defendant City from producing and selling electricity to private consumers without first filing schedules of rates and printing and posting the same as required by §§ 33, 34 of the Public Utilities Act of June 30, 1913. (Laws 1913, p. 459.) The bill was dismissed on demurrer by the court of first instance. An appeal was taken to the Supreme Court where the decree was affirmed on rehearing, after a previous decision the other way. The Public Utilities Act and the Municipal Ownership Act (Laws 1913, pp. 455) were enacted by the State of Illinois within a few days of each other and, according to the Supreme Court of the State, as parts of a single plan. The former excepts municipal corporations from its requirements and the latter allows cities to go into this business among others and to fix the rates, which in the plaintiff's case are subject to the approval of the State Public Utilities Commission. The plaintiff contends that the exception of municipal corporations from the Public Utilities Act is void under the Fourteenth Amendment and that the Act should be enforced as if the exception were not there.

It might perhaps be a sufficient answer to the plaintiff's case that the Supreme Court has intimated after careful consideration that the Utilities Act must stand or fall as a whole, so that if the plaintiff's attack upon the exception were sustained the whole statute would be inoperative and the only ground of suit would fail. The plaintiff attempts to reargue the question, but upon this point the decision of the State court would be final and would control. However, as the Supreme Court did not stop at that point, but, assuming that under the law of Illinois the plaintiff had a standing to demand the relief sought if its case was otherwise good, went on to decide the validity of the exception, we think it proper to follow the same course and to deal with the constitutional question raised.

The plaintiff's argument shortly stated is that in selling electricity a city stands like any other party engaged in a commercial enterprise and that to leave it free in the matter of charges while the plaintiff is subject to the Public Utilities Board is to deny to the plaintiff the equal protection of the laws. But we agree with the Supreme Court of the State that the difference between the two types of corporation warrants the different treatment that they have received.

The private corporation, whatever its public duties, is organized for private ends and may be presumed to intend to make whatever profit the business will allow. The municipal corporation is allowed to go into the business only on the theory that thereby the public welfare will be subserved. So far as gain is an object it is a gain to a public body and must be used for public ends. Those who manage the work cannot lawfully make private profit their aim, as the plaintiff's directors not only may but must. The Supreme Court seems to interpret the Municipal Ownership Act as limiting the charges allowed to what will be sufficient to meet outlays and expenses of every kind, thus emphasizing the purely public nature of the interests concerned and excluding the latitude for wrong that the plaintiff fears. The court further says that the municipalities can exercise their power to make all needful rules and regulations only by ordinances and resolutions as in other public action. It calls attention to the fact that the accounts are regulated by law and open to the public eye, and that the consumers in this as in the other case may have a resort to the courts.

The plaintiff did not venture to contend that the submission of similar duties of different bodies to different tribunals was of itself unconstitutional, or that the fixing of rates might not be entrusted to city councils. But the fact that the municipality owned the plant for which its council fixed the rate was supposed to disqualify its officers, at least when other plants were submitted to the judgment of strangers. But a city council has no such interest in the city's electric plant as to make it incompetent to fix the rates. Whatever the value of the distinction between the private and public functions of the municipality, the duty of its governing board in this respect as we have said is public and narrowly fixed by the Act. The conduct of which the plaintiff complains is not extortion but, on the contrary, charging rates that draw the plaintiff's customers away. The standard for these rates, however, according to the Supreme Court, is fixed by the legislature. If the rates had been fixed by law at the present amounts it would be vain to deny their validity. The trouble with the plaintiff's argument is that it attempts to go behind the interpretation that the Supreme Court has given to the Acts concerned and to overlook the delicate distinction between the private and public capacities of municipal corporations. It is unnecessary to refer to the numerous cases upon classification by State laws in order to show that the distinction in question here is very far from being so arbitrary that we can pronounce it bad.

Decree affirmed.

Springfield Gas & Electric Co. v. City of Springfield
257 U. S. 66

VIII. ON STATE TAXATION

Taxing a Stock Exchange Seat

(*Citizens' National Bank* v. *Durr*, 1921)

[THE COURT HELD THAT THE STATE OF OHIO MIGHT CONSTITUTIONally impose a property tax on one of its residents by reason of his ownership of a seat in the New York Stock Exchange. The State court was warranted in finding, Mr. Justice Pitney said, that the membership was personal property which, being without fixed situs, might be taxed by the State of the owner's domicile. Mr. Justice Holmes expressed his doubts:]

THE QUESTION whether a seat in the New York Stock Exchange is taxable in Ohio consistently with the principles established by this Court seems to me more difficult than it does to my brethren. All rights are intangible personal relations between the subject and the object of them created by law. But it is established that it is not enough that the subject, the owner of the right, is within the power of the taxing State. He cannot be taxed for land situated elsewhere, and the same is true of personal property permanently out of the jurisdiction. It does not matter, I take it, whether the interest is legal or equitable, or what the machinery by which it is reached, but the question is whether the object of the right is so local in its foundation and prime meaning that it should stand like an interest in land. If left to myself I should have thought that the foundation and substance of the plaintiff's right was the right of himself and his associates personally to enter the New York Stock Exchange building and to do business there. I should have thought that all the rest was incidental to that and that that on its face was localized in New York. If so, it does not matter whether it is real or personal property or that it adds to the owner's credit and facilities in Ohio. The same would be true of a great estate in New York land.

As my brothers Van Devanter and McReynolds share the same doubts it has seemed to us proper that they should be expressed.

*Citizens' National Bank of Cincinnati, Administrator of Anderson
v. Durr, as former auditor, et al.*
257 U. S. 99, 110

Taxing a Trust Fund in Another State

(*Safe Deposit & Trust Co.* v. *Virginia*, 1929)

[A CITIZEN OF VIRGINIA TRANSFERRED STOCKS TO A MARYLAND TRUST company in trust for his minor sons, also domiciled in Virginia. After the donor died, the trust company continued to pay taxes to Maryland and challenged the validity of a Virginia statute purporting to tax the securities. The Court held that by this statute Virginia was attempting "to tax things wholly beyond her jurisdiction or control in violation of the Fourteenth Amendment." Mr. Justice McReynolds wrote the opinion. In a concurring opinion Mr. Justice Stone was joined by Mr. Justice Brandeis. Mr. Justice Holmes dissented:]

THE SPECIAL Court of Appeals was plainly right in holding that the deed of trust conferred an absolute gift upon the two beneficiaries, perhaps, though I doubt it, subject to be divested upon a condition subsequent. Gray, *Perpetuities*, 1st ed., § 108. If the beneficiaries could be taxed at all they could be taxed for the whole value of the property, because the whole title was in them, even if liable to be divested at some future time in a not very probable event.

I am of opinion that on principle they can be taxed. In the first place I do not think that it matters that the owners, residing in Virginia, have only an equitable title. To be sure the trustee having the legal title and possession of the bonds in Maryland may be taxed there. But that does not affect the right of Virginia by reason of anything that I know of in the Constitution of the United States. . . .

I see no other fact to cut down Virginia's power. It is true that the conception of domicil has been applied to tangible personal property and it now is established that a State cannot tax the owner of such property if it is permanently situated in another State. But hitherto the decisions have been confined to tangibles that in a plain and obvious way owed their protection to another power.... It seemed to me going pretty far to discover even that limitation in the Fourteenth Amendment. It opens vistas to extend the restriction to stocks and bonds in a way that I cannot reconcile with *Blodgett* v. *Silberman*, 277 U. S. 1. Taxes generally are imposed upon persons, for the general advantages of living within the jurisdiction, not upon property although generally measured more or less by reference to the riches of the person taxed, on grounds not of fiction but of fact. ... The notion that the property must be within the jurisdiction puts the emphasis on the wrong thing. The owner may be taxed for it although it never has been within the State. ... It seems to me going still further astray to rely upon the *situs* of the debt. A debt is a legal relation between two parties and, if we think of facts, is situated at least as much with the debtor against whom the obligation must be enforced as it is with the creditor. To say that a debt has a *situs* with the creditor is merely to clothe a foregone conclusion with a fiction. The place of the property is not material except where inability to protect carries with it inability to tax. But that is an exceptional consequence. One State may tax the owner of bonds of another State, although it certainly contributes nothing to their validity. ... It is admitted that Maryland could tax the trustee in this case although most at least of the securities handed over were beyond the power of Maryland to affect in any substantial way. The equitable owners of the fund were in Virginia and I think they could be taxed for it there. I do not understand that any merely technical question is raised on the naming of the trustee instead of the *cestuis que trust* as the party taxed. Nor is there any question of the amount. Throughout the record, by the court and by the trustee, the single issue is stated to be whether the fund can be reached. In the words of the trustee it is: "Has such corpus, so created and held, a taxable *situs* in Virginia within the sanction of section one of the 14th Amendment to the Constitution of the United States?" I think the judgment should be affirmed.

Safe Deposit & Trust Co. of Baltimore v. Commonwealth of Virginia
280 U. S. 83, 96

Another Tax Across State Lines

(*Farmers' Loan & Trust Co.* v. *Minnesota,* 1930)

[A RESIDENT OF NEW YORK DIED, LEAVING AS PART OF HIS ESTATE bonds issued by the State of Minnesota and two of its cities. The testamentary transfer was taxed by New York. The Supreme Court of Minnesota, relying on a recent case in the United States Supreme Court, held that a Minnesota statute imposing an inheritance tax might constitutionally be applied to the same transfer. Its judgment was reversed, Mr. Justice McReynolds writing the opinion of the Court. Mr. Justice Stone wrote a separate opinion, concurring in the result. Mr. Justice Brandeis concurred in the dissenting opinion of Mr. Justice Holmes:]

THIS IS a proceeding for the determination of a tax alleged to be due to the State of Minnesota but objected to by the appellant as contrary to the Fourteenth Amendment of the Constitution of the United States. The tax is imposed in respect of the transfer by will of bonds and certificates of indebtedness of the State of Minnesota and bonds of two cities of that State. The testator died domiciled in New York and the bonds were there at the time of his death. The Supreme Court of the State upheld the tax, *In re Estate of Taylor,* 176 Minn. 634, and the executor appeals.

It is not disputed that the transfer was taxable in New York, but there is no constitutional objection to the same transaction being taxed by two States, if the laws of both have to be invoked in order to give it effect. It may be assumed that the transfer considered by itself alone depends on the law of New York, but if

ON STATE TAXATION

the law of Minnesota is necessary to the existence of anything beyond a piece of paper to be transferred then Minnesota may demand payment for a privilege that could not exist without its help. It seems to me that the law of Minnesota is a present force necessary to the existence of the obligation, and that therefore, however contrary it may be to enlightened policy, the tax is good.

No one would doubt that the law of Minnesota was necessary to call the obligation into existence. Other States do not attempt to determine the legal consequences of acts done outside of their jurisdiction, and therefore whether certain acts done in Minnesota constitute a contract or not depends on the law of Minnesota alone. I think the same thing is true of the continuance of the obligation to the present time. It seems to me that it is the law of Minnesota alone that keeps the debt alive. Obviously at the beginning that law could have provided that the debt should be extinguished by the death of the creditor or by such other event as that law might point out. It gave the debt its duration. The continued operation of that law keeps the debt alive. Not to go too far into the field of speculation but confining the discussion to cities of the State and the State itself, the continued existence of the cities and the readiness of the State to keep its promises depend upon the will of the State. If there were no Constitution the State might abolish the debt by its fiat. The only effect of the Constitution is that the law that originally gave the bonds continuance remains in force unchanged. But it is still the law of that State and no other. When such obligations are enforced by suit in another State it is on the footing of recognition, not of creation. . . . Another State, if it is civilized, does not undertake to say to the debtor now that we have caught you we will force an obligation upon you whether you still are bound by the law of your own State or not. I believe this to be the vital point. Unless I am wrong the debt, wherever enforced, is enforced only because it is recognized as such by the law that created it and keeps it still a debt. No doubt sometimes obligations are enforced elsewhere when the statute of limitations has run at home. But such decisions when defensible stand on the ground that the limitation is only procedural and does not extinguish the duty. If the statute extinguishes the debt by lapse of time no foreign jurisdiction that intelligently understood its function would attempt to make the debtor pay.

I will not repeat what I said the other day in *Safe Deposit & Trust Co.* v. *Virginia, ante,* concerning the attempt to draw conclusions from the supposed *situs* of a debt. The right to tax exists in this case because the party needs the help of Minnesota to acquire a right, and that State can demand a *quid pro quo* in return. . . .

I do not dwell on the practical necessity of resorting to the State in order to secure payment of State or municipal bonds. Even if the creditor had a complete and adequate remedy elsewhere, I still should think that a correct decision of the case must rest on whether I am right or not about the theoretical dependence of the continued existence of the bonds upon Minnesota law.

Blackstone v. *Miller,* 188 U. S. 189, supports my conclusions and I do not think that it should be overruled. A good deal has to be read into the Fourteenth Amendment to give it any bearing upon this case. The Amendment does not condemn everything that we may think undesirable on economic or social grounds.

Mr. Justice Brandeis agrees with this opinion.

The Farmers' Loan & Trust Co., Executor, v. *Minnesota*
280 U. S. 204, 216

A Sky-Limit to "Due Process"

(*Baldwin* v. *Missouri*, 1930)

[MR. JUSTICE M'REYNOLDS AGAIN WAS SPOKESMAN FOR THE COURT IN holding a State tax unconstitutional. A resident of Illinois left bonds and bank credits in Missouri which were held not taxable in Missouri; enforcement of that State's transfer or inheritance taxes was held to violate the due process clause of the Fourteenth Amendment. Mr. Justice Holmes again dissented. This time both Justices Brandeis and Stone agreed with him:]

ALTHOUGH THIS decision hardly can be called a surprise after *Farmers' Loan & Trust Co.* v. *Minnesota* [see page 270] and *Safe Deposit & Trust Co.* v. *Virginia* [see page 267], and although I stated my views in those cases, still, as the term is not over, I think it legitimate to add one or two reflections to what I have said before. I have not yet adequately expressed the more than anxiety that I feel at the ever increasing scope given to the Fourteenth Amendment in cutting down what I believe to be the constitutional rights of the States. As the decisions now stand, I see hardly any limit but the sky to the invalidating of those rights if they happen to strike a majority of this Court as for any reason undesirable. I cannot believe that the Amendment was intended to give us *carte blanche* to embody our economic or moral beliefs in its prohibitions. Yet I can think of no narrower reason that seems to me to justify the present and the earlier decisions to which I have referred. Of course the words "due process of law," if taken in their literal meaning, have no application to this case; and while it is too late to deny that they have been given a much more extended and artificial signification, still we ought to remember the great caution shown by the Constitution in limiting the power of the States, and should be slow to construe the clause in the Fourteenth Amendment as committing to the Court, with no guide but the Court's own discretion, the validity of whatever laws the States may pass. In this case the bonds, notes and bank accounts were within the power and received the protection of the State of Missouri; the notes, so far as appears, were within the considerations that I offered in the earlier decisions mentioned, so that logically Missouri was justified in demanding a *quid pro quo;* the practice of taxation in such circumstances I think has been ancient and widespread, and the tax was warranted by decisions of this Court.... (I suppose that these cases and many others now join *Blackstone* v. *Miller* on the *Index Expurgatorius*—but we need an authoritative list.) It seems to me to be exceeding our powers to declare such a tax a denial of due process of law.

And what are the grounds? Simply, so far as I can see, that it is disagreeable to a bondowner to be taxed in two places. Very probably it might be good policy to restrict taxation to a single place, and perhaps the technical conception of domicil may be the best determinant. But it seems to me that if that result is to be reached it should be reached through understanding among the States, by uniform legislation or otherwise, not by evoking a constitutional prohibition from the void of "due process of law," when logic, tradition and authority have united to declare the right of the State to lay the now prohibited tax.

Mr. Justice Brandeis and Mr. Justice Stone agree with this opinion.

[Mr. Justice Stone wrote a separate dissenting opinion in which Justices Holmes and Brandeis joined.]

Baldwin et al. v. *Missouri*
281 U. S. 586, 595

IX. Excerpts from Various Opinions

THE ACTION does not appear to have been arbitrary except in the sense in which many honest and sensible judgments are so. They express an intuition of experience which outruns analysis and sums up many unnamed and tangled impressions; impressions which may lie beneath consciousness without losing their worth.

Chicago, B. & Q. Ry. Co. v. *Babcock*
204 U. S. 585, 598

SOME DOUBTS have been expressed as to the source of the immunity of a sovereign power from suit without its own permission, but the answer has been public property since before the days of Hobbes (*Leviathan*, c. 26, 2). A sovereign is exempt from suit, not because of any formal conception or obsolete theory, but on the logical and practical ground that there can be no legal right as against the authority that makes the law on which the right depends. *"Car on peut bien recevoir loy d'autruy, mais il est impossible par nature de se donner loy."* Bodin, *Republique,* 1, c. 8. Ed. 1629, p. 132; Sir John Eliot, *De Jure Maiestatis,* c. 3. *"Nemo suo statuto ligatur necessitative."* Baldus., *De Leg. et Const., Digna Vox* (2d ed., 1496, fol. 51b. Ed. 1539, fol. 61).

Kawananakoa v. *Polybank*
205 U. S. 349, 353

PHILOSOPHY may have gained by the attempts in recent years to look through the fiction to the fact and to generalize corporations, partnerships and other groups into a single conception. But to generalize is to omit, and in this instance to omit one characteristic of the complete corporation, as called into being under modern statutes, that is most important in business and law. A leading purpose of such statutes and of those who act under them is to interpose a nonconductor, through which in matters of contract it is impossible to see the men behind.

Donnell v. *Herring-Hall-Marvin Safe Co.*
208 U. S. 267, 273

IT IS TRUE that Spain in its earlier decree embodied the universal feudal theory that all lands were held from the Crown, and perhaps the general attitude of conquering nations toward people not recognized as entitled to the treatment accorded to those in the same zone of civilization as themselves. It is true also that in legal theory sovereignty is absolute, and that as against foreign nations, the United States may assert, as Spain asserted, absolute power. But it does not follow that as against the inhabitants of the Philippines the United States asserts that Spain had such power. When theory is left on one side sovereignty is a question of strength and may vary in degree. How far a new sovereign shall insist upon the theoretical relation of the subjects to the head in the past and how far it shall recognize actual facts are matters for it to decide.

The Province of Benguet was inhabited by a tribe that the Solicitor General, in his argument, characterized as a savage tribe that never was brought under the civil or military government of the Spanish Crown. It seems probable, if not certain, that the Spanish officials would not have granted to any one in that prov-

EXCERPTS FROM VARIOUS OPINIONS

ince the registration to which formerly the plaintiff was entitled by the Spanish laws, and which would have made his title beyond question good. Whatever may have been the technical position of Spain, it does not follow that, in the view of the United States, he had lost all rights and was a mere trespasser when the present Government seized his land. The argument to that effect seems to amount to a denial of native titles throughout an important part of the island of Luzon, at least, for want of ceremonies which the Spaniards would not have permitted and had not the power to enforce.

The acquisition of the Philippines was not like the settlement of the white race in the United States. Whatever consideration may have been shown to the North American Indians, the dominant purpose of the whites in America was to occupy the land. It is obvious that, however stated, the reason for our taking over the Philippines was different. No one, we suppose, would deny that, so far as consistent with paramount necessities, our first object in the internal administration of the islands is to do justice to the natives, not to exploit their country for private gain. By the Organic Act of July 1, 1902, c. 1369, § 12, 32 Stat. 691, all the property and rights acquired there by the United States are to be administered "for the benefit of the inhabitants thereof." It is reasonable to suppose that the attitude thus assumed by the United States with regard to what was unquestionably its own is also its attitude in deciding what it will claim for its own. The same statute made a bill of rights embodying the safeguards of the Constitution, and, like the Constitution, extends those safeguards to all. It provides that "no law shall be enacted in said islands which shall deprive any person of life, liberty, or property without due process of law, or deny to any person therein the equal protection of the laws." § 5. In the light of the declaration that we have quoted from § 12, it is hard to believe that the United States was ready to declare in the next breath that "any person" did not embrace the inhabitants of Benguet, or that it meant by "property" only that which had become such by ceremonies of which presumably a large part of the inhabitants never had heard, and that it proposed to treat as public land what they, by native custom and by long association, one of the profoundest factors in human thought, regarded as their own.

Cariño v. *Insular Government*
212 U. S. 449, 457

IT IS common in extradition cases to attempt to bring to bear all the factitious niceties of a criminal trial at common law. But it is a waste of time. For while of course a man is not to be sent from the country merely upon demand or surmise, yet if there is presented, even in somewhat untechnical form according to our ideas, such reasonable ground to suppose him guilty as to make it proper that he should be tried, good faith to the demanding government requires his surrender. . . . We are bound by the existence of an extradition treaty to assume that the trial will be fair.

Glucksman v. *Henkel*
221 U. S. 508, 512

I TAKE IT that probably many, certainly some, rules of law based on less than universal considerations are made absolute and universal in order to limit those over-refined speculations that we all deprecate, especially where such rules are based upon or affect the continuous relations of material things. The right that is given to inflict various inconveniences upon neighboring lands by building or digging, is given, I presume, because of the public interest in making improvement free, yet it generally is made absolute by the common law. It is not thought worth while to let the right to build or maintain a barn depend upon the speculations of a

jury as to motives. A defect in the highway, declared a defect in the interest of the least competent travellers that can travel unattended without taking legal risks, or in the interest of the average man, I suppose to be a defect as to all. And as in this case the distinction between the inevitable and the negligent escape of sparks is one of the most refined in the world, I think that I must be right so far, as to the law in the case supposed. * * *
I do not think we need trouble ourselves with the thought that my view depends upon differences of degree. The whole law does so as soon as it is civilized. . . . Negligence is all degree—that of the defendant here degree of the nicest sort; and between the variations according to distance that I suppose to exist and the simple universality of the rules in the Twelve Tables or the Leges Barbarorum, there lies the culture of two thousand years.

LeRoy Fibre Co. v. Chicago, Milwaukee & St. Paul Ry.
232 U. S. 340, 353

It would be a surprising extension of the Fourteenth Amendment if it were held to prohibit the continuance of one of the most universal and best known distinctions of the mediaeval law. From the *exceptio spolii* of the Pseudo-Isidore, the Canon Law and Bracton to the assize of novel disseisin the principle was of very wide application that a wrongful disturbance of possession must be righted before a claim of title would be listened to—or at least that in a proceeding to right such a disturbance a claim of title could not be set up; and from Kant to Ihering there has been much philosophising as to the grounds. But it is unnecessary to follow the speculations or to consider whether the principle is eternal or a no longer useful survival. The constitutionality of the law is independent of our views upon such points.

No doubt circumstances have changed. The proof of title does not depend upon difficult evidence, technical procedure, or the duel. Usually a few sheets of paper copied from the registry and costing but a trifle will establish the right, often with less trouble than it takes to prove possession. But these are not the only considerations. The State is within its constitutional power when it limits the sphere of self-help. It may protect an established possession against disturbance by anything except process of law. It may attach such consequences to the disturbance as it sees fit, short of cruel and unusual punishment. If it ordains a *restitutio in integrum* or its equivalent in money it not only is adopting a familiar remedy, but, with the conditions attached in Louisiana, does not go so far as it might.

Grant Timber Co. v. *Gray*
236 U. S. 133, 134

M<small>EN MUST</small> turn square corners when they deal with the Government. If it attaches even purely formal conditions to its consent to be sued those conditions must be complied with. *Lex non praecipit inutilia* (Co. Lit. 127*b*) expresses rather an ideal than an accomplished fact. But in this case we cannot pronounce the second appeal a mere form.

Rock Island R. R. Co. v. *United States*
254 U. S. 141, 143

T<small>HE</small> Fourteenth Amendment, itself a historical product, did not destroy history for the States and substitute mechanical compartments of law all exactly alike. If a thing has been practiced for two hundred years by common consent, it will need a strong case for the Fourteenth Amendment to affect it, as is well illustrated by *Ownbey* v. *Morgan*, 256 U. S. 94, 104, 112. . . . Such words as "right" are a constant solicitation to fallacy. We say a man has a right to the land that he has bought and that to subject a strip six inches or a foot wide to liability to use for

EXCERPTS FROM VARIOUS OPINIONS

a party wall therefore takes his right to that extent. It might be so and we might be driven to the economic and social considerations that we have mentioned if the law were an innovation, now heard of for the first time. But if, from what we may call time immemorial, it has been the understanding that the burden exists the land owner does not have the right to that part of his land except as so qualified and the statute that embodies that understanding does not need to invoke the police power.

Of course a case could be imagined where the modest mutualities of simple townspeople might become something very different when extended to buildings like those of modern New York. * * * In a case involving social history as this does, we should be slow to overrule the decision of courts steeped in the local tradition, even if we saw reasons for doubting it, which in this case we do not.

Jackman v. *Rosenbaum Co.*
260 U. S. 22, 31

THIS COURT has stated many times the deference due to the understanding of the local courts upon matters of purely local concern. It is enough to cite *De Villanueva* v. *Villanueva*, 239 U. S. 293, 299. . . . This is especially true in dealing with the decisions of a court inheriting and brought up in a different system from that which prevails here. When we contemplate such a system from the outside it seems like a wall of stone, every part even with all the others, except so far as our own local education may lead us to see subordinations to which we are accustomed. But to one brought up within it, varying emphasis, tacit assumptions, unwritten practices, a thousand influences gained only from life, may give to the different parts wholly new values that logic and grammar never could have got from the books.

Diaz v. *Gonzalez*
261 U. S. 102, 105

NEITHER ARE WE troubled by the question where to draw the line. That is the question in pretty much everything worth arguing in the law. . . . Day and night, youth and age are only types. But the distinction between the cases put of a gift from the corpus of the estate payable in instalments and the present seems to us not hard to draw, assuming that the gift supposed would not be income. This is a gift from the income of a very large fund, as income. It seems to us immaterial that the same amounts might receive a different color from their source. We are of opinion that quarterly payments, which it was hoped would last for fifteen years from the income of an estate intended for the plaintiff's child, must be regarded as income within the meaning of the Constitution and the law. It is said that the tax laws should be construed favorably for the taxpayers. But that is not a reason for creating a doubt or for exaggerating one when it is no greater than we can bring ourselves to feel in this case.

Irwin v. Gavit
268 U. S. 161, 168

IT IS SAID that when the meaning of language is plain we are not to resort to evidence in order to raise doubts. That is rather an axiom of experience than a rule of law, and does not preclude consideration of persuasive evidence if it exists. If Congress has been accustomed to use a certain phrase with a more limited meaning than might be attributed to it by common practice, it would be arbitrary to refuse to consider that fact when we come to interpret a statute. But, as we have said, the usage of Congress simply shows that it has spoken with careful precision, that its words mark the exact spot at which it stops, and that it distinguishes between the damages caused by the collision and the later loss caused by the delay in paying for the first,—between damages

EXCERPTS FROM VARIOUS OPINIONS

and "the allowance of interest on damages," as it is put by Mr. Justice Bradley in *The Scotland,* 118 U. S. 507.

Boston Sand & Gravel Co. v. *United States*
278 U. S. 41, 48

MANY MODERN improvements must be expected to take their toll of life. When a railroad is built experience teaches that it is pretty certain to kill some people before it has lasted long. But a court cannot condemn a legislature that refuses to allow the toll to be taken even if it thinks that the gain by the change would compensate for any such loss.

Nashville, Chattanooga & St. Louis Ry. v. *White*
278 U. S. 456, 459

IT ALREADY has been decided that the defendants are doing a wrong to the complainants and that they must stop it. They must find out a way at their peril. We have only to consider what is possible if the State of Illinois devotes all its powers to dealing with an exigency to the magnitude of which it seems not yet to have fully awaked. It can base no defenses upon the difficulties that it has itself created. If its constitution stands in the way of prompt action is must amend it or yield to an authority that is paramount to the State.

Wisconsin v. *Illinois*
281 U. S. 179, 197

THE INTERPRETATION of constitutional principles must not be too literal. We must remember that the machinery of government would not work if it were not allowed a little play in its

[285]

joints. In deciding whether a corporation is denied the equal protection of the laws when its creator establishes a more extensive venue for actions against it than is fixed for private citizens, we have to consider, not a geometrical equation between a corporation and a man, but whether the difference does injustice to the class generally, even though it bear hard in some particular case, which is not alleged or proved here.... This it is for the corporation to make out. The range of the State's discretion is large.... The question seems to be answered by *Cincinnati Street Ry. Co. v. Snell,* 193 U. S. 30, 36, 37, which lays down that, if the protection of fundamental rights by equal laws equally administered is enjoyed, the Constitution does not forbid allowing one person to seek a forum from which another in the same class is excluded. But without asserting a universal proposition, it is obvious that there is likely to be such a difference between the business done by a corporation and that done by a private person that the State may well take it into account when it permits a corporation to be formed.

Bain Peanut Co. of Texas, et al. v. Pinson, et al.
282 U. S. 499, 501

NEW YORK proposed to divert a large amount of water from the above-named tributaries of the Delaware and from the watershed of that river to the watershed of the Hudson River in order to increase the water supply of the City of New York. New Jersey insists on a strict application of the rules of the common law governing private riparian proprietors subject to the same sovereign power. Pennsylvania intervenes to protect its interests as against anything that might be done to prejudice its future needs.

We are met at the outset by the question what rule is to be applied. It is established that a more liberal answer may be given than in controversy between neighbor members of a single

EXCERPTS FROM VARIOUS OPINIONS

State. . . . Different considerations come in when we are dealing with independent sovereigns having to regard the welfare of the whole population and when the alternative to settlement is war. In a less degree, perhaps, the same is true of the *quasi*-sovereignties bound together in the Union. A river is more than an amenity, it is a treasure. It offers a necessity of life that must be rationed among those who have power over it. New York has the physical power to cut off all the water within its jurisdiction. But clearly the exercise of such a power to the destruction of the interest of lower States could not be tolerated.

And on the other hand equally little could New Jersey be permitted to require New York to give up its power altogether in order that the river might come down to it undiminished. Both States have real and substantial interests in the river that must be reconciled as best they may be.

The different traditions and practices in the different parts of the country may lead to varying results but the effort always is to secure an equitable apportionment without quibbling over formulas.

New Jersey v. *New York*
283 U. S. 336, 342

X. SELECTED MASSACHUSETTS OPINIONS

In Defense of Labor Legislation

(*Commonwealth* v. *Perry,* 1891)

[A MASSACHUSETTS STATUTE, PROVIDING THAT NO EMPLOYER WITHhold any part of the wages of an employee, engaged at weaving, for imperfections in the work, was held unconstitutional. Mr. Justice Knowlton, writing for the court said: "There are certain fundamental rights of every citizen which are recognized in the organic law of all our free American States. A statute which violates any of these rights is unconstitutional and void, even though the enactment of it is not expressly forbidden. Article I of the Declaration of Rights in the Constitution of Massachusetts enumerates among the natural, inalienable rights of men the right "of acquiring, possessing, and protecting property." . . . This right, he said, "includes the right to make reasonable contracts." Mr. Justice Holmes dissented:]

I HAVE the misfortune to differ from my brethren. I have submitted my views to them at length, and, considering the importance of the question, feel bound to make public a brief statement, notwithstanding the respect and deference I feel for the judgment of those from whom I differ.

In the first place, if the statute is unconstitutional as construed by the majority, I think it should be construed more narrowly and literally, so as to save it.

Taking it literally, it is not infringed, and there is no withholding of wages when the employer only promises to pay a reasonable price for imperfect work, or a price less than the price paid for perfect work, and does pay that price in fact.

But I agree that the act should be construed more broadly,

and should be taken to prohibit palpable evasions, because I am of opinion that, even so construed, it is constitutional, so far as any argument goes which I have heard.

The prohibition, if any, must be found in the words of the constitution, either expressed or implied, upon a fair and historical construction. What words of the United States or State constitution are relied on?

The statute cannot be said to impair the obligation of contracts made after it went into effect. . . . So far as has been pointed out to me, I do not see that it interferes with the right of acquiring, possessing, and protecting property any more than the laws against usury or gaming. In truth, I do not think that that clause of the Bill of Rights has any application. It might be urged, perhaps, that the power to make reasonable laws impliedly prohibits the making of unreasonable ones, and that this law is unreasonable. If I assume that this construction of the constitution is correct, and that, speaking as a political economist, I should agree in condemning the law, still I should not be willing or think myself authorized to overturn legislation on that ground, unless I thought that an honest difference of opinion was impossible, or pretty nearly so.

If the statute does no more than to abolish contracts for a *quantum meruit*, and recoupment for defective quality not amounting to a failure of consideration, I suppose that it only puts an end to what are, relatively speaking, innovations in the common law, and I know of nothing to hinder it. But I do not confine myself to technical considerations.

I suppose that this act was passed because the operatives, or some of them, thought that they were often cheated out of a part of their wages under a false pretense that the work done by them was imperfect, and persuaded the legislature that their view was true.

If their view was true, I cannot doubt that the legislature could deprive the employers of an honest tool which they were using for a dishonest purpose, and I cannot pronounce the legislation void, as based on a false assumption, since I know nothing about the matter one way or the other.

The statute, however construed, leaves the employers their remedy for imperfect work by action.

The objection that this remedy is practically worthless is, I apprehend, no less true, although for different reasons, if the workman's wages should be detained unjustly.

My opinion seems to me to be favored by *Hancock* v. *Yaden,* 121 Ind. 366; Slaughter-House Cases, 16 Wall. 36, 80, 81.

Commonwealth v. *Perry*
155 Mass. 117, 123

A Policeman in Politics

(*McAuliffe* v. *New Bedford,* 1892)

This is a petition for mandamus to restore the petitioner to the office of policeman in New Bedford. He was removed by the mayor upon a written complaint, after a hearing, the mayor finding that he was guilty of violating the thirty-first rule of the police regulations of that city. The part of the rule which the petitioner seems certainly to have violated is as follows: "No member of the department shall be allowed to solicit money or any aid, on any pretense, for any political purpose whatever." There was also evidence that he had been a member of a political committee, which likewise was prohibited. Both parties agree that the city had accepted chapter 319 of the Acts of 1890, by virtue of which the members of the police force held office "during good behavior, and until removed by the mayor * * * for cause deemed by him sufficient, after due hearing." It is argued by the petitioner that the mayor's finding did not warrant the removal; that the part of the rule violated was invalid, as invading the petitioner's right to express his political opinions; and that a breach of it was not a cause sufficient, under the statute.

One answer to this argument, assuming that the statute does not make the mayor the final judge of what cause is sufficient, and that we have a right to consider it, (*Ham* v. *Board of Police,* 142 Mass. 90, 95; *Osgood* v. *Nelson,* L. R. 5 H. L. 636, 649) is that there is nothing in the constitution or the statute to prevent the city from attaching obedience to this rule as a condition to the office of policeman, and making it part of the good conduct required.

The petitioner may have a constitutional right to talk politics, but he has no constitutional right to be a policeman. There are few employments for hire in which the servant does not agree to suspend his constitutional rights of free speech as well as of idleness by the implied terms of his contract. The servant cannot complain, as he takes the employment on the terms which are offered him. On the same principle the city may impose any reasonable condition upon holding offices within its control. This condition seems to us reasonable, if that be a question open to revision here.

The petitioner also argues that he has not had due hearing. The first ground for this argument is some testimony reported that the mayor said that he did not care about the evidence; he knew what McAuliffe had been doing; he knew all about it. A sufficient answer to this is that the fact is not found by the judge who tried the case, and, if necessary to support his findings, we should have to assume that he did not believe the evidence. Next, it is said that the charges against the petitioner were not stated specifically, and that when specifications were called for they were refused. The judge was well warranted in finding that the mayor did all that justice required. The complaint was tolerably full, although no doubt, under some circumstances, further specifications properly ought to be demanded. The petitioner attended on notice at the first day appointed for a hearing, and asked for no specifications, and offered no evidence. There was evidence that he said to the mayor at the hearing, "I admit I am guilty. What's the penalty?" and also said to the mayor at another interview that, if he was going to be removed, he would like to know it, so that he could resign. At an adjourned hearing before the mayor, the petitioner attended with counsel, and his counsel asked for specifications. The mayor refused the request, whereupon the petitioner refused to proceed, and the mayor declared the hearing closed. Under the circumstances, we cannot say that he was wrong.

The next suggestion, that no notice was given to the petitioner that a proceeding to remove him from his office was intended, does not require much answer. The petitioner had notice of the proceedings, and must be taken to have known their possible consequences. According to the evidence, he used language to the mayor expressly contemplating those consequences. Finally, it is said that the case should first have been investigated before the committee on police, as provided by rule 24 of the police regulations. But since the passage of the Act of 1890, if not before, we have no doubt of the power of the mayor to hear all cases on the removal of a police officer in the first instance himself.

Petition dismissed.

McAuliffe v. Mayor, etc., of City of New Bedford
155 Mass. 216

A Referendum on Woman Suffrage

(*In re Municipal Suffrage to Women*, 1894)

[A MAJORITY OF THE SUPREME JUDICIAL COURT OF MASSACHUSETTS held in an advisory opinion, replying to the State House of Representatives, that in an act granting woman suffrage it was unconstitutional to provide that the act take effect upon its acceptance by a majority of the voters. Four justices saw nothing in the State constitution showing that the people desired any referendum; on the contrary, the people put the responsibility of government upon their representatives, and the legislative power could not be delegated by the legislature to any other body. Mr. Justice Holmes dissented on all points raised. Justices Barker and Knowlton also dissented.

Three questions were raised by the House of Representatives: "(1) Is it constitutional, in an act granting to women the right to vote in town and city elections, to provide that such act shall take effect throughout the commonwealth upon its acceptance by a majority of the voters of the whole commonwealth? (2) Is it constitutional to provide in such an act that it shall take effect in a city or town upon its acceptance by a majority vote of the voters of such city or town? (3) Is it constitutional, in an act granting to women the right to vote in town and city elections, to provide that such an act shall take effect immediately upon its acceptance by a majority of the voters of the whole commonwealth, including women specially authorized to register and to vote on this question alone?" Mr. Justice Holmes answered:]

To THE HONORABLE the House of Representatives of the Commonwealth of Massachusetts.

In reply to your order, I respectfully submit the following answer:

If the questions proposed to the justices came before us as a court, and I found myself unable to agree with my brethren, I should defer to their opinion, without any intimation of dissent. But the understanding always has been that questions like the present are addressed to us as individuals, and require an individual answer.

It is assumed in the questions that the legislature has power to grant women the right to vote in town and city elections. I see no reason to doubt that it has that power.

1. I admit that the constitution establishes a representative government, not a pure democracy. It establishes a General Court, which is to be the law-making power. But the question is whether it puts a limit upon the power of that body to make laws. In my opinion, the legislature has the whole law-making power, except so far as the words of the constitution, expressly or impliedly, withhold it, and I think that, in construing the constitution, we should remember that it is a frame of government for men of opposite opinions, and for the future, and therefore not hastily import into it our own views, or unexpressed limitations derived merely from the practice of the past. I ask myself, as the only question, what words express or imply that a power to pass a law subject to rejection by the people is withheld? I find none which do so. The question is not whether the people of their own motion could pass a law without any act of the legislature. That, no doubt, whether valid or not, would be outside the constitution. So, perhaps, might be a statute purporting to confer the power of making laws upon them. But the question, put in a form to raise the fewest technical objections, is whether an act of the legislature is made unconstitutional by a proviso that, if rejected by the people, it shall not go into effect. If it does go into effect, it does so by the express enactment of the representative body. I see no evidence in the instrument that this question ever occurred to the framers of the constitution. It is but a short step further to say that the constitution does not forbid such a law. I agree that the discretion of

the legislature is intended to be exercised. I agree that confidence is put in it as an agent. But I think that so much confidence is put in it that it is allowed to exercise its discretion by taking the opinion of its principal, if it thinks that course to be wise. It has been asked whether the legislature could pass an act subject to the approval of a single man. I am not clear that it could not. The objection, if sound, would seem to have equal force against all forms of local option. But I will consider the question when it arises. The difference is plain between that case and one where the approval required is that of the sovereign body. The contrary view seems to me an echo of Hobbes' theory that the surrender of sovereignty by the people was final. I notice that the case from which most of the reasoning against the power of the legislature has been taken by later decisions states that theory in language which almost is borrowed from the *Leviathan*. *Rice* v. *Foster*, 4 Har. (Del.) 479, 488. Hobbes urged his notion in the interest of the absolute power of King Charles I., and one of the objects of the constitution of Massachusetts was to deny it. I answer the first question, "Yes." I may add that, while the tendency of judicial decision seems to be in the other direction, such able judges as Chief Justices Parker, of Massachusetts, Dixon, of Wisconsin, Redfield, of Vermont, and Cooley, of Michigan, have expressed opinions like mine.

2. If the foregoing view of the power of the legislature is right, I am of opinion that the second question also should be answered, "Yes." I find nothing which forbids the legislature to establish a local option upon this point, any more than with regard to the liquor laws. Under the circumstances, I do not argue this or the following question at length.

3. The act suggested by the third question is open to the seeming objection that it might take a part of their power out of the hands of the present possessors, without their assent, except as given by their representatives. But if, as I believe, the legislature could give to women the right to vote, if they accepted it by a

preliminary vote, and could impose as a second condition that the grant should not be rejected by the voters of the Commonwealth, I do not see why it might not combine the two conditions into one, although, as a result, the grant might become a law against the will of a majority of the male voters. I answer this question, also, "Yes."

In re Municipal Suffrage to Women
160 Mass. 586, 594

Licenses for Speeches on Boston Common

(*Commonwealth* v. *Davis*, 1895)

[A MAN MADE A SPEECH ON BOSTON COMMON WITHOUT HAVING OBtained a permit from the mayor. This was a violation of an ordinance which prohibited the making of public addresses on public grounds without such permit. Exceptions were taken and overruled. Mr. Justice Holmes wrote the opinion of the court:]

THE ONLY question raised by these exceptions which was not decided in the former case of *Com.* v. *Davis*, 140 Mass. 485, is one concerning the construction of the present ordinance. That such an ordinance is constitutional is implied by the former decision, and does not appear to us open to doubt. To say that it is unconstitutional means that, even if the legislature has purported to authorize it, the attempt was vain. The argument to that effect involves the same kind of fallacy that was dealt with in *McAuliffe* v. *New Bedford*, 155 Mass. 216. [See page 294 of this volume.] It assumes that the ordinance is directed against free speech generally (as in *Village of Des Plaines* v. *Boyer*, 123 Ill. 348, the ordinance held void was directed against public picnics and openair dances generally), whereas in fact it is directed toward the modes in which Boston Common may be used. There is no evidence before us to show that the power of the legislature over the common is less than its power over any other park dedicated to the use of the public, or over public streets, the legal title to which is in a city or town. . . . As representative of the public, it may and does exercise control over the use which the public may make of such places, and it may and does delegate more or less of such control to the city or town immediately concerned. For the legislature absolutely or conditionally to forbid public speaking in a highway or public park is no more an infringement of the rights of a member of the public than for the owner of a private house to forbid it in his house. When no proprietary right interferes, the legislature may end the right of the public to enter upon the public place by putting an end to the dedication to public uses. So it may take the lesser step of limiting the public use to certain purposes. See Dill Mun. Corp. §§ 393, 407, 651, 656, 666; *Commissioners v. Armstrong*, 45 N. Y. 234, 243, 244.

If the legislature had power, under the constitution, to pass a law in the form of the present ordinance, there is no doubt that it could authorize the city of Boston to pass the ordinance, and it is settled by the former decision that it has done so. As a matter of history, we suppose, there is no doubt that the town, and, after it, the city, always regulated the use of the common, except so far as restrained by statute. It is settled also that the prohibition in such an ordinance, which would be binding if absolute, is not made invalid by the fact that it may be removed in a particular case by a license from a city officer, or a less numerous body than the one which enacts the prohibition. . . . It is argued that the ordinance really is directed especially against free preaching of the gospel in public places, as certain western ordinances, seemingly general, have been held to be directed against the Chinese. But we have no reason to believe, and do not believe, that this ordinance was passed for any other than its ostensible purpose, namely, as a proper regulation of the use of public grounds.

It follows that, as we said at the outset, the only question open is the construction of the present ordinance. We are of opinion that the words, "no person shall make any public address," in the Revised Ordinances of 1892 (chapter 43, § 66), have as broad a meaning as the words, "no person shall deliver a sermon, lecture, address or discourse," in the Revised Ordinances of 1883 (chapter

37, § 11), under which *Com. v. Davis,* 140 Mass. 485, was decided. See Rev. Ord. 1885, c. 42, § 11. Whether lecture, political discourse, or sermon, a speech on the common, addressed to all persons who choose to draw near and listen, is a public address; and the omission of the superfluous words in the last revision is only a matter of style, and the abridgment properly sought for in codification.

Exceptions overruled.

Commonwealth v. *Davis*
162 Mass. 510

Combinations of Labor Against Capital

(*Vegelahn* v. *Guntner*, 1896)

[PICKETING WAS HELD BY THE SUPREME JUDICIAL COURT OF Massachusetts to be "an unlawful interference with the rights both of employer and of employed." Mr. Justice Allen wrote that intimidation is not limited to threats of violence: "there also may be a moral intimidation which is illegal." The motive of the pickets, the fact that their acts might be punishable as a crime, and the absence of contracts did not stand in the way of an injunction. Chief Justice Field, dissenting, remarked that "the practice of issuing injunctions in cases of this kind is of very recent origin" and he did not think the jurisdiction of a court of equity extended to enjoining picketing unless there was a destruction or threatened destruction of property. He supported a report handed up by Mr. Justice Holmes, who also dissented:]

IN A CASE like the present, it seems to me that, whatever the true result may be, it will be of advantage to sound thinking to have the less popular view of the law stated, and therefore, although, when I have been unable to bring my brethren to share my convictions, my almost invariable practice is to defer to them in silence, I depart from that practice in this case, notwithstanding my unwillingness to do so, in support of an already rendered judgment of my own.

In the first place, a word or two should be said as to the meaning of the report. I assume that my brethren construe it as I meant it to be construed, and that, if they were not prepared to do so, they would give an opportunity to the defendants to have it amended in accordance with what I state my meaning to have been. There was no proof of any threat or danger of a patrol exceeding two men, and as, of course, an injunction is not granted except with reference to what there is reason to expect in its absence, the question on that point is whether a patrol of two men should be enjoined. Again, the defendants are enjoined by the final decree from intimidating by threats, express or implied, or physical harm to body or property, any person who may be desirous of entering into the employment of the plaintiff, so far as to prevent him from entering the same. In order to test the correctness of the refusal to go further, it must be assumed that the defendants obey the express prohibition of the decree. If they do not, they fall within the injunction as it now stands, and are liable to summary punishment. The important difference between the preliminary and the final injunction is that the former goes further, and forbids the defendants to interfere with the plaintiff's business "by any scheme * * * organized for the purpose of * * * preventing any person or persons who now are or may hereafter be * * * desirous of entering the [plaintiff's employment] from entering it." I quote only a part, and the part which seems to me most objectionable. This includes refusal of social intercourse, and even organized persuasion or argument, although free from any threat of violence, either express or implied. And this is with reference to persons who have a legal right to contract or not to contract with the plaintiff, as they may see fit. Interference with existing contracts is forbidden by the final decree. I wish to insist a little that the only point of difference which involves a difference of principle between the final decree and the preliminary injunction, which it is proposed to restore, is what I have mentioned, in order that it may be seen exactly what we are to discuss. It appears to me that the judgment of the majority turns in part on the assumption that the patrol necessarily carries with it a threat of bodily harm. That assumption I think unwarranted, for the reasons which I have given. Furthermore, it cannot be said, I think, that two men, walking together up and down a sidewalk, and speaking to those who enter a certain shop, do necessarily and always thereby convey a threat of force. I do not think it possible to discriminate, and to say that two workmen, or even two representatives of an organization of workmen, do; especially when they are, and are known to be, under the injunction of this court not to do so. See Stimson, *Labor Law*, 60, especially pages 290, 298-300; *Reg.* v. *Shepherd*, 11 Cox, Cr. Cas. 325. I may add that I think the more intelligent workingmen believe as fully as I do that they no more can be permitted to usurp the State's prerogative of force than can their opponents in their controversies. But, if I am wrong, then the decree as it stands reaches the patrol, since it applies to all threats of force. With this I pass to the real difference between the interlocutory and the final decree.

I agree, whatever may be the law in the case of a single defendant (*Rice* v. *Albee*, 164 Mass. 88), that when a plaintiff proves that several persons have combined and conspired to injure his business, and have done acts producing that effect, he shows temporal damage and a cause of action, unless the facts disclose or the defendants prove some ground of excuse or justification; and I take it to be settled, and rightly settled, that doing that damage by combined persuasion is actionable, as well as doing it by falsehood or by force. . . .

Nevertheless, in numberless instances the law warrants the intentional infliction of temporal damage, because it regards it as justified. It is on the question of what shall amount to a justification, and more especially on the nature of the considerations which really determine or ought to determine the answer to that question, that judicial reasoning seems to me often to be inadequate. The true grounds of decision are considerations of policy and of social advantage, and it is vain to suppose that solutions can be attained merely by logic and general propositions of law which nobody disputes. Propositions as to public policy rarely are unanimously accepted, and still more rarely, if ever, are capable of unanswerable proof. They require a special training to enable anyone even to form an intelligent opinion about them.

In the early stages of law, at least, they generally are acted on rather as inarticulate instincts than as definite ideas, for which a rational defense is ready.

To illustrate what I have said in the last paragraph: It has been the law for centuries that a man may set up a business in a small country town, too small to support more than one, although thereby he expects and intends to ruin someone already there, and succeeds in his intent. In such a case he is not held to act "unlawfully and without justifiable cause," as was alleged in *Walker* v. *Cronin* and *Rice* v. *Albee*. The reason, of course, is that the doctrine generally has been accepted that free competition is worth more to society than it costs, and that on this ground the infliction of the damage is privileged. . . . Yet even this proposition nowadays is disputed by a considerable body of persons, including many whose intelligence is not to be denied, little as we may agree with them.

I have chosen this illustration partly with reference to what I have to say next. It shows without the need of further authority that the policy of allowing free competition justifies the intentional inflicting of temporal damage, including the damage of interference with a man's business by some means, when the damage is done, not for its own sake, but as an instrumentality in reaching the end of victory in the battle of trade. In such a case it cannot matter whether the plaintiff is the only rival of the defendant, and so is aimed at specially, or is one of a class all of whom are hit. The only debatable ground is the nature of the means by which such damage may be inflicted. We all agree that it cannot be done by force or threats of force. We all agree, I presume, that it may be done by persuasion to leave a rival's shop, and come to the defendant's. It may be done by the refusal or withdrawal of various pecuniary advantages, which, apart from this consequence, are within the defendant's lawful control. It may be done by the withdrawal of, or threat to withdraw, such advantages from third persons who have a right to deal or not to deal with the plaintiff, as a means of inducing them not to deal with him either as customers or servants. . . . I have seen the suggestion made that the conflict between employers and employed was not competition. But I venture to assume that none of my brethren would rely on that suggestion. If the policy on which our law is founded is too narrowly expressed in the term "free competition," we may substitute "free struggle for life." Certainly, the policy is not limited to struggles between persons of the same class, competing for the same end. It applies to all conflicts of temporal interests.

I pause here to remark that the word "threats" often is used as if, when it appeared that threats had been made, it appeared that unlawful conduct had begun. But it depends on what you threaten. As a general rule, even if subject to some exceptions, what you may do in a certain event you may threaten to do—that is, give warning of your intention to do—in that event, and thus allow the other person the chance of avoiding the consequence. So, as to "compulsion," it depends on how you "compel." . . . So as to "annoyance" or "intimidation." . . . In *Sherry* v. *Perkins*, 147 Mass. 212, it was found as a fact that the display of banners which was enjoined was part of a scheme to prevent workmen from entering or remaining in the plaintiff's employment, "by threats and intimidation." The context showed that the words as there used meant threats of personal violence and intimidation by causing fear of it.

So far, I suppose, we are agreed. But there is a notion, which latterly has been insisted on a good deal, that a combination of persons to do what any one of them lawfully might do by himself will make the otherwise lawful conduct unlawful. It would be rash to say that some as yet unformulated truth may not be hidden under this proposition. But, in the general form in which it has been presented and accepted by many courts, I think it plainly untrue, both on authority and principle. . . . There was combination of the most flagrant and dominant kind in *Bowen* v. *Matheson* [14 Allen, 499] and in the *Steamship Co. Case* [(1892) App. Cas. 25], and combination was essential to the success achieved. But it is not necessary to cite cases. It is plain from the slightest consideration of practical affairs, or the most superficial reading of industrial history, that free competition means combination, and that the organization of the world, now going on so fast, means an ever-increasing might and scope of combination. It seems to me futile to set our faces against this tendency. Whether beneficial on the whole, as I think it, or detrimental, it is inevitable, unless the fundamental axioms of society, and even the fundamental conditions of life, are to be changed.

One of the eternal conflicts out of which life is made up is that between the effort of every man to get the most he can for his services, and that of society, disguised under the name of capital, to get his services for the least possible return. Combination on the one side is patent and powerful. Combination on the other is the necessary and desirable counterpart, if the battle is to be carried on in a fair and equal way. I am unable to reconcile *Temperton* v. *Russell* (1893) 1 Q. B. 715, and the cases which follow it, with the *Steamship Co. Case*. But *Temperton* v. *Russell* is not a binding authority here, and therefore I do not think it necessary to discuss it.

If it be true that workingmen may combine with a view, among other things, to getting as much as they can for their labor, just as capital may combine with a view to getting the greatest possible return, it must be true that, when combined, they have the same liberty that combined capital has, to support their interests by argument, persuasion, and the bestowal or refusal of those advantages which they otherwise lawfully control. I can remember when many people thought that, apart from violence or breach of contract, strikes were wicked, as organized refusals to work. I suppose that intelligent economists and legislators have given up that notion today. I feel pretty confident that they equally will abandon the idea that an organized refusal by workmen of social intercourse with a man who shall enter their antagonist's employ is unlawful, if it is dissociated from any threat of violence, and is made for the sole object of prevailing, if possible, in a contest with their employer about the rate of wages. The fact that the immediate object of the act by which the benefit to themselves is to be gained is to injure their antagonist does not necessarily make it unlawful, any more than when a great house lowers the price of goods for the purpose and with the effect of driving a smaller antagonist from the business. Indeed, the question seems to have been decided as long ago as 1842, by the good sense of Chief Justice Shaw, in *Com.* v. *Hunt,* 4 Metc. (Mass.) 111. I repeat, at the end, as I said at the beginning, that this is the point of difference in principle, and the only one, between the interlocutory and final decree; and I only desire to add that the distinctions upon which the *final* decree was framed seem to me to have coincided very accurately with the results finally reached by legislation and judicial decision in England, apart from what I must regard as the anomalous decisions of *Temperton* v. *Russell* and the cases which have followed it. . . .

The general question of the propriety of dealing with this kind of case by injunction I say nothing about, because I understand that the defendants have no objection to the final decree if it goes no further, and that both parties wish a decision upon the matters which I have discussed.

Vegelahn v. *Guntner et al.*
167 Mass. 92, 104

Inducing a Breach of Contract

(*May* v. *Wood*, 1898)

[THE PLAINTIFF WAS EMPLOYED AS A COMPANION AT A SALARY OF four dollars a week and on the understanding that her employer would provide for her a legacy of $700. After the plaintiff was discharged from the employment and the provision in the will was revoked, action was brought against alleged conspirators for spreading malicious statements about the servant and inducing the dismissal. Chief Justice Field said for the majority that the conspiracy charge was immaterial and that "it is essential that the statements made should be substantially set out in the declaration" so that the court might judge whether the alleged effect could be attributed to the remarks. Mr. Justice Holmes' dissenting opinion follows:]

I CANNOT agree with the decision of the majority, and, as the law in cases of this sort is somewhat unsettled, I think it may be useful that I should state my views. I regard it as settled in this Commonwealth, and as rightly settled, whether it be consistent with *Allen* v. *Flood* (1898) App. Cas. 1, or not, that an action will lie for depriving a man of custom,—that is, of possible contracts,—as well when the result is effected by persuasion as when it is accomplished by fraud or force, if the harm is inflicted simply from malevolence, and without some justifiable cause, such as competition in trade.... See *Vegelahn* v. *Guntner*, 167 Mass. 92, 99, 105. I think that it does not matter what motive to abstain from dealing is given to the possible customer, whether it be fear or simply prejudice, if the motive be effectual, or whether it be produced by falsehood, or without it, by malevolently intended advice. I think it plain that the fact that the conduct of the possible customer in abstaining from dealing is lawful does not affect the liability of the person who induced him to do so, although this person is remoter from the damage complained of. I think this a principle which not only is obviously sound, but is established by the cases first cited above, by the recognition of loss of custom as an element in damages (*Walker* v. *Cronin*, 107 Mass. 555, 565; Odgers, Sland. & L. [2nd Ed.] pp. 298, 307, 309, c. 10, subds. 2, 3), and by the doctrine that a man who utters a slander may be liable for the privileged repetition of it, if reasonably to be expected, when he would not be liable unless he actually intended it, if the repetition were itself a wrong. . . .

A fortiori, under similar conditions and limitations an action will lie for inducing the breach of an actual contract. . . . As in the former case [*Walker* v. *Cronin*], the ground of liability is not false statements, but the intentional causing of temporal damage, without justifiable cause, by any means contemplated as effectual, and, proving so in the event. One of the means alleged in the present declaration, namely, inducing Mary A. Wood to believe that the plaintiff was a dangerous person and unfit associate, might have been accomplished without uttering a falsehood, and might have been alleged as the only means without impairing the count.

I cannot make it plainer than it is upon simply reading the declaration that this is an action of the kind just supposed. It is not an action for slander with special damages, but it is an action for malevolently and without justifiable cause inducing a third person to break a contract. That is the gist of the action. And falsehood or slander is material only as one out of many possible, and two alleged, means of bringing about the wrong. It is one degree more remote than where the slander itself is the thing complained of, and by all analogy, when referred to, need not be set out specifically, as when slander is the gist. See the form of declaration held good on demurrer in *Lumley* v. *Gye*, 2 El. & Bl. 216. . . .

Of *Rice* v. *Albee,* 164 Mass. 88, I will only say that, whether the decision be right or wrong, the reasoning always has seemed to me inadequate, but that, however that may be, in that case the action was for preventing the making of a contract, not for causing the breach of one already made. I do not understand that it was intended to overrule previous decisions, or to dissent from cases like *Lumley* v. *Gye,* which previously had been approved by the court.

I deal only with the ground which I understand to be relied on in the judgment of the court. I suppose that nothing else is open on the special demurrer (*Parker* v. *Huntington,* 2 Gray. 124, 126, 128); but I will add that the declaration, although informal, plainly means that the defendants not only conspired to do, but did, the acts by reason of which, as it is alleged, Wood was induced to break her contract with the plaintiff. If the defendants wanted a more formal allegation, they should have specified the defect in their demurrer. . . .

Knowlton and Morton, JJ., authorize me to say that they agree with the foregoing.

May v. *Wood, et al.*
172 Mass. 11, 14

Unlawful Methods of Unionizing

(*Plant* v. *Woods*, 1900)

[THE DEFENDANTS, MEMBERS OF ONE UNION, ATTEMPTED TO PERSUADE employers to urge their employees who belonged to a rival union to join their organization. It was found that the defendants had resolved to resort to strikes and boycotts to carry out their purpose. The Supreme Judicial Court of Massachusetts granted an injunction. Mr. Justice Hammond, writing for the court, found that although the defendants had committed no acts of violence, their threat "was coercive in its effect upon the will." He said: "The necessity that the plaintiffs should join this association is not so great, nor is its relation to the rights of the defendants, as compared with the right of the plaintiffs to be free from molestation, such as to bring the acts of the defendants under the shelter of the principles of trade competition." Chief Justice Holmes dissented:]

WHEN A QUESTION has been decided by the court, I think it proper, as a general rule, that a dissenting judge, however strong his convictions may be, should thereafter accept the law from the majority and leave the remedy to the legislature, if that body sees fit to interfere. If the decision in the present case simply had relied upon *Vegelahn* v. *Guntner* [see page 304], I should have hesitated to say anything, although I might have stated that my personal opinion had not been weakened by the substantial agreement with my views to be found in the judgments of the majority of the House of Lords in *Allen* v. *Flood*, [1898] A. C. 1. But much to my satisfaction, if I may say so, the court has seen fit to adopt the mode of approaching the question which I believe to be the correct one, and to open an issue which otherwise I might have thought closed. The difference between my brethren and me now seems to be a difference of degree, and the line of reasoning followed makes it proper for me to explain where the difference lies.

I agree that the conduct of the defendants is actionable unless justified. *May* v. *Wood* [see page 311] and cases cited. I agree that the presence or absence of justification may depend upon the object of their conduct, that is, upon the motive with which they acted. *Vegelahn* v. *Guntner*, pp. 105, 106. I agree, for instance, that if a boycott or a strike is intended to override the jurisdiction of the courts by the action of a private association, it may be illegal. . . .

On the other hand, I infer that a majority of my brethren would admit that a boycott or strike intended to raise wages directly might be lawful, if it did not embrace in its scheme or intent violence, breach of contract, or other conduct unlawful on grounds independent of the mere fact that the action of the defendants was combined. A sensible workingman would not contend that the courts should sanction a combination for the purpose of inflicting or threatening violence or the infraction of admitted rights. To come directly to the point, the issue is narrowed to the question whether, assuming that some purposes would be a justification, the purpose in this case of the threatened boycotts and strikes was such as to justify the threats. That purpose was not directly concerned with wages. It was one degree more remote. The immediate object and motive was to strengthen the defendants' society as a preliminary and means to enable it to make a better fight on questions of wages or other matters of clashing interests. I differ from my brethren in thinking that the threats were as lawful for this preliminary purpose as for the final one to which strengthening the union was a means. I think that unity of organization is necessary to make the contest of labor effectual, and that societies of laborers lawfully may employ in their preparation the means which they might use in the final contest.

Although this is not the place for extended economic discussion, and although the law may not always reach ultimate economic conceptions, I think it well to add that I cherish no illusions as to the meaning and effect of strikes. While I think the strike a lawful instrument in the universal struggle of life, I think it pure phantasy to suppose that there is a body of capital of which labor as a whole secures a larger share by that means. The annual product, subject to an infinitesimal deduction for the luxuries of the few, is directed to consumption by the multitude, and is consumed by the multitude, always. Organization and strikes may get a larger share for the members of an organization, but, if they do, they get it at the expense of the less organized and less powerful portion of the laboring mass. They do not create something out of nothing. It is only by divesting our minds of questions of ownership and other machinery of distribution, and by looking solely at the question of consumption,— asking ourselves what is the annual product, who consumes it, and what changes would or could we make,—that we can keep in the world of realities. But, subject to the qualifications which I have expressed, I think it lawful for a body of workmen to try by combination to get more than they now are getting, although they do it at the expense of their fellows, and to that end to strengthen their union by the boycott and the strike.

Paul J. Plant, et al. v. Henry K. Woods, et al.
176 Mass. 492, 504

INDEX

Advertising, 217
Alienation of land, 96
Aliens, 195
Allen, Mr. Justice, 304
American Bank & Trust Co. v. Fed. Reserve Bank, 158
Arizona Employers' Liability Cases, 41
Assessments, 10, 20
Attractive nuisance, 232

Baldwin v. *Missouri*, 273
Banking, 20, 113, 158
Barker, Mr. Justice, 297
Bentham, 6
Biddle v. *Perovich*, 236
Blacklist, 127
Block v. *Hirsh*, 53; cited, 60
Blodgett v. *Holden*, 190
Bodin, 277
Boycotts, 166, 314
Brandeis, Mr. Justice, 43, 190, 267, 270, 274; dissenting from opinions by Holmes, 66, 112, 227, 242
Brewer, Mr. Justice, 7, 79, 150, 200, 254
Brown, Mr. Justice, 9
Brown v. *United States*, 228
Buck v. *Bell*, 67
Butler, Mr. Justice, 70, 121, 190, 242

Casey v. *United States*, 239
Cedar Rapids Gas Co. v. *Cedar Rapids*, 255
Central Lumber Co. v. *South Dakota*, 28
Chinese, 25, 195
Citizens' National Bank v. *Durr*, 265
Civil Service Act, 171
Clarke, Mr. Justice, 43, 112, 231, 234
Coercing a jury, 224
Combinations in restraint of trade, 34, 125, 137, 143, 147, 153, 158, 163, 166
Commerce clause, 34, 86, 109, 119
Commonwealth v. *Davis*, 301
Commonwealth v. *Perry*, 291

Commutation of sentence, 236
Competition, 28, 125, 145, 308-9
Congressional authority, 96, 101, 113, 185, 190
Conspiracies, 137, 147
Constitutionality, 19, 190, 281, 285
Contempts, 75, 177, 201
Contracts, 4, 16, 21, 59, 66, 80, 106, 139, 143, 255, 291, 311
Copyright Act, 175
Criminal procedure, 91, 177, 204, 221, 236
Curtis, Mr. Justice, 199

Day, Mr. Justice, 45, 175, 200, 227, 235
Daylight saving, 116
"Delusive exactness," 12
Deportation, 195
"Draconian doctrine," 234
Due process, 3, 14, 20, 28, 31, 44, 46, 53, 59, 62, 67, 71, 80, 91, 106, 153, 158, 185, 190, 199, 200, 204, 210, 245, 255, 265, 267, 270, 273

Economic beliefs of judges, 5, 272, 273, 292
Education, 14
Eleventh Amendment, 118
Emergency legislation, 53, 59
Eminent domain, 31
Equal protection of the laws, 3, 8, 10, 14, 25, 28, 34, 44, 67, 80, 259, 282
Erie R. R. Co. v. *Public Utility Comsrs.*, 46
Eureka Pipe Line Co. v. *Hallanan*, 109
Evidence, 239
Executive process, 91
Extradition, 280
Eyeglass business, 71

Farmers' Loan & Trust Co. v. *Minnesota*, 270; cited, 273
Farming, 8, 154, 166
Federal Reserve Board, 113, 158
Field, Chief Justice, 304, 311

INDEX

Fifteenth Amendment, 210
Fifth Amendment, 65, 158, 190, 199, 214
First Amendment, 78
Ft. Smith Lumber Co. v. *Arkansas,* 44
Fourteenth Amendment, 3, 8, 10, 14, 20, 25, 28, 31, 41, 44, 46, 53, 59, 62, 67, 71, 75, 80, 86, 91, 106, 153, 204, 210, 245, 255, 259, 265, 267, 270, 273, 281, 282
Fourth Amendment, 201
Frank Case, cited, 207, 209
Free speech, 75, 301
Fuller, Chief Justice, 90, 254

Galveston, Harrisburg, &c., Ry. Co. v. *Texas,* 86
Gompers v. *United States,* 177
Good character, 221
Government inducing crime, 241-2
Grade crossings, 46
Greer v. *United States,* 221

Hammond, Mr. Justice, 314
Harlan, Mr. Justice, 19, 79, 90, 254
Harrison Anti-Narcotic Act, 239
Hobbes, 277, 299
Holding companies, 44
Homestead Act, 96
Horning v. *District of Columbia,* 224
Hudson Water Co. v. *McCarter,* 80
Hughes, Mr. Justice, 27, 143

Ihering, 281
Imbeciles, 67
Immigration, 195
Immunity from suit, 277
Income tax return, 213
Insurrection, 91
International Harvester Co. v. *Kentucky,* 153; cited, 57
Interstate commerce, 34, 49, 51, 84, 86, 106, 109, 116, 125, 152, 153, 166
Interstate Ry. Co. v. *Massachusetts,* 14

Johnson grass, 8
Judicial notice of social and economic data, 5, 27, 103, 283
Jurisdiction, 101, 114, 118, 228, 240, 265, 267
Jury trials, 92, 204, 224, 228, 240

Kant, 281
Knowlton, Mr. Justice, 291, 297, 313
Kohler Act, 62

Labor—combinations, 163, 304, 314; legislation, 291; picketing, 304; strikes and boycotts, 314; wages, 163, 291; under martial law, 93
Lamar, Mr. Justice, 27
Laundries, 25
Legislative leeway, 5, 9, 12, 13, 17, 21, 22, 26, 29-30, 32, 40, 54, 63, 89, 245, 285
Liability, employers', 41
Libel, 217
Liquor traffic, 213
"Logical extreme," 17, 21, 82
Louisville & Nashville v. *Barber Asphalt Co.,* 10

McAuliffe v. *New Bedford,* 294; cited, 301
McCulloch v. *Maryland,* cited, 9
McFarland v. *Amer. Sugar Co.,* 34
McKenna, Mr. Justice, 9, 43, 45, 58, 61, 85, 90, 223
McReynolds, Mr. Justice, 43, 45, 52, 58, 61, 96, 115, 118, 209, 227, 242, 266, 267, 270, 273

Marcus Brown Co. v. *Feldman,* 59
Marshall, Chief Justice, 105, 183
Martial law, 91
Mass. State Grange v. *Benton,* 116
May v. *Wood,* 311; cited, 314
Migratory Bird Treaty, 101
Miles Medical Co. v. *Park,* 143
Miller, Mr. Justice, 41
Mining, 62
Missouri v. *Duncan,* 113
Missouri v. *Holland,* 101
Missouri, K. & T. Ry. Co. v. *May,* 8
Mob domination, 204
Monopoly, 34, 125
Moore v. *Dempsey,* 204
Morton, Mr. Justice, 313
Mt. Vernon Cotton Co. v. *Alabama Power Co.,* 31; cited, 55
Moyer v. *Peabody,* 91
Municipal ownership, 259
Music rolls, 175

Narcotics, 239
Nash v. *United States,* 147
National Ass'n of Window Glass Mfrs. v. *United States,* 163
National Prohibition Act, 213
Negligence, 281

[318]

INDEX

Advertising, 217
Alienation of land, 96
Aliens, 195
Allen, Mr. Justice, 304
American Bank & Trust Co. v. Fed. Reserve Bank, 158
Arizona Employers' Liability Cases, 41
Assessments, 10, 20
Attractive nuisance, 232

Baldwin v. Missouri, 273
Banking, 20, 113, 158
Barker, Mr. Justice, 297
Bentham, 6
Biddle v. Perovich, 236
Blacklist, 127
Block v. Hirsh, 53; cited, 60
Blodgett v. Holden, 190
Bodin, 277
Boycotts, 166, 314
Brandeis, Mr. Justice, 43, 190, 267, 270, 274; dissenting from opinions by Holmes, 66, 112, 227, 242
Brewer, Mr. Justice, 7, 79, 150, 200, 254
Brown, Mr. Justice, 9
Brown v. United States, 228
Buck v. Bell, 67
Butler, Mr. Justice, 70, 121, 190, 242

Casey v. United States, 239
Cedar Rapids Gas Co. v. Cedar Rapids, 255
Central Lumber Co. v. South Dakota, 28
Chinese, 25, 195
Citizens' National Bank v. Durr, 265
Civil Service Act, 171
Clarke, Mr. Justice, 43, 112, 231, 234
Coercing a jury, 224
Combinations in restraint of trade, 34, 125, 137, 143, 147, 153, 158, 163, 166
Commerce clause, 34, 86, 109, 119
Commonwealth v. Davis, 301
Commonwealth v. Perry, 291

Commutation of sentence, 236
Competition, 28, 125, 145, 308-9
Congressional authority, 96, 101, 113, 185, 190
Conspiracies, 137, 147
Constitutionality, 19, 190, 281, 285
Contempts, 75, 177, 201
Contracts, 4, 16, 21, 59, 66, 80, 106, 139, 143, 255, 291, 311
Copyright Act, 175
Criminal procedure, 91, 177, 204, 221, 236
Curtis, Mr. Justice, 199

Day, Mr. Justice, 45, 175, 200, 227, 235
Daylight saving, 116
"Delusive exactness," 12
Deportation, 195
"Draconian doctrine," 234
Due process, 3, 14, 20, 28, 31, 44, 46, 53, 59, 62, 67, 71, 80, 91, 106, 153, 158, 185, 190, 199, 200, 204, 210, 245, 255, 265, 267, 270, 273

Economic beliefs of judges, 5, 272, 273, 292
Education, 14
Eleventh Amendment, 118
Emergency legislation, 53, 59
Eminent domain, 31
Equal protection of the laws, 3, 8, 10, 14, 25, 28, 34, 44, 67, 80, 259, 282
Erie R. R. Co. v. Public Utility Comsrs., 46
Eureka Pipe Line Co. v. Hallanan, 109
Evidence, 239
Executive process, 91
Extradition, 280
Eyeglass business, 71

Farmers' Loan & Trust Co. v. Minnesota, 270; cited, 273
Farming, 8, 154, 166
Federal Reserve Board, 113, 158
Field, Chief Justice, 304, 311

INDEX

Fifteenth Amendment, 210
Fifth Amendment, 65, 158, 190, 199, 214
First Amendment, 78
Ft. Smith Lumber Co. v. *Arkansas,* 44
Fourteenth Amendment, 3, 8, 10, 14, 20, 25, 28, 31, 41, 44, 46, 53, 59, 62, 67, 71, 75, 80, 86, 91, 106, 153, 204, 210, 245, 255, 259, 265, 267, 270, 273, 281, 282
Fourth Amendment, 201
Frank Case, cited, 207, 209
Free speech, 75, 301
Fuller, Chief Justice, 90, 254

Galveston, Harrisburg, &c., Ry. Co. v. *Texas,* 86
Gompers v. *United States,* 177
Good character, 221
Government inducing crime, 241-2
Grade crossings, 46
Greer v. *United States,* 221

Hammond, Mr. Justice, 314
Harlan, Mr. Justice, 19, 79, 90, 254
Harrison Anti-Narcotic Act, 239
Hobbes, 277, 299
Holding companies, 44
Homestead Act, 96
Horning v. *District of Columbia,* 224
Hudson Water Co. v. *McCarter,* 80
Hughes, Mr. Justice, 27, 143

Ihering, 281
Imbeciles, 67
Immigration, 195
Immunity from suit, 277
Income tax return, 213
Insurrection, 91
International Harvester Co. v. *Kentucky,* 153; cited, 57
Interstate commerce, 34, 49, 51, 84, 86, 106, 109, 116, 125, 152, 153, 166
Interstate Ry. Co. v. *Massachusetts,* 14

Johnson grass, 8
Judicial notice of social and economic data, 5, 27, 103, 283
Jurisdiction, 101, 114, 118, 228, 240, 265, 267
Jury trials, 92, 204, 224, 228, 240

Kant, 281
Knowlton, Mr. Justice, 291, 297, 313
Kohler Act, 62

Labor—combinations, 163, 304, 314; legislation, 291; picketing, 304; strikes and boycotts, 314; wages, 163, 291; under martial law, 93
Lamar, Mr. Justice, 27
Laundries, 25
Legislative leeway, 5, 9, 12, 13, 17, 21, 22, 26, 29-30, 32, 40, 54, 63, 89, 245, 285
Liability, employers', 41
Libel, 217
Liquor traffic, 213
"Logical extreme," 17, 21, 82
Louisville & Nashville v. *Barber Asphalt Co.,* 10

McAuliffe v. *New Bedford,* 294; cited, 301
McCulloch v. *Maryland,* cited, 9
McFarland v. *Amer. Sugar Co.,* 34
McKenna, Mr. Justice, 9, 43, 45, 58, 61, 85, 90, 223
McReynolds, Mr. Justice, 43, 45, 52, 58, 61, 96, 115, 118, 209, 227, 242, 266, 267, 270, 273

Marcus Brown Co. v. *Feldman,* 59
Marshall, Chief Justice, 105, 183
Martial law, 91
Mass. State Grange v. *Benton,* 116
May v. *Wood,* 311; cited, 314
Migratory Bird Treaty, 101
Miles Medical Co. v. *Park,* 143
Miller, Mr. Justice, 41
Mining, 62
Missouri v. *Duncan,* 113
Missouri v. *Holland,* 101
Missouri, K. & T. Ry. Co. v. *May,* 8
Mob domination, 204
Monopoly, 34, 125
Moore v. *Dempsey,* 204
Morton, Mr. Justice, 313
Mt. Vernon Cotton Co. v. *Alabama Power Co.,* 31; cited, 55
Moyer v. *Peabody,* 91
Municipal ownership, 259
Music rolls, 175

Narcotics, 239
Nash v. *United States,* 147
National Ass'n of Window Glass Mfrs. v. *United States,* 163
National Prohibition Act, 213
Negligence, 281

[318]

INDEX

Negroes, 204, 210
N. Y. Trust Co. v. *Eisner,* 185
Newspapers, 75, 217
Nixon v. Herndon, 210
Noble State Bank v. *Haskell,* 20; cited, 55
Otis v. *Parker,* 3

Packers & Stockyards Act, 166
Pardons, 236
Patterson v. *Colorado,* 75
Peck v. *Tribune Co.*, 217
Peckham, Mr. Justice, 7, 13, 200
Pennsylvania Coal Co. v. *Mahon,* 62
Philippine Islands, 278
Picketing, 304
Pipe lines, 109
Pitney, Mr. Justice, 43, 105, 112, 152, 184, 203, 231, 265
Plant v. *Woods,* 314
Police power, 17, 18, 21-23, 46, 53, 59, 64, 66, 82
Political solicitation, 171, 294
Possession, 281
Prentis v. *Atlantic Coast Line,* 245
Presidential authority, 236
Presumption, 221, 239
Price-fixing, 128, 143, 147, 153
Primaries, 210
Prohibition, 214
Public utility regulation, 14, 46, 245, 255, 259
Publication, 75, 177, 217

Quong Wing v. *Kirkendall,* 25; cited, 44

Railroads, 8, 10, 14, 46, 86, 106, 245, 255, 259, 277, 281, 282, 285
Rate-making, 245, 255, 259
Referendum, 297
Rent, 53, 59
Re-sale price, 143
Retreat, 228
Revenue Act of 1924, 190
Rights, qualified, 160-1, 282-3
Riparian rights, 80, 286
Roschen v. *Ward,* 71
Ruddy v. *Rossi,* 96

Safe Deposit & Trust Co. v. *Virginia,* 267; cited, 273
Sanford, Mr. Justice, 190, 242
Search and seizure, 201

Self-incrimination, 213
Sherman Act, 38, 125, 137, 143, 147, 163
Silverthorne Lumber Co. v. *United States,* 201
Socialism, 58
Sovereignty, 277, 278
Springfield Gas Co. v. *Springfield,* 259
Statute of limitations, 177, 272
Sterilization, 67
Stock Exchange seat taxed, 265
Stock sales on margin, 3
Stone, Mr. Justice, 190, 267, 270, 274
"Structural habits," 18
Suffrage for women, 297
Superior Oil Co. v. *Mississippi,* 119
Sutherland, Mr. Justice, 115, 209
Swift & Co. v. *United States,* 125; cited, 144

Taft, Chief Justice, 90, 235; as President, 236
Taking of property, 18, 21, 24, 31, 53, 62, 82, 291
Taxation, 10, 18, 25, 44, 86, 106, 109, 119, 132, 185, 190, 265, 267, 270, 273, 284
Tenth Amendment, 101
Thirteenth Amendment, 61
Treaty, supremacy of, 101
Trespass, 232
Trust funds, 113, 267

United States v. *Amer. Livestock Co.,* 166
United States v. *Ju Toy,* 195
United States v. *Kissel,* 137; cited, 181
United States v. *Sullivan,* 213
United States v. *Thayer,* 171
United Zinc Co. v. *Britt,* 232

Value, defined, 156
Van Devanter, Mr. Justice, 43, 45, 52, 58, 61, 105, 121, 184, 190, 226
Vegelahn v. *Guntner,* 304; cited, 314, 315

Wages, 163, 291
Wallace v. *Hines,* 106
Water power, 31
Water supply, 80, 286
White, Chief Justice, 9, 13, 43, 52, 58, 61, 90, 203, 227
White-Smith Music Co. v. *Apollo Co.,* 175
Wills, 113, 185, 270, 311

[319]